COACH

COACH

25 WRITERS REFLECT ON
PEOPLE WHO MADE A DIFFERENCE

Edited by

Andrew Blauner

Foreword by Bill Bradley

WARNER BOOKS

NEW YORK BOSTON

Copyright information continued on page 289.

Warner Books

Time Warner Book Group
1271 Avenue of the Americas, New York, NY 10020
Visit our Web site at www.twbookmark.com.

Printed in the United States of America

First Edition: October 2005
10 9 8 7 6 5 4 3 2 1

Library of Congress Cataloging-in-Publication Data
Coach : 25 writers reflect on people who made a difference in their lives / edited by Andrew Blauner.— 1st ed.
     p. cm.
     ISBN 0-446-57745-6
   1. Coaches (Athletics)—United States—Anecdotes. 2. Coaching (Athletics)—United States—Anecdotes. I. Blauner, Andrew.
     GV711.C56 2005
796.07'7—dc22   2004030865

Book design by Giorgetta Bell McRee

For my mother and my father
For Amanda

Contents

BILL BRADLEY
Foreword ix

GEORGE VECSEY
"The Old Man" 1

E. M. SWIFT
"Why Be Last, Son?" 15

PAT CONROY
"My Losing Season" 29

BUZZ BISSINGER
"When I Was Young" 41

JOHN EDGAR WIDEMAN
"Passing It On" 47

ANDREW SOLOMON
"Prudent Fitness: A Panegyric" 55

JOHN MCPHEE
"VBK" 69

FRANCINE PROSE
"Physical Education" 75

JOHN IRVING
"Underdog" 87

THOMAS BELLER
"Something Special" 93

CHARLES MCGRATH
"Ironing" 109

DAVID MARANISS
"The Coach Who Wasn't There" .113

FRANK DEFORD
"The Depression Baby" 125

DARIN STRAUSS
"Long Island Shaolin" 147

GEORGE PLIMPTON
"Golf Lessons" 163

LAUREN SLATER
"Tripp Lake" 175

TOURÉ
"The Last of the Great Dreamers" 187

BENJAMIN CHEEVER
"The Boy They Cut" 199

ROBERT LIPSYTE
"To Althea, From the Net" 211

JANE LEAVY
"Coaching Bob" 217

JONATHAN AMES
"The Duel" 231

CHRISTINE BRENNAN
"Our Miss O" 239

BOB WOLFF
"Making It to the Majors" 251

IRA BERKOW
"Back to Basics" 261

BUD COLLINS
"Fit to Be Tied" 275

Foreword

BY BILL BRADLEY

LEADERSHIP MEANS GETTING PEOPLE TO THINK, believe, see, and do what they might not have without you. It means possessing the vision to set the right goal and the decisiveness to pursue it single-mindedly. It means being aware of the fears and anxieties felt by those you lead even as you urge them to overcome those fears. A great coach embodies these qualities and transforms them into a force that can effect powerful changes in those they lead.

My high school coach, the only man who would ever be "the coach" to me, was like a monk, withdrawn personally and unsociable in town circles; unreachable by the power of the company, the church, the bank, or the mayor; rigid with discipline and sparse with compliments; inspiring to boys like me, cruel to those unprepared or unwilling. Never did he confuse his roles. He was not the college counselor, family adviser, tutor, athletic businessman, or budding politician. He aspired only to be the coach. It was a calling. If in my years as a New York Knick there would be thousands of words written about passing and teamwork and hitting the open man, it would not be new. It would be the "coach's" game, which by age seventeen was second nature to me.

The really great coaches engage their players in a quest to be the best. Some bark their orders; others are more like machines, with a clipboard full of practice drills. In the right player-coach relationship, a quiet "well done" can go a long way. By talking candidly about the problems of adolescence or the vagaries of the parent-child relationship some high school coaches extend their reach to life off the court. Their players may never become pros, but because they learned the values of the game they are better prepared for life. Many people in all walks of life will tell you that their lives were turned around by a coach who took an interest in their total well-being. But, no matter your relationship with that person who will always be "the coach" for you, you will hear their words like a record every time you meet challenges or set out to accomplish goals. It is only then that you fully realize how they shaped you and how their vision still drives you.

In this book you will find powerful stories about the ways in which a coach changed the direction of someone's life and coaxed that person into taking a harder, more rewarding path. There are also a few recollections of coaches who had a negative effect on an individual's life. As you read the words of each writer, you will see that the story of a "coach" and their "player" serves as an allegory that illustrates the most basic, but most important aspects of human interaction. These individual stories taken together form a narrative of value that shows us the powerful reward of vision, hard work and the belief that together we can be something bigger and better than if we never listened to, learned from or engaged with the people we encounter in our lives.

———————————————

BILL BRADLEY has been a three-time basketball All-America at Princeton, an Olympic gold medalist, a Rhodes scholar, and a professional player for ten years with the New York Knicks during which time they won two NBA championships. He served in the U.S. Senate from 1979 to 1997, and in 2000 he was a candidate for the Democratic nomination for President of the United States. He is the author of several books, including *Life on the Run* and *Values of the Game*.

COACH

The Old Man

BY GEORGE VECSEY

THE OLD MAN TALKS TO ME EVERY DAY, in that raspy whisky voice of his.

He would clamp his paw on your forearm, like one of those so-called Denver Boots the police put on the tires of illegally parked cars. You could not pry him off.

"Wait a minute," he would bellow. "I'm trying to tell you something."

What was Casey Stengel trying to tell us? Usually, something practical relating to baseball, but often it was about the weirdness of baseball, the intricacies of it, like life itself.

The Old Man used to say, "Every day in baseball you see something you never saw before."

Early in the 2004 season, on national television, Roger Clemens of the Houston Astros was pitching to Barry Bonds of the San Francisco Giants. The broadcasters said it was the first time in baseball history that a pitcher with 300 victories had ever pitched to a slugger with 600 home runs.

Right away I thought: "The Old Man."

It happens a lot. A ball takes a squirrelly path, a player commits a gaffe, and I find myself muttering, "I've never quite seen *that* before."

Strange things happened around Casey, and he was alive enough and alert enough to sputter or laugh about them.

Of all the managers and coaches I've been around, Casey

Stengel taught me the most. I was part of that motley band Casey called "my writers." Some of his ballplayers were wise enough to learn from him, too.

"You knew when he was being funny," said Ron Swoboda, who played one season for Casey with the Mets, and still treasured it four decades later. "And you knew when he was serious."

Swoboda was under no illusions, then or now. He was a raw kid with a bit of power, and he was the best Casey had. The Old Man had managed DiMaggio and Berra and Mantle, and now he had a player he called "Suh-boda."

But somehow or other, Casey Stengel, in his four years with the dreadful Mets, performed a more amazing job than he had with the lordly Yankees. For this new franchise he created an image of lovability that has barely eroded decades later.

Managers and coaches are often handed the burden of being role models, doing that job for the rest of society. Molding character was not exactly Casey's goal in life. He was no kindly Mr. Chips. He referred to himself as "the slickest manager in baseball"—and he expected others to be slick, too.

Ron Swoboda learned that lesson in 1965. He was a husky rookie out of Baltimore, not yet twenty-one years old, bright and outspoken, but in baseball experience still a busher.

In an early-season game in old Busch Stadium in St. Louis, the Mets had a three-run lead in the ninth. Swoboda was playing right field as the rain ended and a strong sun emerged, directly in his eyes.

"The smart thing would have been to call time and get my sunglasses," Swoboda recalled in 2004. "But I figure, 'One more out, I can handle it.' Then Dal Maxvill hits a little flair that either would have been a single or I would have caught it, but I lose sight of it, and I have no clue how to play it, so three runs score and the game is tied.

"I know I screwed up," Swoboda recalled, "and I come up to bat the next inning and I make out and by now I am an emotional bomb. I stomp on my old fiberglass helmet. I'm gonna crush it. But the open end is facing up, and my foot gets caught, and it closes around my foot and I'm jumping around on my other foot."

The description from somebody in the dugout was that Swoboda resembled "a demented chicken."

"Casey comes up the stairs like he's twenty-five," Swoboda recalled, "and he grabs me with his good hand. He had broken his wrist that spring, and I figure he's going to hit me with his cast. He's yelling, 'When you screwed up the fly ball, I didn't go into your locker and break your watch, so don't you break the team's equipment!' Then he said, 'Go sit down!'

"You know the movie *A League of Their Own,* where Tom Hanks says, 'There's no crying in baseball'? Bullshit. I sat there and cried. I figured my career was over."

Only later did Swoboda figure out that Casey had affection for him, the way he did for a few of his brighter young players. He could be tough on the Youth of America, but he was preparing them.

It made him nuts if ballplayers didn't listen. He loved to tell the story about when he was managing the Yankees in 1951 and escorted young Mickey Mantle out to right field before an exhibition in Ebbets Field in Brooklyn. Casey wanted to show Mantle the complexities of the wall, but Mantle mostly stared at him, unable to fathom that his manager had once patrolled this very field.

"He thinks I was born old," Casey muttered to "my writers," who functioned as his Greek chorus. The writers' job was to hum appropriately when he made a good point.

Casey's outlook was based on his experiences. He'd been to Europe and Japan before it was convenient. He was born in the late nineteenth century and he still buzzes in my head early in the twenty-first century.

People said he spoke in Stengelese, a dialect straight out of Lewis Carroll's "Jabberwocky." Other times he spoke blunt Anglo-Saxon that had earthy folk wisdom to it.

In his monologues, he called other people "Doctor," so we referred to him as "the Doctor." If we debated him, he would frequently say, "You're full of shit and I'll tell you why." He was the first person I remember who used the term "you asshole" as a debating point, without incurring harsh feelings—no easy trick. And when the umpires' decisions and logic went against the Mets in those early gruesome years, Casey used to say, "They screw us because we're horseshit." And he was right. The umpires did, and the Mets were.

He could ramble on, if he wanted to. In 1958, he captivated a Senate hearing into the fairness of baseball's antitrust exemption, filibustering until the senators laughingly begged for mercy.

Casey's testimony is an American classic, right up there with Nixon's "Checkers" speech and Marilyn Monroe singing "Happy Birthday, Mr. President," well worth seeking out with a simple Google search. Somehow, if you listened long enough, you figured it out.

Charles Dillon Stengel (born July 30, 1890, in Kansas City, Missouri) took a circuitous route to being one of the immortal sports figures in his country. He was a quite decent outfielder in the National League and then he was burdened with the stigma of failure as a manager. In nine horrendous seasons with the Brooklyn Dodgers and Boston Braves, he never once finished in the top half of the eight-team league.

He then managed well enough in the fast Pacific Coast League to earn the Yankees' call in 1949. Joe DiMaggio and many of the older Yankees thought he was a clown, a minor leaguer, but he soon showed he had enough nerve to run the Yankees his way.

"He had his funny moments with the Yankees, but he wasn't this lovable old clown, either," said Swoboda, who later became a broadcaster and a student of his sport, particularly Casey's career.

"He was a tough old bastard," Swoboda added.

Foisted upon the older Yankees, Stengel showed no fear of

improvising and tinkering and taking command. He ran a platoon system at some positions like left field, alternating a left-handed hitter like Gene Woodling with the right-handed Hank Bauer. Neither of these crusty warhorses liked being platooned, except when they cashed their World Series check almost every autumn. He even put the great DiMaggio on first base for one game, just to prove he could.

In World Series games, he was not afraid to go a long way with hot relief pitchers like Joe Page, or use one of his best starters, Allie Reynolds, in relief, or bring in an obscure pitcher like Bob Kuzava in a tight situation. He was utterly fearless, and he answered to no one.

His main disciple with the Yankees was a scrappy little infielder named Billy Martin, who had known Stengel back in the Pacific Coast League.

"I love that old man with the ball in his sock," Martin would say, referring to a lump on Casey's ankle, a souvenir from having been hit by a taxi one rainy night in Boston. (One columnist nominated the cabbie as the man who did the most for Boston sports that year.)

Martin loved Casey right up to the moment Martin was involved in a brawl in a nightclub, the Copacabana, along with several more valuable Yankees. The Yankees' front office traded Martin away, but Martin blamed Casey and did not talk to him for a decade.

There was very little parental about Casey Stengel. Casey and his wife, Edna Lawson Stengel, did not have children, for reasons only they knew. People did not discuss such things back then. She had been an actress in New York, but they settled near her affluent banking family in Glendale, California. I remember her as willowy, cultured, and friendly, a grand old lady in my youthful eyes, and formidable enough to deflate some of Casey's bluster.

I encountered Casey during his last pennant run in 1960. I was twenty years old, just graduating from Hofstra College, and my boss at *Newsday*, Jack Mann, thought it was time for me to cover my first major league game up at Yankee Stadium.

It was a day game, and by 11 a.m. Casey was chattering to the writers in the dugout, blending tales from the olden days with fresh insights into the previous night's game. He was in the process of moving Clete Boyer into the regular lineup at third base, benching the veteran Gil McDougald, and he discussed it at great length, with apologies to nobody.

The pregame drill is very different today in the age of the microphone and the camera and the tight security. Joe Torre conducts a useful fifteen-minute update to the media swarm before the game, seated in the dugout while the Yankee Stadium sound system blares its inanities.

Back then, Casey held court. On my first day covering the Yankees, I was so fascinated with him that I sat in the dugout and gaped, not noticing that I was the only writer left.

Finally Casey turned to me and said, "Young man, you'll have to leave now because otherwise I'll have to put you in the starting lineup." It was about five minutes to game time.

His action revealed the essential Stengel. He could have made me feel like an idiot for staying too long, but he let me off the hook with a joke. He was not like some managers then and now who delight in bullying a newcomer. He saved his best stuff for his bosses, or his stars, or lions of the media like Dick Young or Howard Cosell, or critics like Jackie Robinson.

(Robinson—who had been the favorite player in my Dodger-centric household—criticized Stengel in his Mets years, saying Casey tended to snooze in the dugout. "Tell Robi'son he's Chock full o' Nuts," Stengel blurted, aptly referring to the coffee company Robinson had represented.)

Most of the Yankees kept their distance, judging Casey as one lucky eccentric to be able to manage the Berras, Fords, and Mantles.

Casey would not win a popularity contest in his clubhouse.

Clete Boyer will never forget kneeling in the on-deck circle in the second inning of the first game of the 1960 World Series.

Then he heard the Old Man shout, "Hold the gun!" Casey was sending up Dale Long to hit for Boyer, because the Yankees had fallen behind, 3–1, and had two runners on base. The Old Man's move was not only unorthodox, it was cold.

The Yankees lost that Series in seven games, and Stengel was blasted for not starting his ace, Whitey Ford, until the third game. Ford wound up pitching two shutouts, in the third and sixth games, and critics said he theoretically could have pitched three times if he had opened the Series.

The Yankees dismissed Casey immediately afterward. He said he would never again make the mistake of turning seventy.

On his body of work—ten pennants and seven World Championships in twelve seasons with the Yankees—Stengel was now one of the great managers in baseball history. He could have stomped off to California and lived very nicely representing his brother-in-law's banks.

However, he was not ready for the civilian world. He still needed "the baseball business" at least as much as it needed him. He was saving up a last act as manager that was, in its own way, more spectacular than his time with the Yankees.

Casey returned to Yankee Stadium in the fall of 1961 to attend a World Series game with the Cincinnati Reds. I remember the buzz as he strode through the cheering crowd of New Yorkers, his formerly gray hair now shockingly reddish. (Milton Gross of the *New York Post* referred to Casey as "Bixby," the name of a shoe polish of the distant past.)

New York got Casey back in 1962, after the New York Mets had been formed in an expansion draft.

There had been a terrible gap in New York after the Dodgers moved to Los Angeles and the Giants moved to San Francisco after the 1957 season. There was nothing like today's glut of televised games and sports highlight shows to keep up with Mays, Clemente, Aaron, and Robinson.

In 1962, the National League stars were coming back to New York to play the Mets, who included some of the worst culls and rejects from other farm systems. Would haughty New York tolerate a dismal baseball team? That was why the man with the rubbery face and the equally flexible syntax had been brought back from California.

"There was a huge longing for National League ball," Swoboda said. "Casey bought time by taking advantage of this."

Casey's job was to teach baseball, win a game here and there, entertain desperate New Yorkers, and sell some tickets. He tried the flim-flam approach at times. Dismissing a young pitcher during spring training of 1962, Casey said the Mets wanted to compete for the pennant and could not afford inexperienced players.

This was pure poppycock. Most of the time, Stengel caustically referred to how "the attendance got trimmed," meaning, in his lexicon, that the paying customers had been shortchanged.

Casey also fought publicly with his general manager, George M. Weiss, who had been his boss with the Yankees and had now rescued him from enforced retirement. Casey probably was grateful. But whenever the frugal Weiss tried to retain a player in whom he had invested a few dollars, Stengel thundered that the player was "a fraud."

I can picture him naked, a tough old bird in his early seventies, his Mets uniform lying discarded on the floor of his office, while he pounded his burly chest and proclaimed the entire franchise was "a fraud."

Casey was doing something no other man in "the baseball business" had ever done—he was managing and performing vaudeville at the same time. He was creating a personality for a bad baseball team in the toughest market in the country. He was inventing the New York Mets on the fly.

"He sacrificed some of his legend to keep the media and the fans from turning on the team," Swoboda said.

At the same time, Casey was talking baseball to the fans, the writers, and the players.

"Why wouldn't ya wanna . . . ?" was Casey's Socratic prelude to a lecture about some nuance of his business.

The writers and fans tended to get more out of Casey than many of his players. Casey discovered this one day during batting practice when he was delivering a lecture on the batting technique he called "the butcher boy"—chopping downward to knock the ball through a hole in the infield.

Casey looked around at the blank looks of his own players. Then he spotted one pair of alert, intelligent eyes watching his every move, absorbing his every word.

Unfortunately, those eyes belonged to Maury Wills, the shortstop for the Dodgers, the Mets' opponent later in the day. Wills had already won one World Series in 1959 with his resourcefulness, and was not above eavesdropping on Casey's seminar. Needless to say, the Old Man did not run Wills off. He was a baseball man, teaching baseball.

Some Mets appreciated him. One was Richie Ashburn, the feisty old center fielder who ran into walls, fought with umpires, batted .306, and brought out the humorous side of an itinerant first baseman named Marvelous Marv Throneberry, who became the personification of the Mets—inept, but also comical. Ashburn hated to lose, and he understood that the Old Man did, too. Nobody blamed him when he bailed for a broadcasting job after one season.

Another player who totally got Casey was Rod Kanehl, a vagabond utility player whom Casey had once noticed years earlier at the Yankees' minor league complex. Casey kept him around the Mets for three seasons because Kanehl hustled and would play any position (seven, ultimately). Kanehl also took up Casey's standing offer of $50 for getting hit by a pitch with the bases loaded.

A midwesterner like Stengel, Kanehl felt the same fascination with the big city that Stengel once had. As a young Dodger, Stengel had enticed teammates into the rudimentary subway system, blithely losing them and forcing them to find their way back to their hotel. Kanehl also acted as subway tour guide to other Mets, who called him "the Mole." Kanehl absorbed Casey's wisdom; he just didn't have enough talent to execute the lessons.

Casey did not escape criticism. In addition to the old sleeping-in-the-dugout charge—why wouldn't you want to snooze out of sheer escapism?—Casey was said to confuse players' identities. One former Met has said that Casey once ordered "Blanchard" to pinch-hit and that the coaches had to tactfully tell Casey that Johnny Blanchard was still employed across the Harlem River with the Yankees. More likely, Casey just mixed up names. He had two pitchers named Bob Miller that first season, so he called one of them "Nelson," either by design or accident.

A nap or a wrong name didn't matter much. The Mets won 40 games and lost 120 in that first season, with two games mercifully rained out.

Casey was managing the worst team in the history of baseball. "You could look it up," Casey often said, a phrase he either borrowed from Ring Lardner, or Ring Lardner borrowed from him.

One catch phrase for that 1962 Mets team was created by a boisterous raconteur with a gift for language. I am speaking here not of Casey Stengel but of Jimmy Breslin.

A gifted writer from New York, Breslin showed up on assignment from *Sports Illustrated* one hot, humid July weekend of 1962. The Mets threw a seventy-second birthday party for Casey in the Chase Park Plaza Hotel, then the garden spot of St. Louis. (The headwaiter had once pitched batting practice before Cardinals games; Casey treated him like an equal, even imitating his pitching form.)

Casey spent the reception standing up, drink in hand, commenting on the multi-ineptitudes of his team. Blessed with youthful kidneys, I stayed by his elbow the entire evening.

A year later, a Breslin book came out, entitled *Can't Anyone Here Play This Game?* a plea ostensibly uttered by Casey during his long monologue that evening in St. Louis.

Not long afterward, Breslin called me for a phone number or something and at the end I said, "Jimmy, just curious, I was at that party for Casey, never left his side, and I don't remember him ever saying, 'Can't anyone here play this game?'"

Long pause.

"What are you, the FBI?" Breslin asked.

Breslin has since admitted he just might have exercised some creative license. Casey never complained about being mis-quoted. He would have said it if he had thought of it.

I stuck as close as possible to Casey those years. I wasn't look-ing for a parent or a mentor but I think I was just wise enough to know I would never meet anybody like him again.

There have been entire volumes devoted to those wonderful early days of Casey and the Mets. (I wrote one myself, long out of print, entitled *Joy in Mudville*.) If I could distill the entire four years into one madcap experience, it would be the night of May 4, 1964, in Milwaukee.

By this time, the Mets were marginally better, partially be-cause Casey had spotted a scrappy second baseman named Ron Hunt in spring training of 1963, and installed him at the top of the lineup. On this nippy night in Milwaukee, Hunt tried to score with two outs in the ninth, but was tagged out at home in a rough collision. Then he and the catcher, Ed Bailey, began to mix it up, as both teams milled around home plate.

In the midst of the scrum, a Milwaukee infielder named Denis Menke felt a pair of powerful arms trying to pry him away from the plate. Menke shrugged the man loose. Then he looked down at his assailant and saw the Mount Rushmore profile of the Mets' manager, tangled in a bunch of legs. Menke envisioned the next day's front page—"Menke Kills Casey Stengel"—and helped pick up the Old Man, who was still sputtering.

After order was restored, Casey totally denied having been anywhere near the fight. However, a couple of his players raved about the combativeness of the Old Man. Casey's story was discredited when he stripped to take a shower, revealing a few new bruises and scrapes.

After getting tossed around like that, most seventy-three-year-old men might retire to their hotel room and take a long hot bath. Casey went out drinking with his writers. We found some bar, where Casey gave a vivid imitation of a tornado that hit Milwaukee twenty years earlier, his battered body getting blown across the barroom by the imaginary high winds.

When the bar closed, eight of us found a rib joint, which turned out to be the hangout of a motorcycle gang. At first I was a little concerned we might be in for trouble, until one of the cyclists spotted Casey and came over with his girlfriend, who appeared to be sixteen years old, and respectfully asked for an autograph.

Casey, who had gotten bored with his writers, now engaged the motorcyclists in a debate over whether the Braves were willing to trade their brilliant but aging shortstop, Roy McMillan.

"Now, you want to give me McMillan, who is thirty-three, and we don't know if he can throw. Then who do you want, Hook?"

(Jay Hook was a sweet Northwestern graduate with advanced degrees in physics, who could explain why a curveball curved, but could not throw one.)

"Hook has won a lot of games for me and he has a lovely family," Casey told the motorcyclists. "Edna says I can't trade him. Would you like to talk to Edna for me?"

Casey and the cyclists talked baseball for about an hour or so, until the writers began falling asleep on the bar.

The next morning I dragged myself down to the coffee shop around nine o'clock. There was the Old Man, finishing a full breakfast, talking baseball with the customers.

As I think about Casey these days, I am struck by the vast amount of alcohol consumed by him and his traveling chorus. Alcohol had no hold over me but in those days you drank to be sociable. I had not yet figured out that you can sip a club soda and lime rather than a scotch and soda, and will feel much better the next morning.

Casey used to say, "Whiskey makes you sick when you're well—and well when you're sick."

He also had an expression for people who lost their composure when they drank too much: "Whiskey-slick." Even with his amazing constitution, Casey could become garrulous or argumentative, might need a friendly arm to get him from the taxi to the hotel elevator.

Having a lot of friends who are alcoholics, recovering or otherwise, I would say that Casey was nowhere near the state of powerlessness that defines alcoholism. The Old Man surely drank a bit, but at the same time he was skillfully ducking or answering questions from his writers.

He kept up his guard, but occasionally you would see a glimpse of emotion. Casey had a great deal of respect for Fred Hutchinson, the burly manager of the Reds, who had once battled the Yankees as a pitcher with the Tigers. I will never forget Casey shuddering when he spotted his friend and rival, emaciated from cancer, being taken around the ballpark on a golf cart in 1964. There was no joking from the Old Man that day. The next year, Hutchinson was dead.

That same spring Casey broke a wrist when he slipped on a wet patch during an exhibition game. Then, late at night on July 25, 1965, Casey fell and broke his hip, and needed an artificial ball inserted in his hip socket. On August 30, he called a press conference to say he would resume managing but would not return the following season. At that conference, he horrified Edna by abruptly crossing one leg over another to demonstrate what a good job the surgeons had done.

"Casey!" she blurted, the way wives will.

They stayed home in Glendale after 1965, although Casey was a fixture every spring training in Florida. My daughter, now a sports columnist with the *Baltimore Sun*, can recall being a little girl, sitting on a barstool at the old Colonial Inn at St. Petersburg Beach, holding a ginger ale and chatting with that nice old couple, Casey and Edna.

In 1969, Casey was around to celebrate the Mets' improbable World Championship, with Gil Hodges now the manager. Ron Swoboda, the Youth of America, made an epic diving catch in right field to help win one game.

The final years were not kind. One season Casey visited the Mets and confided that Edna was fine—"from the neck down," meaning her wit and reason were gone.

Casey died in 1975 and Edna lived three years longer. I see them every day. My wife has made a large montage of our family photographs and she included a photo of Casey and Edna circa 1965, in a hansom cab, he doffing a top hat, she chucking him under the chin, a striking mixture of aging prophet and ageless beauty.

To this day, when I am taking an iconoclastic stance in my column, I remember asking the Old Man why he was not afraid.

"I can make a living telling the truth," he would bellow.

I think of him every day.

GEORGE VECSEY, sports columnist with the *New York Times*, covered his first Yankee game in 1960, a month before his twenty-first birthday. He is the author of over a dozen books, including *Joy in Mudville*, a history of the Mets, published in 1970, with Casey Stengel as its central figure.

Why Be Last, Son?

BY E. M. SWIFT

IN THE EARLY 1970S SOMEONE MADE A TAPE recording of Frank Ward teaching wrestling to a group of first graders. I open with this, not because wrestling was an important element in Coach Ward's repertoire, nor because he became a local legend at the Lake Forest (Illinois) Country Day School by working with first graders. A history teacher and the athletic director between 1959 and 1982, the barrel-chested Ward was best known for coaching football and baseball to seventh, eighth, and ninth graders. He wore a brush cut and carried himself with a military bearing, having been a decorated infantryman in both World War II and Korea. His imposing physical presence was offset by a warmth and twinkle in his eyes and a disarming sense of humor. He frequently ended history class with long, funny stories about army life. He called the quizzes he sprung on us "quizzicals." The big test at the end of the term was a "testicle."

Why the tape was made is something of a mystery, but the recording captures Coach Ward's voice better than anything I've run across. It may help the reader understand how this extraordinary man was able to engender the loyalty and devotion of a generation of boys who later proved they were worthy of his life's work. It may even help some readers understand why Coach Ward eventually alienated a small but vocal set of sheltering parents, an alienation that led to his premature retirement. Certainly those who knew him will recognize in the tape Coach Ward's spirit, his love of nonsensical nicknames, his gruff, dramatic voice, and his ability to make the most meaningless competition into a Homeric struggle demanding courage and sacrifice.

"We're going to do a little wrestling," the tape begins. "Weinerman Henry, out here in the middle. Whites Woloson, right here. Get on all fours. Now when I say wrestle, wrestle. The idea is: Can you move fast? Who is fast? That's what we're trying to find out. Now wrestle! Use your hands. That's it. Jeez, he gave that man an awful going over. Don't take that, Whites Woloson. [The boy is apparently crying.] You all right? You're all right. You're a tough cookie, Whitey. You're one tough cookie, Whites Woloson. Take a rest, you two. A mush job for Mouse Henry. Ha! Ha! Ha!"

Coach Ward would take one of his ham-sized palms and rub it vigorously and affectionately over a boy's face when administering a "mush job." It was the physical embodiment of tough love.

"Sid Gorter and Charlie Hough, out in the middle. Get on all fours. Now wrestle! The power of Charlie Hough! He's trying to wear his man out, a typical Monty Hough trick. He's a regular Jack Hough. [Jack Hough was Charlie's older brother.] Oh, Sid, you're taking an awful beating. Get on your stomach, Sid. He can't pin you when you're on your stomach. Roll on your stomach. Beautiful effort made by Sid, he almost had him. Oooh. It could be all over. It's curtains for Sid. Here's your winner. The power of Charlie Hough is brutal."

You can hear the other first graders squealing with delight in the background. Coach Ward's passion was infectious. "These two men, Whites Stauber and friend. Ready? Wrestle! Holy cow! Kent's all over his man. He's tearing Whites Stauberman apart! Whites Stauberman won't take that. He will not take that. He's going right after a pin. Hold it, hold it. Beautiful rolling in there. Whitey J. Stauberman learned to roll while fighting steers out West. Pin his arms down, Kent. Now squeeze him. He's going to squeeze the stomach right out of him. Move the legs! He's going to ride his man down. Fifty seconds to go in this bout. The clock is running. Kent's as fast as a cat. He's as fast as a cat without whiskers. Oh, man! He's got him tied in a knot. He's chasing his man all over the lot. No touching the competitors. Any man touching the competitors will be asked to leave. He almost had him by the big toe! Stay with him, Kent. Ten seconds left. Get on top of him. Go left, Whitey. Go left. Oh! He went right instead of left. This bout's history."

It was this particular class's first introduction to Frank Ward. Some were already being dubbed with nicknames that would stay with them the rest of their lives. David "Sid" Gorter was the first of three Gorter brothers to be called "Sid" by Coach Ward, for no particular reason. Any kid with blond hair became "Whitey." My brother, whose name was Lock, became J. K. Knutterman, who was a sausage maker out of Coach Ward's childhood. He was also called Crazy Legs. The nicknames were a badge of honor, a boy's athletic alter ego. Parents and siblings often adopted them. To this day (forty years after the fact) David Gorter's parents call him Sid.

Frank Ward, like a lot of men of his era, believed in competition. He held chin-up contests, push-up contests, footraces. Sometimes he staged boxing matches. When children compete, there are winners and losers, sometimes tears. But with Coach Ward, whichever camp you landed in, the victorious or the vanquished, there was also fun and laughter. Real laughter. Not happy talk. Not: "Did everyone have fun today?" Feelings were hurt and quickly mended. At the end of the wrestling recording one boy can be heard lamenting that the gym class was too short, too short. Eight years later, as that group left the Day School, nearly all of them would believe the same thing. Their time with Frank Ward was too short, too short. Few of them would ever forget him.

I thought of Coach Ward last fall when I went to see my

eleven-year-old son play school football. He was in sixth grade, a year older than when I began playing for Frank Ward, and it was his first year of tackle in full equipment. I was curious about the level of play. It soon became apparent the kids were working without a playbook. They were making up plays in the huddle, so each huddle lasted about five minutes, with six kids talking at once, arguing about who would get the ball. The coach, a math teacher, was refereeing, silently watching the chaos. There was no blocking, no teaching of fundamentals, no discipline. It was recess in full equipment.

The kids, of course, loved it. Kids can hack around all day. What they learn from it is another matter. I later talked to the school's athletic director about the philosophy behind such a program, and he explained that at the sixth grade level, he didn't want the kids to be too regimented. They had enough regimentation in the classroom. His thinking was, let the boys blow off some steam in the afternoon, have some fun, experiment playing different positions, and in seventh and eighth grade they'd get a real playbook and real coaching and learn real football. It didn't seem to bother him that this formula had produced a string of losing seasons dating back a quarter century. The boys were having fun.

I ran this philosophy past Coach Ward, who's now eighty-four and living in Charlottesville, Virginia. We hadn't talked in several years. He immediately remembered what positions I'd played forty years ago, who my teammates were. He's in wonderful shape, physically and mentally. "My philosophy was that I was on the field as an instructor," Coach Ward said. "The same way an English or math teacher is in the classroom. I was trying to instill something for life. If we just went out to the field and kicked the ball around, had fun, made up some plays, that's the same as if a math teacher said, 'We'll do some multiplication tables for a few minutes, then we'll hack around with numbers. I'll throw out some problems and we'll see if you can get any of them right. Wrong answer? Oh, that's all right. Nice try, fella. At least we're using numbers.'

"I can't conceive of doing something on an athletic field without organization," he said. "We had the fifth and sixth graders use the same playbook as the varsity. It was fun, but it was also serious. Repetition. Repetition is the key to success."

He knew about success. When he retired in 1982, Frank Ward's football teams at LFCDS were 145-47-11. In baseball—he had spent a season in the Pittsburgh Pirates organization as a pitcher—his teams were 198–86. In the fall of 1962 and 1963, his 7th and 8th grade football teams were undefeated and unscored upon, going a combined 14–0. That merited a mention in the "Faces in the Crowd" section of *Sports Illustrated*, which was pretty heady stuff back then. My older brother played on the 1962 team, and I played some defense as a seventh grader on the 1963 squad. When the undefeated streak finally ended on the last play of the last game of the 1964 season on a long Hail Mary pass, breaking a 0–0 tie, Coach Ward reacted with an equanimity that few of us were able to fathom, never mind match. That, too, has endured. On the long, quiet bus ride home from Chicago, he told us how we'd had a great run, to hold our heads up. When the headmaster, Sam Parkman, came into his office that afternoon to ask how we'd done, Coach Ward summed it up with a single phrase: "It's the end of an era, Sam."

"I remember one of the parents saying, 'This isn't good for them,'" Coach Ward reminisced over the phone. "'They're going to get big heads and a distorted view of life.' I told that parent, 'Oh, it's good for them, don't you worry about that. There's nothing wrong with winning. You don't have to do it in a boastful manner, but everyone has to experience success. We all want a pat on the back for the job we do. There's nothing better to build spirit in youth than having success in sports.'"

He was right, of course. All of us who were involved in either or both of those undefeated teams still take pride in the accomplishment. For many, it was the highlight of their athletic careers. We were a small school, about twenty boys to a grade, so almost everyone had to contribute in one way or another to the football team. Some were starters, some were backups, and some were the "loonies" who played special teams. But all were part of the team, and there was no "I" in team—one of the many motivational sayings Coach Ward hung around his locker room, lettered in his perfect, calligraphic hand, ornamented with hand-drawn stars, winged feet, trees, and footballs.

"Enthusiasm creates momentum."

"Always run off the field."

"The difference between champ and chump is you."

It didn't matter if you were the third-string center, or the star running back: the rules were the same. His attention to your development was identical. No one was under his radar. Most of us were spoiled rich kids, raised by nannies, destined to head off to the best private schools in the East. Those were the trappings that gave us big heads and a distorted view of life. Coach Ward was our dose of reality. He made us want to prove ourselves to him. Our success on the football field was the result of what he liked to call "pick and shovel work." He'd remind us of this fact while supervising our blocking and tackling drills, or when he told us we were going to run the sledding hill "till we dropped" at the end of practice. To the slowest runners, he'd exhort, "Why be last, son?" a theme many of his less athletic players would always remember, because while few are blessed with the speed and talent to be first, all of us, through nothing more than determination and will, have the ability to be better than last. The last man was a quitter. Coach Ward insisted only that we try.

And we did try, because if we didn't he had an endless repertoire of comical putdowns that would be repeated and quoted for years. A boy who shied away from contact was a "spineless weenie." A kid who made a mental error was dubbed "Cement Head" and accused of thinking about "Susie Schlitzenheimer," his generic name for any girl. A kid who loafed during practice had been spending too much time at "88 Flavors," his name for the local ice-cream store. "Hells bells, son, forget about your ice-cream cone or you'll have cleat marks up your back!"

A running back who went down too easily must have "tripped in a cleat hole." A poor tackle would elicit a comment like, "That man thinks he's waltzing with Susie Schlitzenheimer. This is football, not dancing school." If a kid had an older brother, Coach Ward's standard line to light his fire was, "You couldn't carry your brother's jockstrap." An overweight lineman unable to do a single chin-up might be dubbed: The Crisco Kid. "Isn't that pathetic?" the coach would say with a merry chuckle, as we watched and hooted while the boy dangled from the chin-up bar. "You are watching the triumph of gravity over blubber. Have you no pride, son? Show some pride!" It might take a small boost, but eventually that boy would do a chin-up, and Coach Ward would celebrate it as if he'd won an Olympic medal.

"I remember one rainy day having to run the obstacle course in the gym," Bill "Whitey" Hunter remembers. He's now forty-eight. "I was having trouble climbing a wall, and he was all over me. He could really get under your skin. It filled me with anger, and all of a sudden I discovered a fifth gear I didn't know I had. I got over the wall, tripped, and did a somersault on the stairs, but managed to finish first. He ran over and grabbed me and gave me a 'mush job,' praising me, which was one of the best feelings I ever had in a competitive environment. He did it personally, not in front of everyone as he often did. It was as if he said, 'If you can finish first with that kind of effort, imagine the other things you can accomplish.' I don't think it was the winning that was important to me that day. It was the discovery that I really had more determination and effort than I thought. To some people it may sometimes have seemed he was making fun of kids, but he did not play favorites, and really what he was doing was molding character."

Coach Ward's jocular barbs were delivered during practices,

never during games, and often broke tension and generated laughs in the midst of a long, hot practice. He could tease, prod, poke fun at, and berate, and we'd willingly come back for more. He never crossed the line into meanness, and his quips were balanced by an equal measure of praise. "He taught all of us to laugh at each other. All of us knew that we could be the subject of the next laugh," Tom Hunter, now fifty, recently said. "Try hard, and when you make the mistake of a lifetime, laugh and learn from it. Don't take yourself too seriously. Frank asked us to risk looking like a fool while playing sports."

"I felt humor added something," Coach Ward says now. "Knute Rockne used to say when things get tense, you need to relieve that, to make a little joke, get the boys to laugh. We had this fella, Ralph Brown, who was a little wingback. We kept practicing a reverse to him, and he kept fumbling. Time after time. He's embarrassed, he's feeling down, and I remember thinking I'd better say something. So I went up to him and said, 'Ralph, give me your hands. Let me look at them. Oh, there you go. That explains it. No wonder you're fumbling the ball, son. You don't have fingers. Those are nubs. This man has nubs for fingers. Okay, let's run it again.' Everyone laughs, and he relaxes, and from that day forward he's Nubs Brown."

In the winter Coach Ward led hikes on Saturday morning through the ravines of Lake Forest. Kids, parents, and fellow teachers accompanied him. He had that magic that made people want to be in his company, and he was a wonderful storyteller. As a high school kid, he'd been one of the young men charged with handling the docking ropes for the dirigible *Hindenburg* when it exploded into flames, killing thirty-five people on board. To hear him describe the flames raining down from the sky, the screams, the terror—you didn't want to miss that. So people got up on those cold winter mornings and hiked. He loved nature and believed in physical conditioning. In the spring he cleared trails through the woods surrounding the school, and had younger kids "run the bunny trail" for exercise during recess. It somehow made jogging more fun. Baseball, with its relaxed pace and peculiar bounces, was a ripe source of humor. An outfielder who misplayed a fly ball had either "lost it in his eyelash" or was "out there picking daisies." A batter who stepped in the bucket was "a Mary Margaret hitter." A line drive pulled foul was greeted with the exclamation, "She's foul, fat, and forty!" A pitcher who walked too many batters was playing "Waltz me around again, Willie." You never knew what was going to come out of his mouth.

He called the suicide squeeze play the "skeezix," and a generation of LFCDS ballplayers can still remember the sign. Coach Ward would stand at the third base box, place both hands below his jockstrap, then yank upward with a pronounced, unsightly hitch. Sandy Stuart, now fifty-three, remembers getting the sign in a game in 1964 and starting inwardly to chuckle. He then missed the bunt, causing the runner to be out at home. "Hells bells, son," Coach Ward told him. "If you can't hit the ball with the bat, stick a leg or arm out there. Take one for the team!"

"With another chance at bat, I would have," Stuart says now. "He wasn't angry. Coach Ward rarely got angry. He just wanted me to focus on the task at hand."

He could get angry, though. He had lines one didn't cross. As a sixth grader I lost my temper after we'd lost an intrasquad baseball game, and in a fit I accused him of lying. His reaction was immediate: "You're done, son," he snapped. "Take a hike and don't come back. Your playing days on this field are over."

I missed the next three days of sports until my homeroom teacher gently suggested that I apologize. I slunk into his office. Coach Ward's door was always open. Near tears, fearful, I told him I was sorry. He listened with understanding in his eyes. "We all make mistakes," he told me, his usual gruffness softened. "You come out this afternoon and apologize to the team, and the whole incident is forgotten. Son, it never happened."

It was, I'm certain, the last time I raised my voice to a coach in anger again.

So we learned. Without even knowing it, we learned. How to win and lose. How to practice. To hustle. To be accountable for our actions. To laugh at our mistakes. After we left the Day School, we went on with our lives, but within each of us Coach Ward's voice lived on, coming forth during competitions and practices in high school, then college, then when we became parents and tried to imitate his teasing, prodding, compassionate manner with our own kids. Coach Ward stayed at LFCDS, turning down opportunities to coach older athletes, turning down better-paying jobs, because he'd found a niche where he knew he was making a difference.

Time passed, and the world started to change around him. Parents became more involved, more vocal, more protective. Teachers and coaches were judged, not by their body of work, but by what they had done for "my" child today. Competition became, if not a dirty word, a word that raised eyebrows of suspicion. Political correctness ramped up. Repetition? Discipline? Spineless weenies? All became out of vogue.

"When I came here there were parents who didn't buy Frank's style, whose kids sat on the bench most of the game," says Jim Marks, who became headmaster of LFCDS in 1981. "It wasn't to the point where he had to go, but the wolves were at the door. He was still very popular, because Frank was Frank. But he was somewhat out of step with the times."

Girls' sports were becoming more important, and, nationally, soccer was on the rise. "At the end of his career, Frank was criticized by a number of parents because 'the times had changed,'" recalls Bob Bullard, a history teacher at LFCDS since 1971, who coached football and baseball with Ward for five years. "Frank could be tough on kids, with a little bit of a 'survival of the fittest' attitude, and tough love wasn't as appreciated as much anymore."

Gently pushed by the new administration, Coach Ward decided to retire early, in 1982, at age sixty-one. The school named a new sports field after him, and gave him a small stipend. He was able to ride off into the sunset as one of the most beloved teachers in the history of the school.

Problem was, his kids couldn't forget him. "There was some serious depression in our class when Frank left," remembers Luke Lincoln, who'd been a seventh grader Ward's final year. He vividly recalls how Ward's successor removed all the team photos from the walls of the school, the neatly stacked footballs and baseballs with the records of every former team he'd coached. All the individual records—longest punt, longest run from scrimmage, longest pass completion. The history and tradition, all gone.

His former players kept talking about him whenever they got together, however, quoting him, wondering how Coach Ward was doing. Once in a while someone would go down to visit him in Lexington, Virginia, where he'd moved. They'd report back how he hadn't changed, he was active in the Senior Olympics, still a physical fitness fanatic, still practicing throwing the discus and putting the shot. He'd saved all his memorabilia from his LFCDS days, photos with team captains, records, playbooks. They were stored in a shed in the back. He was living on a small place in the country with his wife, Jeanne.

This went on for years. Then, in the spring of 2000, Luke Lincoln and his brother-in-law, John Hough, both former players, went to visit. Coach Ward, who was eighty, put lime down on the field in his backyard in anticipation of their arrival so they could hold a mini-Olympics. He narrated the tilt with his usual passion, holding a punting competition, then having them put the shot and throw the discus. It was like when they were kids back in school.

Afterwards they went inside to watch the Masters golf tournament on television.

"He had a grainy, black-and-white TV with rabbit ears,"

Hough remembers. "He couldn't afford cable. This was a man who would have loved the History Channel and ESPN. His car had about 120,000 miles on it, and he couldn't afford to have it fixed. He'd bought it from a shady dealer and was paying a 29 percent interest rate. He wasn't going to complain about anything, but it was obvious he was living on a shoestring."

As they'd been taught to do on the football field as kids, Lincoln and Hough picked up the ball and ran with it. A call went out to Ward's former players, men (and women) between thirty and fifty-five years old, for funds to buy him a new car, a new TV, monthly cable. The response was overwhelming. "They raised so much they couldn't spend it all," says David Gorter. "So they started looking at how else they could help."

"We asked ourselves, how can we pay back a guy who's meant so much to us?" Hough says. "Here was a very social guy living way out in the country, very little social interaction. He was eighty years old, taking care of the place himself. His children weren't around to help him. He was worried what would happen if an illness or injury happened to him or to Jeanne. We wanted to improve his life." They took the Wards to visit an upscale retirement home in Charlottesville, Virginia, called the Colonnades. Did they like it? Would they be interested in moving there? Yes, of course, the Wards responded. But they'd never be able to afford it.

The phone calls began. The letters. They called themselves the Secret Panthers—the Panthers was the team nickname of LFCDS—and in a matter of months 150 donors, in increments between $10 and $10,000, had given $165,000, with additional pledges for $35,000 a year to offset the annual rent for the Wards at the Colonnades. In 2003 they moved in. "Members of every single class he ever coached gave," says David "Sid" Gorter, who helped organize the fund-raising efforts launched by Lincoln and Hough. "Parents gave. Twelve women donated who as girls had had him as a history teacher. It was an incredible, immediate response. It isn't often in life you get to go back and tell somebody who's meant a lot to you, Thank you. If we hadn't done this, everyone who ever played for him would have wished they'd told him that while he was still alive. Now they've done so. This is one of those feel-good stories. It's been win-win."

A Secret Panther dinner was held back in Lake Forest to honor Coach Ward. People flew in from all over the country. Composed, lucid, humorous, and wise, the old mentor went around the table, squeezing shoulders and saying something about every man there. They weren't just his star athletes. They were all ages, and all skill levels. Cement Heads (2) and Whiteys (8), Sids (3) and Seamonoviches (1). "Never much of an athlete," he said to one, "but this man had the heart of a lion."

And to another: "The best third-string center in the history of the school."

Any bitterness he'd once felt about retiring early, the tiny pension he was forced to live on, was entirely gone. He spoke as a man fulfilled, his emotions under control, ever the teacher. "Only the words of a poet could express my feelings for what you gentlemen have done for Jeanne and me," he said. "I can only say there is a God that looks out for people."

Then he spoke about his profession, about coaching young kids. "Football's a slice of life. Most of my guys never went on to play in high school or college, but for the rest of their lives they could watch a bowl game, or an NFL game, and relate. They were able to say, 'At one time in my life, I played football.' The joy is in taking a guy who isn't going to be an athlete and incorporating him into the group. One kid runs like Jesse Owens, and here comes a little guy who has two left feet. God did that. So you take the kid who has two left feet, you say something humorous about him, give him a nickname, something to make the others laugh, and now he's part of the group. I enjoyed working with the younger element. I might have had higher aspirations at one time in my life to coach at a higher level, but if you enjoy something and get wrapped up in it, you don't want to leave it. It becomes ingrained in you. It's happiness. You might make more money coaching at a higher level, but it really doesn't offer you more happiness. I don't think you do the same molding of young people in high school or college that you do in elementary school. That's what I always thought of my job, that I was in the business of molding."

—————————————

E.M. SWIFT is a senior writer at *Sports Illustrated*. He weighed 105 pounds when he played linebacker and fullback for Coach Frank Ward in 1964. He lives in Carlisle, Massachusetts.

My Losing Season

BY PAT CONROY

I WAS AT THE END OF MY SOPHOMORE YEAR at The Citadel when the letter arrived from Bill McCann, the former coach at Virginia, telling me that I had a job as a basketball counselor at Camp Wahoo. This was the first of two summers I dedicated to improving my game and to becoming the kind of player other teams feared. During the previous year, I had begun to understand how far behind my game was, compared to those of my teammates and opponents. The coaching I got in high school had been shaky and haphazard at best. I didn't have a clue about anything I did on the court. I'd learned everything by imitating players better than me. Coach Paul Brandenburg had surprised me by stopping a freshman practice and telling the team that I had the best reverse dribble he'd ever seen. I didn't have the foggiest notion what he was talking about.

For those two summers at Wahoo, in 1965 and '66, I lived in the center of the game through sunburned clinics at which I assisted famous coaches and players teaching the fundamentals to boys as eager as beagle puppies. I listened to men like the incomparable Jerry West explain the rudiments of ballhandling and shooting and defense.

The campers arrived on a Sunday with their parents, and twenty 15-year-old boys were assigned to my dormitory room that first summer. I took to the role of counselor my experience as the oldest brother among seven children. I was easy in the company of young boys, especially the sassy, rebellious ones sent by parents who needed a vacation from their mouthy sons. Camp Wahoo's genius lay in the fact that it kept even the crossest kid exhausted and out of breath.

An odd, unsettling event took place on my very first workday. As I was walking with other counselors and campers toward court number 5, a voice called out, "Conroy!"

I turned around and was shocked to see Mel Thompson, my head coach at The Citadel, smoking a cigarette on the steps. He seemed as surprised to see me. "What the hell you doing here, Conroy?" he asked.

"I needed to work on my game, Coach."

"That's the truth. Who told you about Camp Wahoo?"

"Coach Brandenburg got me the job."

He eyed me obliquely. "He did, huh?" Coach Thompson always looked at you from odd angles, as though there were a tree or a bush blocking his view. "Why didn't you tell me about it?"

"I didn't know you'd ever heard of Camp Wahoo, Coach."

"O.K." He finished his cigarette. "Get out of here, Conroy."

In the two summers I worked at Camp Wahoo, that was the last time Mel Thompson spoke to me, even to say hello. His failure to acknowledge me left me feeling sullied and insulted, especially because he seemed to relate so well to the other counselors, the boys from rival colleges. I would see Coach Thompson's car packed with other coaches and counselors going into town for hamburgers and a movie. I witnessed his laughter but always from a distance, and when he smiled his face was transformed, making it softer, almost handsome. Those two summers in Virginia, I studied my coach as he passed me without a sign of recognition.

In the morning, with the sun rising up from the tidelands, I couldn't wait to take to the court. My days passed in a dreamy blur of pivots, stutter steps, crossover dribbles and outlet passes. That first summer, competing against players of the caliber of West, Hot Rod Hundley, Rod Thorn, Lenny Chappell, John

Wetzel and Art Heyman, my game improved. I was a baitfish struggling upstream with the leaping wild salmon, but I was swimming in the same river and happy to be there.

My second summer—the summer after The Citadel's dreadful 1965–66 season—I returned to Wahoo with an unshakable sense of mission. My time on the bench during my dismal junior year had frustrated me greatly, and the modest dreams I'd entertained as a player were quickly slipping away. I needed to improve my jump shot, learn how to run a basketball team, how to play smothering defense. After Wahoo was finished I signed up to be a counselor at Vic Bubas's camp at Duke as well as the one at Dartmouth run by Doggie Julian and a young Rollie Massimino.

That last blissful summer at Wahoo, I hung on every word spoken by the coaches and pros who conducted the clinics, as though they were bringing me newly discovered gospels that would point the way toward my salvation as an athlete.

In that summer of fiercely contested night games, with the campers filling the stands, the counselors split up into teams and went to war. I have never enjoyed basketball as much as I did then, nor have I ever played it so well or against better players.

Because I passed the ball, I often played on the team selected to highlight the visiting pro. The star that summer was Art Heyman, Duke's fast-talking, gum-chewing All-America who won the player of the year award his senior year, beating out Walt Hazzard and Bill Bradley. When Art entered the room his outrageous big-city ways became the focus of every eye. Art Heyman was to teach us a new sensibility that was then making its presence known in basketball circles across America. With no apologies, Art's game was urban, wise-ass Jewish, no-holds-barred and a hot dog at Nathan's after the game. He seemed to delight in and feed off the hatred of the Southern boys who filled the ranks of counselor—boys out of VPI, Hampden-Sydney, Wake Forest and Richmond, who were much more at ease with the aw-shucks, pass-the-biscuits-ma'am variety of heroism embodied by West and Thorn. Heyman came up to me before the jump ball and whispered, "It's showtime, Peanut. Get me the ball."

For 40 whirlwind minutes I threw passes to the best college basketball player of 1963. Wetzel, the dazzling forward from Virginia Tech who would later play for the Los Angeles Lakers and coach the Phoenix Suns, was first to guard Heyman, and he did it with rabid intensity. He covered Heyman like a sheen of sweat.

UVA's Chip Conner drew the assignment in the second half. Heyman ran his mouth the entire game. He was the first trashtalker I'd ever met, and there's nothing white Southern boys hate more than a trash-talker.

That night the overheated court shimmered with competitive zeal. I brought the ball upcourt, fast, but I was guarded by Spider Lockhart, a 6' 5" jumping jack with long arms who was always a threat to steal the ball. My dribbling—the best part of my game—got me around him. The moment I was free I'd look for Heyman, who was engaged in a wrestling match with Wetzel on the left side of the court. Heyman used his body brilliantly and always got himself in a perfect position. Then with a call of "Right here, Peanut," he'd motion with his huge hand where he wanted the ball.

That night I looked like an All-America point guard when I was flipping the ball to Art Heyman. He scored almost at will. One play stands out in my mind. Heyman stole a pass intended for Wetzel and raced downcourt. Both Conner and Wetzel ran with him.

Both men were faster and better leapers than Art. I'd broken right behind him and found myself filling the center lane, trailing the play by 10 feet.

At the top of the key, Heyman drove hard for the rim, rising upward with Conner and Wetzel. I didn't even see the moment when Heyman at the top of his leap flipped the ball back to me.

Running at full speed, I caught the pass belt high, as soft as an exchange of feathers between children. As the three players crashed to the floor in a pile of tangled limbs, I laid the ball into the hoop without a soul around me. It was the most beautiful and precisely delivered pass I had ever seen.

My task that summer at Camp Wahoo was to learn how to play tough defense. Tom Carmody, who coached at Bethel Park High, outside of Pittsburgh, said that defense took courage and commitment and the heart of a Siberian tiger. I burned that summer with a desire to help my team win games by refusing to let my man score a single point.

I lived for those night games. All I wanted to do was make beautiful passes to my teammates and to shut out the man I was guarding. I stayed low and in my man's face the whole game. Defense became something I dreamed about at night. I stopped Spider Lockhart on Tuesday and Hugh Corless of LaGrange College on Wednesday and the gifted Paul Long of Wake Forest on Thursday.

On Friday night I faced off with Johnny Moates of the University of Richmond, whom I had guarded on occasion in the Southern Conference during the previous two years. The games that summer were an offensive show put on for the enjoyment of the campers, a factor that worked in my favor. None of the pros or the counselors put much effort on the defensive end, except in those rare encounters with the big cats, like Heyman. My sudden dedication to defense struck some of the players as weird. Moates did not like it worth a damn.

I picked Moates up full-court my last night at my beloved Camp Wahoo, and I stuck to him like a wood tick. No one set a screen for him the whole game. No one helped him get open. His frustration turned to anger. The game was an agony for him, and he began to push me away.

"Just play ball, Conroy—this is bulls——," he yelled, then pushed me off him again.

I was not a step away from him the entire game, and Moates

did not score. When the final whistle sounded I was the happiest son of a bitch in the state of Virginia.

After the game I went out into the darkness and looked at the school buildings, watching the campers and counselors drift toward the dormitories. Young boys called my name and reached out to touch me as they flowed past.

Just then, someone slapped my fanny, disrupting my reverie. A large, dark shape moved past me on the left—Mel Thompson, my college coach, smoking, that slap his wordless praise, his acknowledgment of the hard work I'd put in that summer.

We come, then, to last games. We come to the Southern Conference Tournament game against Richmond at the end of the 1966–67 season. The Citadel had gone a dismal 8–16, but there had been optimism in our locker room after the defeat by Davidson in our last game, the thought that we had given a great effort and actually frightened the Wildcats on their court. Before the tournament our practices were lively and our enthusiasm catching. I was convinced we had as good a chance of winning the tournament as anyone. If we could win three games in a row, we could spend the rest of our lives calling ourselves champions.

Louis Chestnut wrote in *The News and Courier* of Charleston that "the Bulldogs will be led into the game by seniors Danny Mohr and Pat Conroy, who will be tasting their final competition. Mohr is a top rebounder who sports a 13.3 scoring average and Conroy, who has not been a starter until this year, has shot for an 11.8 average. The top scorer all season has been junior John DeBrosse. The small (5' 10") floor leader has a 14.4 average." Mr. Chestnut agreed that our team was peaking and could do some damage in the tournament.

When The Citadel was warming up in the Charlotte Coliseum, the place that represented the big time for any Southern guy, I noted something in the layup line that had been peculiarly absent for most of the year: forward Doug Bridges snorting and clapping and dunking with authority, if not fury. When

Bridges was lit up to play his best game, he could score 30 against any team in the country. He was the best athlete on our squad. He had as beautiful a body as I have ever seen. That night Bridges's eyes looked like the place where madness was born. I felt my team coming together at last.

Richmond's captain, Johnny Moates, was the 11th-leading scorer in the nation, with an average of 25 points per game. He had the same look that I had spotted in Bridges's eyes, and I took that to be a bad omen for me. I shook hands with the five Richmond players. Moates regarded me with contempt.

I met him as he crossed half-court each time, his four teammates lining up to pick for him in endless combinations. "Pick left!" I'd hear Bridges cry out behind me. "Pick right, Pat!" De-Brosse screamed. "Double pick!" Mohr cried out as Richmond center Buster Batts came out to set a high-post screen. Moates, 6′1″, lean and long and flowing, dribbled toward me. I went into my defensive crouch, slapped both hands on the shining floor and motioned for Moates to come and get it. Unfortunately, he accepted my invitation.

Sometimes Moates would dribble toward forward Tom Green, who would set a devastating pick, driving his bladelike knee into my left thigh. Fighting over the top of that pick, I would lose one step on Moates and he would go into the air, his eccentric-looking shot held high behind his head.

In one agonizing three-minute stretch in the first half, Moates came at me four times in a row, took me over a series of 10 picks and hit four long-range jumpers and, when I fouled him out of frustration on the last shot, a free throw. My teammates shouted encouragement. "Get 'em, Pat! Fight him, Pat! Fight your ass off!"

After Moates made the nine straight points, I changed my tactics. I realized he was planning to score 60 against me and was fully capable of doing it. I started taunting him: "Hey, Moates, don't you have some other guys on this team? Hey, Green, don't you like to shoot every now and then? I've seen ball hogs in my life, but this guy thinks he's the only guy out here."

"Shut up, Conroy," Moates said as he passed to Green for the first time.

"Wow, give him an assist," I screamed. "Nice pass, Moates. You're not a virgin anymore."

I looked like I knew what I was doing whenever I got the ball to Bridges or Mohr. Bridges played in a special realm that day, as though not subject to laws of physics. Every time I threw the ball to him I simply got out of his way. He made spinning, wheeling jump shots as he faded back toward the out-of-bounds lines, off-balance, uncontrolled.

Under the boards Mohr was scrapping for rebounds against the taller Batts. Our big guys were beating their big guys, keeping us in the game as Moates demonstrated the difference between a first-team All–Southern Conference guard and an also-ran like me. After taking me over three picks, he put up a jump shot that arched more steeply than a rainbow. When it scorched the net I felt like the sky was falling in on me. I heard Coach Thompson scream, "Fight him, Pat! Fight him for everything it's worth. Don't quit on me."

Those words ignited me, and I vowed to put Moates on the floor on his next possession. Then I had a better idea. We had run the court since the opening whistle, fast-breaking every time we touched the ball and keeping the lead for most of the first half. I noticed exhaustion on Moates's face with nine minutes left in the half, and I saw him gasp for breath as he guarded me. "Hey, Moates," I yelled. "You know what I noticed at Camp Wahoo last summer? You can't play defense worth s——."

"I can sure score, though, can't I, Conroy?" he said back.

"But Johnny, how you gonna keep me out of the paint?" And I blew by him, leaving him flat-footed at the top of the key. I was flying into the lane when the 6′8″ Batts moved out to intercept me with his hands held high. I flicked a bounce pass to Mohr, who laid it up. Each time we came downcourt I drove past Moates, and if no one came out to contest me, I laid it up. If Green picked me up, I passed to Bridges or anyone else who was open.

To end the half DeBrosse retrieved a jump ball and hit Mohr near the foul line. Mohr dribbled once, then launched a shot from half-court that swished through the net at the buzzer. Richmond led us 47–45. They had shot an amazing 65.5% from the field. Moates had lit me up for 21 points. I walked into that locker room feeling like the worst defensive player in America.

The Citadel came out in the second half burning and clawing for every loose ball and rebound, and at the 12-minute mark the score was 61–61. Every time Moates guarded me, I drove the lane hard. Richmond players knocked me to the floor again and again. I ended up shooting 14 free throws—a career high—and made 11 of them. Both Harvey Roberts and Larry Patterson fouled out taking me to the floor.

Six times during the game, Green's knee hit my thigh squarely, the pain as bad as anything I'd experienced on the court. It was smart, not dirty, basketball, and it was damaging my game. But I noticed that Moates was fighting for breath at the same time I was running out of gas.

We went ahead. They went ahead. We responded. They answered. The game was tied at 84. We stormed back and went ahead. Green scored. Mohr scored. Batts scored. The game went into overtime.

Gasping for air, I wished the time between the end of regulation and the beginning of overtime would stretch to an hour. When the horn sounded two of our practice players lifted me to my feet. I do not think I could've risen without them.

The overtime period proved to be just as racehorse and chaotic as the first 50 minutes. Our rebounding slowed down, and our big guys ran out of gas under the boards. Though we were the third-best rebounding team in the conference, Richmond's big men began to dominate the boards. Bridges and

Mohr had given everything they had. DeBrosse and I held each other up during foul shots and jump balls.

When Moates took me around Green's pick again, the Richmond forward's left knee knifed into my left thigh, and something tore. Mel called timeout, and I limped to the bench. Moates staggered back to the Richmond bench. My leg hurt so badly I thought I'd be hospitalized that night.

Mel screamed at the big guys to hit the boards, but they stared at him with oxen-like passivity. When the whistle blew again I reached out for teammates and they lifted me off my chair. I almost screamed when I put my full weight on the hurt leg. I grabbed DeBrosse and said, "John, I can't move my leg. You've got to take Moates for me."

"F—— you, Conroy, I'm not taking that son of a bitch," DeBrosse said. "He's your man."

In nausea and pain, I watched an exhausted Moates bring the ball upcourt. I had driven the lane the whole game, and there was nothing he could do but chase me. I had scored 25 points against him, equaling my career high. There were pro scouts in the building that day, and I'm sure they noted the unearthly skills that Moates brought to the task of scoring. I hope they also noted that a guard who could not stop Conroy might have difficulty with Jerry West or Oscar Robertson.

I had my hands on my knees when I saw DeBrosse make his move. Because of his fatigue, Moates was incautious as he dribbled. He was bouncing the ball too high when DeBrosse stuck a hand in and swiped it clean. DeBrosse broke for our basket, and Moates, embarrassed and spent, did not even give pursuit. I took one step out of instinct, then stopped out of exhaustion and lack of character. I stood on Richmond's foul line and watched DeBrosse's triumphant flight down the court. I remember being surprised that he was taking the ball straight in instead of laying it in off the glass. When DeBrosse took off, there was an exaggerated bounce to his leap, as though he had jumped higher than he ever had before, but his form was picture-perfect. I had never seen DeBrosse miss a layup. He released the basketball at the height of his jump. The ball nicked the front of the rim, bounced off the back of the rim, then rolled out to the left. Moates sprinted to retrieve the ball, and Richmond scored to go up by one with less than two minutes to play.

They scored. We scored. With two seconds left, a jump ball was called. Mohr tried to tap it to Bridges but hit it too high, and the ball was rolling out of bounds when the buzzer sounded. We had lost the game 100–98. Our terrible season had come to a fitting end. I stood beneath the lights for the last time, then limped to the locker room.

I sat by my locker for a brief moment. The first sob caught me by surprise, and the second one was so loud that it didn't seem to come from me at all. I wept as I had never wept before in public. I could not stop myself. I was lost in the overwhelming grief I felt at losing my game, losing basketball as a way to define myself in a world that was hostile and implacable to me. I removed my jersey and put my face into the number 22, and my sweat mingled with my tears. I gave it up, gave basketball up, gave my game up, the one I played so badly and adored so completely. Each one of my teammates squeezed my shoulder as he passed on the way to the shower. Basketball had lifted me up and given me friends whom I got to call teammates. The game gave me moments in which I brought crowds of strangers to their feet, calling out my name. The game had allowed me to be carried off the court in triumph. The game had allowed me to like myself a little bit, and at times the game had even allowed me to love the beaten, ruined boy I was.

I have always been a closet weeper. When my father would take me apart as a child, I could not cry in front of him or the beating became, instantly, more savage and dangerous. I learned to disembody myself from the boy who was getting beaten. Later, I would cry for much of the night for that kid whom I abandoned when he was being torn up. I never thought of him as belonging to me.

COACH

The next morning Mel Thompson, who had never offered me a compliment, said in *The News and Courier*, "Pat Conroy gave another great performance. That kid gets more mileage out of his talent than any player I have ever coached."

PAT CONROY is the best-selling author of *The Great Santini*, *The Lords of Discipline*, *The Prince of Tides*, *Beach Music*, and *My Losing Season*.

When I Was Young

BY BUZZ BISSINGER

FOR MOST OF MY LIFE I've never been much of a competitive athlete. Maybe the mistake was in going to Andover, where everybody seemed to be blond and beautiful and six foot ten. At five foot six and Jewish, I felt like a mangy Lilliputian, slow and plodding and out of my league to the gorgeous gentiles who so seamlessly ran and threw and skated. Since sports were compulsory each term, I was reminded daily of my haplessness. I played football into my sophomore year, a 145-pound pulling guard with no choice but to stay low, very very low, aim at ankles in the vain hope nobody would see me coming.

The coach hated me and I hated the coach. He had no use for me, his eyes crisscrossing into exasperated tourniquets whenever he saw me, the clear suggestion that I didn't take it seriously enough, because I guess I didn't. Two hours before game time, I'd psych myself up by walking down to the local Friendly's to engorge myself on Fribbles and Big Beefs and lanky oil-soaked fries on the logical assumption that I was never going to get in until the very end, when the score was 40-to-nothing our favor or their favor. Which left me with no recourse but to toss my cookies during one brutally hot day after he put me out there for the opening kickoff, no doubt aware, in the way that coaches are somehow aware of everything, of my pregame binge.

I went on to Penn, where I latched on to the college newspaper. I became one of those nerds who wrote about sports as some meager substitute for actually playing them. I wrote mostly nasty things about athletes. I did it because I envied them, secretly admired them, felt inadequate around them, and they were smart enough to recognize the motivation. They knew what I wanted, some sort of attention on equal footing, which is exactly why they never gave it to me, treated me with the casual boredom of picking a scab off an old insect bite.

But I had a moment when I was a member of the haves, a part of sports instead of some conflicted voyeur into it. It occurred when I was still in elementary school at the Dalton School in Manhattan, still growing then, my muscle memory and coordination working in a lockstep that surprised and gratified me. I could hit and catch a baseball. I played an earnest guard in basketball. I wasn't a bad running back. I still remember the apex of my athletic career, a misdirection against Trinity in eighth grade on the first play from scrimmage in which I cut to the outside and peeled off 50 yards and could have maybe gone all the way if I hadn't just gotten tired and bailed out of bounds.

Which is why the coach I remember the most, liked the most, wanted to please the most, worshipped the most, was Coach Boyers.

I haven't seen or talked to Coach Boyers since I was thirteen, a passage of thirty-seven years. I'm pretty sure that he's no longer coaching at Dalton. For all I know he may no longer be alive. But I remember him in the way that memory is most useful, through my own psychological needs, which is also to say that much of what I do remember may not even be accurate. But in a journalistic career of seeing coaches up close and personal in all sorts of different phases, elementary and high school and college and pro, it is Coach Boyers who stands out the most to me. I just think of him as a coach, The Coach, probably because he also intersected with my own brief period of grace. He recognized me, saw some talent there, or at least I think he saw some talent there, and even if it's all apocryphal, I find my life much more pleasant thinking that he did since all boys at birth really do want to be athletes.

I remember the whistle around his neck, the cold lump of silver nestled between the breastplates. I remember the way he blew it, that short perfect shrieky shrill able to freeze anxious and rambunctious elementary school kids dead in their tracks within a hundred-mile radius. I remember him being tall. I remember Coach Boyers with a thick mop of black hair, although I also confess I may well be confusing him with Clete Boyer, who played a mean third base for the Yankees during the same time frame of the 1960s. I even remember the smell of him, liniment with just a little splash of sweat sock and sneaker.

I also remember that voice, strong, stentorian, brief in its output and stinting of praise. He understood the coaching yin and yang, inaccessibility a form of attraction, throaty and hearty but never too friendly. When he said something to you, anything really, it left you floating on air at the dinner table.

PARENTS: How was school today?

CHILD: Really really good.

PARENTS (pleased, relieved, surprised): Well that's wonderful. What happened?

CHILD: Coach Boyers said something to me.

PARENTS (slightly quizzical): Well that's nice. What did Coach Boyers say?

CHILD: He told Curtis and me to stop screwing around and put our sneakers back on or else he'd throw us out of the gym.

PARENTS (now quite concerned): That's it?

CHILD (dreamily): That's it.

Coach Boyers could be strict when we screwed around with our sneakers, or tried to stuff our socks down each other's shirts, or sought out a particularly easy mark for a stealth wedgie, or ran around the gym in circles like little speed freaks. He didn't like it when we didn't listen, and generally being little spoiled pissants of privilege from the upper east and west sides of Manhattan, there were times when we didn't listen. But he squelched it like a dictator, because all good coaches are dictators, intuitively know the line between wanting kids to have an okay time and wanting kids to fear you just a little bit because it might be reflected in their physical performance. He believed in kids. I remember that about him as well. He didn't simply go through the motions with us. He never seemed bored, never had that hazy faraway look in his eyes of, Please God, if there is a God, please please teleport me to somewhere else because I don't think I can bear another second of watching these morons play dodgeball.

He took sports seriously, viewed it as an exquisite way of expression in the same way that art and music were exquisite forms of expression. So he insisted that we take it seriously. He taught us how to care about sports, to honor it, feel the thrill of it, that competition, healthy competition, whether it was dodgeball or basketball or football, was sanctity for the soul. He had that camp counselor voice capable of rousing even the fish out of the lake for 6 a.m. breakfast, but as far as I can remember he never abused it or used it gratuitously. There was always a little wink in his eye, the small but comforting sense that, Hey, I may be the coach and you may be the players, but we're still in this together. Sort of . . .

Although it sounds hopelessly outdated in today's world where sports has become a ridiculous matter of life and death at every stage of youth, he made competing fun. He understood the proper alchemy of emphasis. I will always feel a certain indebtedness to Coach Boyers for that. I will always feel a certain gratitude, just as I also feel compelled to explain after nearly forty years that the only reason my sneakers were off was because my shoelaces were untied and Curtis, being Curtis, knew a good opportunity when he saw one.

———————————————

BUZZ BISSINGER is a Pulitzer Prize winner and the author of the bestselling book *Friday Night Lights*, about the impact of high school football on a small town in Texas. He is also the author of *Three Nights in August*, a book on the art and craft of a major league baseball manager, published by Houghton Mifflin.

Passing It On

BY JOHN EDGAR WIDEMAN

ED FLEMING, WHOM I'D LAST SEEN . . . when . . . where . . . now here in Warden's in his charcoal gray, fashionable, gangster-shouldered suit in the midst of a crowd of mourners congregated just inside the entrance of Parlor A.

After we'd talked a minute or so and he had to go back inside and I needed to return to Omar, he said, "Uh-huh. My mom lived on Finance. For a good long while before she passed. Heard her speak highly of Mrs. French. And Mrs. French your grandmother, huh. Hmmm. I never knew that. Heard my mother praise Mrs. French many times. Good to see you, man. You take care of yourself now, John. Don't be a stranger. Holler next time you're in town."

John. I don't believe I'd ever heard Ed Fleming say my first name. A baptism of sorts, in Warden's of all places. He'd always called me Wideman on the court. The surname detached, objectified, like when it's entered in a scorebook. *Wideman.* A clean slate for each new game. Every game you're obligated, challenged to fill the line of empty slots following your name with field goals attempted and made, foul shots hit or missed, personal fouls, rebounds, steals, turnovers, assists, blocked shots. Who Wideman *is* is drastically simplified. You are the numbers, period. Nothing else matters—where you came from, who your daddy or grandmammy might be—you're just a player. *Wideman.* The numbers—over a course of a game, over the course of a season, a career—accumulate or not, may resonate or not when another player says your name. You get used to people observing the last-name-only convention until *Wideman*'s a tag that doesn't exactly belong to you or anyone. *Wideman* only signifies the numbers racked up, then wiped clean so your name's a question mark each time a game begins. And unfair though it may be, the sole numbers really mattering are always the ones in progress—when they're skimpy, they peg you as a chump, forget how you kicked ass the game before or the last dozen games.

On the playground no uniforms and numbers identify you. A single name's enough on Homewood court, and if it's your surname, *Wideman*, it's said with little intentional chill of depersonalization, the way a referee calls you by your uniform number, foul on *Ten*, in high school or college games. Strictly business on the playground too, when somebody chooses you in the meatmarket picking of teams for the first serious run of the day. Alternating choices till a limit of ten spots filled, the two guys choosing—they earn the privilege by being the first to hit a foul shot—call you by your last name or maybe a nickname: Got Smith—Gimme Pooky—Got Jones—Take Sky. You can go years, a lifetime, playing alongside guys and know them only by their court handles. Read something in a newspaper about one of your basketball buddies, and never know it's him, *Snobs*, inside the disguise of a whole, proper name. You'll have to hear the good news or bad news over again on the sidelines from somebody who tells the story with the court name in place. *D'you hear about Snobs, man.*

Ed Fleming had always called me Wideman in my coming-up days. For him to acknowledge a life for me off the court would have been highly improbable back then. Why would he care who I was. Or who I thought I was. He was a legend. He ruled. He was a grown man, born into a different age set, with different running buddies who'd come up hoping together, getting in and out of trouble together, and obviously no outsider could enter that cohort, just like nobody could leave it. Because I was precocious on the court, my age-group friends seldom accompanied me when I played ball. In some ways it meant I stuck out like a sore thumb. I didn't mind being a special case, didn't like the loneliness. No crew to hang with on walks to the court or back home again. No chance to replay games in our words, from our rookies' perspective. No opportunity to boast or tease each other or badmouth some old head turkey who thought he was God's gift. Over time I'd discover half the fun of playground ball resided in these rituals that extended the game, the imagined recreations like a good preacher retelling Adam and Eve, jazzing up his version with parables and homilies and metaphor not only to stitch together a way to live in the world but exemplify a style of doing it with his words. No crew meant I had not one to watch my back unless an older player chose to look out for me. Literally a look. One look was all it took to dissuade a bully from coming down too hard on the youngblood. Rules, consequences communicated in a single glance from one of the enforcers like Ed Fleming nobody's hardly going to the mat to challenge.

To some of his peers he was *Ed* or *Fleming*. Always *Ed Fleming* in my mind. Both names necessary, three inseparable syllables, more incantation or open-sesame mantra than a name. A mini–sound bite like those heroic epithets identifying characters—Ox-eyed Hera, Swift-heeled Achilles—whose adventures I followed in the *Golden Book of Greek Myth* or in *Classics Illustrated* comic versions of the *Iliad* and *Odyssey*. See the guy down low, backing into the *key, pat, pat, pat,* demanding inch by inch the space he needs. That's not just any old Ed or Fleming. He's *the* Ed Fleming. Implacable. Irresistible. Each dribble a hammerstroke staking out his claim. *Pat, pat.* Both names, all three syllables spoken internally, honored, even when I don't say them aloud. Even now, forty years later in Warden's, when I call him *Ed,* the single, naked sound coming out of my mouth almost as surprising for me to hear as hearing *John* pass through Ed Fleming's lips.

To my father, Edgar, he would have been *Fleming*, one of a vintage crop of good, young players rising up behind him. Fleming, Stokes, and their teammates, winners at Homewood's Westinghouse High of the state title, kids good enough to groom and be wary of simultaneously, especially the Fleming boy since one day soon he might also encroach upon *Eddie*, my father's court name. My father, Edgar Wideman, would have taken a prodigy like Ed Fleming under his wing, tested him, whipped on him unmercifully, protected him with hard stares if anybody got too close to actually damaging the precious talent, the fragile ego and vulnerable physique of a large, scrappy, tough kid just about but not quite ready to handle the weight and anger of adult males who used the court to certify their deepest resources of skill, determination, heart, resources they could publicly exhibit and hone few other places in a Jim Crow society. Homewood court a threshing ground, and the weak better not stray too close to the blades. The mean could find release for some of the best things in themselves, and of course, that included dangerous stuff too. Play not exactly play. No-no-no. Winning and losing cut deep. Very, very deep. Yet ability, a refined repertoire of hoop skill enabling you to win more often than lose, not the thing that gave you a passing or failing grade on the court. The real examination results, the score that counts so much it keeps the play, for all its ferocity, about more than winning or losing, registers inside each player. When you step on or off the court, how do other players look at you and you at them. What name do they call you by, how is the saying of your name inflected. Among the infinitely nuanced possibilities a particular pronunciation might suggest, which one is communicated to you, to others when you're greeted, when you are picked for a squad, when players talk about you and you're not around, when they are not around and you talk to yourself about the court, about the game, replaying the action in your mind on that private, private screen at home at night, in bed, recalling a whole hot afternoon and you have to fill in the slots, the blanks, where your name goes into the imagining. What is it, how is it said.

To Ed Fleming, *Wideman* would be the respected name of one of the old heads who broke him in and also the name of a kid coming in behind him. Wideman *père*. Wideman *fils*. Did he ever have trouble distinguishing us, keeping us straight. Did he concern himself with policing such a fine line. Something he once said to me indicated he didn't always differentiate. In Great Time what goes round comes round. After hip-checking me *blam* into the fence just behind the poles and backboard when we were both after a loose ball, or maybe it was when he lifted me off my feet and tossed me a yard or so from the sweet spot I thought I was strong enough to deny him, bodying him away from it for a couple of seconds till he decided to show me that day what he could bring to bear if he really needed a spot as much as I needed him out of it, Ed Fleming whispered words to this effect: Your daddy was extra rough on me, and boy, I'm sure gonna return the favor. Gonna give you a hard row to hoe, son, and don't start crybabying or calling fouls neither, not today, youngblood. If you can't stand the heat, get out of the kitchen.

So Ed Fleming's hoop war with my father was not over in one generation. He revisited it through me. Hard truths imprinted on Edgar Wideman's will and flesh by some anonymous bunch of old guys hoping, then imprinted by my father on Ed Fleming, coming home to roost in my bruised feelings and meat, the knobby-boned body I prayed daily would hurry up and get padded by muscle like Ed Fleming's.

What my father had reaped and sown would sprout up again when the weather turned warm enough for outdoor runs to commence at Homewood court. The game, its lore and lessons. For instance, *Never forget*—not where you came from nor what's coming up behind you, a lesson concretely applied when you're dribbling the ball, leading a fast break attack on an opponent's basket, when it's a matter of peripheral vision, of the Janus look backward and forward so you're aware of who's in front of you and behind, also mapping 360 degrees all the other players' positions on the court, the kaleidoscoping shifts, the evolving opportunities and hazards your rush to the hoop engenders. More abstractly applied, the lesson reminds you to take seriously your place in time, in tradition, within the community of players. Ed Fleming and the other vets teaching me to take my time, no matter the speed I'm traveling. Teaching me to be, not to underreach or overreach myself. Either way you cheated the game, cheated your name, the name in progress, the unfolding narrative, told and retold, backward, forward, sideways, inside out. Of who you would turn out to be as you played.

I learned, among other things, to recognize and be grateful for a helping hand, learned it might not be exactly the kind of hand I thought I wanted, maybe it would be a rough hand, a bitter pill, but I was learning to appreciate different hands on their different terms. Above all learning not to be so intent on moving forward I turned my back on the ones behind who might need my hand or have one to offer.

Learned about time as I was learning the game. Because the game is time. Not time out from the real business of life. Not simply play time. Time. Like good gospel music, the game brings time, tells time, announces the good news that there is Great Time beyond clock time and this superabundance, this sphere where you can be larger than you are, belongs to nobody. It's too vast. Everlasting. *Elsewhere.* Yet you can go there. It's in your hands. White people nor nobody else owns it. It's waiting for you to claim it. The game conjures Great Time, gives it and takes it away. Clock time, linear time irrelevant while the game's on—two teams might battle fifteen minutes to complete a run or twice as long or till dark hides the court forever if neither side pushes ahead by two baskets in a deuce (win by two) contest. The game trumps time, supersedes it. Good hoop, like good rhythm-and-blues music, alerts you to what's always there, abiding, presiding, master of ceremonies ready to empower your spirit and body, the beat lurking, dancing in all things whether you're conscious of its presence or not. Great Time your chance to be. To get down. Out. To do it right. Right on time. The game, again like gospel music, propogates rhythm, a flow and go, a back beat you can tune in to so time's lonely, featureless stretch feels as charged, as sensuous, as accessible a medium as wind or water. You don't really own game time, but the fit feels so close to perfect you can't help believing on occasion it belongs to you.

JOHN EDGAR WIDEMAN was born in Washington, D.C., and raised in the Homewood section of Pittsburgh. He attended the University of Pennsylvania, where he was elected to Phi Beta Kappa and became an All–Ivy League forward on the basketball team, and studied philosophy as a Rhodes scholar at Oxford University. Currently teaching at Brown University, he has taught at numerous other universities, including the University of Pennsylvania, where he founded and chaired the African American Studies Department. He is the first writer to win the PEN/Faulkner Award twice, in 1984 for *Sent for You Yesterday* and in 1990 for *Philadelphia Fire*. His nonfiction book *Brothers and Keepers* received a National Book Critics Circle nomination, and his memoir *Fatheralong* was a finalist for the National Book Award. Most recently, he was awarded an O. Henry Award for best short story of the year in 2000 and the Rea Prize for short fiction in 1998. *God's Gym* is his twentieth book.

Prudent Fitness:
A Panegyric

BY ANDREW SOLOMON

I ALWAYS HATED EXERCISE. When I asked my mother once whether she thought I had suffered any early traumas, she told me that learning to walk had been my greatest ordeal. "You spoke so early and so easily," she said, "and it took you so long to be coordinated enough to make it across a room." That was my legacy. And because I never liked doing things at which I could not excel, I remained long stranded in words over motion. We live in a changed world, one in which the benefits of exercise are commonplace. If my parents were transposed with their young children into the twenty-first century, they would insist on exercise, I am sure. Forty years on, there might as well have been a social revolution. But when I was little it wasn't one of the health matters that obsessed my mother and father. Not smoking was very important, and so were eating right and staying thin. Exercise was a taste that some people had and others— including us—lacked.

When I was in elementary and high school, I would beg my mother for gym excuses, coming up with all kinds of reasons and pretexts: my hair hurt; or I needed to spend that period studying for a chemistry test; or I had lost my athletic shorts. I hated my gym teachers: they were the villains of my worst nightmares. There was the snide Mr. Slaybaugh, handsome and tough, who demanded push-ups and push-ups, as though they were a ransom. There was Mr. Lombardi, thick as two planks, for whom I was subhuman in my inability to play football; he barely knew my name after eight years of painful interaction. There was Mr. Beisinger, who I in retrospect think was rather a nice man, though that possibility never crossed my mind at the time; he made me run. Mr. Anderson was just a thug with a whistle. Their names and faces are etched forever in my memory: Mr. Quinn (wrestling—at least I had the advantage of being a featherweight in those days); Mr. Kramp (who implausibly coached the swim team); Mr. Brown (endlessly correcting my forehand). I can see in my mind's eye the private tennis teachers too, to whom my mother optimistically sent me, assuring me that knowing the game was a great social asset. There was also the guy my parents hired when I was in second grade, Dana—I called him my gym tutor. He decided to teach me soccer because no one else in those days was trying to learn soccer and so I might conceivably have an advantage in the game. But that too came to naught.

When I graduated from high school, I swore I would never again go to the gym. I had a languid career as an undergraduate: I slept a lot, and ate a lot, and drank a lot, and read and wrote a lot, and the miracle of a lucky metabolism kept me slender on this regimen, and I hadn't yet begun to think about muscula-ture—my own, really, or that of other people. I suppose I thought that having a beautiful body, like having a gift for math-ematics, would be lovely but had nothing to do with who I was, or with my circle of friends. I had one friendly acquaintance who visited the gym almost daily, and had the looks to prove it—indeed, pictures of him in university athletic gear were at a later date available from the Shocking Gray catalog, which sold mildly homoerotic images to middle Americans and shipped them in plain brown wrappers so that pesky mailmen and neighbors wouldn't find out what was afoot. Paul tried to per-suade me that the gym was fun, and I dallied with the idea of at least checking it out, but gym was still in my mind a euphemism for hell, and I finished four square years of study without ever even finding out where the door to the building was or how to get a locker there. All this coincided with a sensual life in which being young was such an asset that having a wholly undeveloped body was scant hindrance. I wasn't yet seeking relationships with my peers, and to the predatory crowd I accommodated, what I had was more than enough. Physical pleasure was thrilling but quick and passing. I was for all intents and purposes disembodied.

When I finished grad school, however, and went forth into the real world, I had to accept the waning of my precocity, and it was at about this time that I graduated into mainstream sexuality. I had my first serious boyfriend, and we were both tall and lean and neither of us was muscular and we were both young, and I was living in England, where the body culture had not yet accelerated. Until that time, I had asked very little of my body, except that it contain my mind and heart. I was all feelings and intellect; I believed that I had a soul that was barely contingent on the flesh. Then suddenly, I wanted to be physically of the physical world. But I also wanted to be a Nobel laureate, and to own a yacht, and the physical world seemed to me as obscure as such achievement and position, to be a reality in which others had commerce but which would to me be forever obscure.

A few years later I moved to New York, and at about that time, when I was twenty-eight, I expressed to a dear friend my frustration with the body-conscious gay culture of New York, and she said, "If you want your body to be happy in sex and on display, you have to pay some attention to it. Try exercise. You might find that it's worth it." It was something of a revelation. As I looked around at the powerful bodies that flaunted themselves on the Chelsea streets, I suddenly wondered whether I could look like that, and what it would feel like, and what possibilities it would open up. I had heard much of the joy of being in shape and wondered how it would feel to climb five flights of stairs without getting winded. It was like imagining a different person, a person I had never thought to be. I had always been a great believer in self-invention, however, and I decided to undertake a smooth transformation.

A college acquaintance was going out with a guy who did some personal training, and at a party she had one night, I got into a conversation with him about his practice. He said he thought I had good potential. "Look at those long, lean muscles you have. You could build them up," he said. No one had ever even suggested that. "And you'd feel better. It's not healthy, the sedentary life." I remember the first time I went skydiving, and the leap into the blue was no more startling to me than the leap into that first conversation with Dièry Prudent. It was the first step in a shift of my relationship to authority and my relationship to my own mass. I said I wasn't sure, didn't know, had to think. He proposed that we try a session. He said he would come to my house and that we could do an initial assessment there. I was relieved that my inadequacies wouldn't have to be flaunted in a room full of adept strangers, the disheartening gym of my imagination. We settled on a Tuesday, and I looked forward to it with an unsettled anxiety like that of entering a new psychiatric treatment or career.

Dièry is mesmeric. Tall and strong and self-assured, he has a quality of profound conviction, a quiet authority that is persuasive but not obnoxious. He was born in Haiti and has skin so black that it seems almost blue. He has a shaved head of noble proportions and large eyes and thick, clearly delineated lips. He has a perfect body, the muscles all arranged as neatly as they were in the anatomy model we studied in ninth grade biology class. He maintains himself the way a museum maintains its art, or a restaurant its food. His voice comes from quite deep in him, and he forms his words with precision; he has no particular accent, but his speech is specific to him and like no one else's. He is one of those people who accomplishes by whispering what less impressive people accomplish by yelling. I envied his then-girlfriend, later his wife, but it was an affectionate envy rather than a lascivious one; it was not that I wanted to have Dièry, but that I took innate pleasure in the contemplation of his personal beauty and elegance, enjoyed being in his thrall. And I admired his aura of serenity, which made me think that from physical power might come inner peace. From our first meeting, he had a quiet optimism about my body that I had never known myself. He knew intuitively what I could and couldn't do, and he set a realistic pace, and didn't drive me too soon to do too much. But he made me believe in possibilities, and he held fitness and musculature out to me like promises. I was, in fact, a weakling, the sort of weedy young man who struggles to get his suitcase off the baggage claim carousel and dumps it awkwardly on the luggage cart as quickly as possible. I hated having to carry anything anywhere. I went to the beach and watched people swim from the indolent safety of a lounge chair; I usually kept my shirt on. I felt that there was no point standing when one might sit, and no point sitting if one could lie down. I was skinny by birth, with long arms that were about the same girth below the shoulder that they were at the wrist, and toothpick legs, and a flat chest with no particular lines or demarcations on it. I had the tautness of youth, but there was no strength in my body. Dièry acted from the start as though I were dormant where I had thought I was dead. The strength of that confidence was re- markable—the belief seemed to matter even more than the qualities in which he believed. Dièry's father was a sometime preacher, and Dièry inherited the ability to persuade others into faith itself.

Let us be quite honest: I started this whole business out of vanity rather than out of concern for health. As I've grown older, the vanity has come to seem a bit futile, and the maintenance of good health has become increasingly necessary, but the original impulse was founded in the visual. Dièry does not judge by sur- faces, but he likes both beauty and rigor, and was game to in- dulge my wish for a dream body. We targeted, at first, the muscle groups that would show the most, and did biceps and chest repeatedly. The rest we snuck in as necessary to make me strong enough to look stronger. We had to work on the most basic things: the idea of good form, for example, and the right ways to breathe. I learned to recognize good and bad pain, the kind without which there was no gain and the kind that signaled we had gone too far. I learned to like the good pain—not the pain in the moment of reaching, but the pain that lingered afterwards and made me feel that my body was alive and that I was doing things to it. I remember those first sessions, and the sense that I was entering a new realm of experience. It turned out that genes were against me, and that even a great deal of exercise would never give me the rippling physique of a Calvin Klein model. The way my body looks has changed, but it does not approach the Platonic ideals I once had in mind. Nonetheless, my feeling about my body has altered dramatically. I take my shirt off on the beach. I am ready for sex when it comes. I no longer think of my physical self as the weak link to my emotional and intellectual self.

It would be rhetorically satisfying to say that Dièry and I interacted in a pure realm of physicality, but that would be a lie. Part of Dièry's success with me—a large part—has to do with the fact that he has many of the qualities I have traditionally admired. He is someone whose intelligence would have allowed him to function very well in the realms where I spend most of my time, but who chose to devote himself to corporeal vitality instead. I had long held the defensive belief that people who were smart enough to read and write at an advanced level would of course choose doing so over a life of the body, which seemed to me to be lower on some great totem pole of superior and inferior activities. But Dièry is as quick as anyone I know. He occasionally writes articles for newspapers, and even to my fussbudget eye, he is a lively, lucid, incisive writer. His conversation sparkles. His language is elegant. His eye for narrative is impeccable. Further, he is a person of rare insight, who can express that insight persuasively. It helped that he had these qualities and it helped that he valued them; I couldn't have gone through the abject humiliation of exposing my physical weakness to someone who wasn't able to understand and appreciate, to some extent to share, my strengths.

It took a long time for me to understand Dièry as pre-Cartesian. It wasn't that he had chosen the body over the mind, but that he didn't see such a great gap between them. The fact that he could bench-press 240 pounds and also write a poem didn't seem anomalous to him. I know that there are many trainers who could have done as good a job as he did of helping me to build up my strength, and that would have been terrific, but with them I might not have found this model for an integrated self, and that has been perhaps his greatest gift to me. The way he has bestowed it—through example and instruction—has been uncommonly generous. In learning from him, I found a great intimacy. When I first met Dièry, I did not think of being his friend. I thought that we were from different planets. Over time, I awakened to his kindness, to a certain stern sweetness that glimmered in our sessions together. And then bit by bit I became aware that in choosing to be a personal trainer, he had opted to be not only physical, but also, more broadly, caretaking. Dièry can't bear to leave anyone's suffering or flaws untended. This quality can be extremely aggravating: he will come to my house and helpfully tell me what is wrong with it, and he will edit parts of my life that I was happy to leave as they were. He has summed up the shortcomings of my various romantic partners with a disagreeable acuity. He can be a busybody, and he is incredibly bossy. But he also waters the plants in my garden, because he notices that they are thirsty and can't bear to leave them to fight the heat of the sun (as I can). He pats my dog. He notices my moods, and makes way for them.

For Dièry, personal training is a ministry. He can be tough on making me do my crunches, but he also has a surprising tenderness. He cares deeply about my well-being, and when I am ailing, he is there to heal me. Sometimes when I'm not performing up to par, he will get impatient. "We're here to work," he'll say. But sometimes, very occasionally, he'll say, "Your heart's not in this today," and give me a massage instead. On those occasions I sometimes want to say, "No, I can really do it, watch me"— but some part of the emotional dynamic between us involves my deferring to his sudden gentleness.

There are three cardinal intimacies assigned to people I pay: the dentist, who puts his hands in my mouth; the psychiatrist, who meddles with my mind and expects total honesty; and the trainer, who tells me what to do, and I do it. I have never supposed that the psychiatrist or the dentist were friends, though I am fond of both of them. But with Dièry, the lines around the intimacy are blurrier. At times, the relationship seems intensely erotic—not because it has any actual sexual content or even desire, but because the subjugation and physicality are so plangent. I couldn't do this with a person who bored me.

We found a commonality in emotion. Dièry, for all his gloss and finish, has grappled with depression from time to time, and I will always remember how, when I was suffering from catastrophic depression in the months after my mother's death, Dièry would coax me along, painful step by step, to keep physical movement in my life. That is part of what got me through. I will never forget the time he came over just before I was supposed to do a reading from my novel. I was in an acute depressive episode, a gibbering mess, wracked with sobs, barely able to move. I remember how Dièry ran a bath for me and put me in it and sprayed me down with cold water to bring me up to speed. I had by then learned to trust him enough to be childlike with him. That hadn't been an easy path. When I was growing up, someone once asked me what I'd like to be when I grew up, and I said I wanted to be intimidating. I tend to deal with uncomfortable subjects—such as physical fitness—with chill austerity. I put forth a cliff-front. With Dièry, I allow myself to be shockingly vulnerable. All my imperfections, physical and cerebral, are on ample display. It runs contrary to my nature, and it happens through a great deal of determination on my part, but all the self-discipline in the world wouldn't allow me to do it with most people. I can't lift my portcullis alone. Words keep me safe; few people can get around them and to the nonverbal part of me.

It has become oddly unclear for whom I am doing all this exercise. Presumably it is for myself, but I cannot bring myself to do it when I am traveling, or when Dièry is traveling. To do so feels like talking to myself, almost a little crazy. Exercise exists for me as a form of dialogue; the onanistic pleasures of the body seem substantially less attractive to me than the communicative ones. I sometimes work out with Dièry, looking all the while at the clock, hoping he'll leave. This is madness: I am paying him to stay. I should have the buyer's right to ignore him. But though my imprisonment is voluntary, its rules are absolute. I seldom say no. Dièry is not only the guide for but also the occasion of my exertions. The relationship appears to be embarrassing because it involves the sublimation of my ego, but I don't find it embarrassing as I live it. I don't like having people tell me what to do, and I ordinarily avoid situations in which I am ordered around, but I seek out this one. Dièry definitely plays the carrot and the stick; he often exhorts me to do more, keep going, not give up, but he can also seem disappointed, as though his every hope of happiness hung on my managing four more reps. And sometimes he can be short with me, irritable if he feels I am not trying. He has a particular hand gesture that he uses when I'm on the exercycle, a sort of rotating of his finger rapidly to suggest rapid rotation of the wheel, that makes me feel like a trained seal or a miscreant dog. I put up with it. Dièry is for me a figure of authority, and I submit to the power I vest in him.

I am a person who fights against structure. I grew up in a household in which everything was orderly and scheduled. My mother could tell you three weeks in advance what she was doing, what time she was doing it, and what she was planning to wear to it. I, on the contrary, like to make plans, then change them, respond to the moment, leave for a weekend in Europe on four hours' notice, and so on. Part of the purpose in becoming a writer was to have the absolute maximum of freedom. If I woke up on a Wednesday and the weather was nice, I could go off and take a walk, and if I had a deadline I could stay up all night to meet it. I could go to bed at 10 p.m. one night and at 5 a.m. the next. But having a personal trainer doesn't work like that. Dièry and I had to settle a time between us, and I had to stick with it. For twelve years now, I have seen Dièry at 11 a.m. five or six days a week when I am in New York. Because I hate getting up to an alarm—it feels like too brutal a way to start the day—I tend to let Dièry come and wake me up. I go to bed most nights around 3 a.m. and get up when Dièry arrives. He is the first person I see, having slept through my partner's earlier departure.

In the beginning, it was all weights, and a little stretching. Bench presses, flies, squats, lunges, unilateral and bilateral curls (I wanted to do a gay weight-lifting book called *Curling Iron*), crunches, super-crunches, jackhammer crunches, twisties, rotators, overhead presses, pullovers, tricep extensions, clean-and-jerks, bent-over rows, upright rows, standing upright rows, shrugs, incline presses, close grips, wide grips, deadlifts, bent-knee deadlifts—the list seems nearly infinite, and just writing it makes my muscles twinge. Over time, we began to incorporate aerobic exercise and now we spend half the session keeping my heartbeat high (pulse 150 if we can). I ride an exercise bicycle and Dièry cheers or prods me on. I know this seems to outsiders like a waste of his time; I should be able to do the aerobic work by myself, but I can't. It takes the interest of another person to sustain my own interest.

I am still about eighteen pounds over my ideal weight. I have tried dieting, and diet pills too. It hasn't been a big success. To have both to do something I don't like doing and to give up something I very much liked doing seems too much. I gladly exercise and eat, and could well not exercise and not eat, but having to exercise and not eat seems too high a price to pay for any kind of beauty. Dièry and I talk about my weight whenever it goes down, and leave the subject whenever it goes up, fluctuating in a ten-pound region over periods of weeks or months. I can feel his look at my belly, and from time to time he has tried to talk me through my eating habits—but there, privacy reigns. I feel I am vulnerable enough to Dièry without adding this insult to the injury. I know about diet, and when and how and to what degree I act on that knowledge, I reserve to myself.

There are three unsought consequences of working with Dièry. First is the jazz. Dièry is passionate about jazz and knows a great deal about it. My course of jazz instruction has been an accessory to my course of physical fitness training. We listen to music and he talks about it and his interest is enlivening, and I know a galaxy that I didn't know twelve years ago, especially about his particular hero, James Moody. We talk about jazz, and then we talk about race. I have many other close friends who are black, and one of my godsons is half black; in general, I treat and experience race as invisible. With Dièry, race is a direct topic of conversation. Because he is a visibly strong black male, he is perceived as threatening, and this has led him to a variety of racial humiliations—from the typical story of not being able to get a taxi to narratives of police brutality. In his tales, I have come to see a more divided world than I had previously recognized. I have more fully appreciated the pain that those divisions cost.

I always looked down on women who confided all their secrets to their hairdressers. I felt that intimacy was an earned privilege and that it lost its meaning if it was shared too freely, especially with a paid captive audience. I tend to have a polite formality with people who work with or for me. But the friendship with Dièry became profound because I like and admire him so much and the mitigating factors—that I followed his orders, that he accepted my money—seemed ultimately to balance each other out. It has taken on a certain unique depth because of its dailyness. I sometimes feel as though his life and mine are soap operas that most people catch occasionally and on the fly, but that we catch in each other day after day. I see him first thing when I get up and am not always in the mood for confidences, but he is my North Star, steady and constant. The fact that we are so occupied with my weightlifting takes up some of the conscious energy that so often impedes confidences. And I have taken a role in his life too, his longest, steadiest client, who sees him most frequently (except when traveling). Time and our ages have caught up with us. I no longer push up that maximum weight at which I once so ecstatically arrived. I slog through these days, and do lots of repetitions with lighter weights to strengthen particular small muscle groups, to improve that occasional ache in my back, or to help the weak shoulder on which I had surgery. We have achieved a rare understanding, predicated on what is at last a balanced power.

If you had told me, in those days of Mr. Slaybaugh and Mr. Beisinger, that one day I would be hiring my own gym teacher to come daily to my house to put me through my paces, that it would become one of my primary activities and expenses, I would have laughed out loud. I could not have conceived, then, of the gift Dièry was to give me, the gift of my own body. I had no idea what lay ahead, that just as my body was beginning to age, I would come to a happier relationship with it than I had ever had, that even as it waned, I would get so much more from it.

———————————

ANDREW SOLOMON studied at Yale University and then at Jesus College, Cambridge. His first novel, *A Stone Boat* (Faber, 1994), was a runner-up for the *L.A. Times* First Fiction prize and was on the *Village Voice* best-seller list. His most recent book, *The Noonday Demon: An Atlas of Depression,* has won him eleven national awards, including the 2001 National Book Award, and is being published in twenty-one languages. It was also a finalist for the Pulitzer Prize. It has been a *New York Times* best-seller and has also been a best-seller in seven foreign countries. He is a fellow of Berkeley College at Yale University and is a member of the New York Institute for the Humanities and the Council on Foreign Relations. He maintains residences in London and New York.

VBK

BY JOHN MCPHEE

BRADLEY CALLS PRACTICALLY ALL MEN "MISTER" whose age exceeds his own by more than a couple of years. This includes any N.B.A. players he happens to meet, Princeton trainers, and Mr. Willem Hendrik van Breda Kolff, his coach. Van Breda Kolff was a Princeton basketball star himself, some twenty years ago, and went on to play for the New York Knickerbockers. Before returning to Princeton in 1962, he coached at Lafayette and Hofstra. His teams at the three colleges have won two hundred and fifty-one games and lost ninety-six. Naturally, it was a virtually unparalleled stroke of good fortune for van Breda Kolff to walk into his current coaching job in the very year that Bradley became eligible to play for the varsity team, but if the coach was lucky to have the player, the player was also lucky to have the coach. Van Breda Kolff, a cheerful and uncomplicated man, has a sportsman's appreciation of the nuances of the game, and appears to feel that mere winning is far less important than winning with style. He is an Abstract Expressionist of basketball. Other coaches have difficulty scouting his teams, because he does not believe in a set offense. He likes his offense free-form.

Van Breda Kolff simply tells his boys to spread out and keep the ball moving. "Just go fast, stay out of one another's way, pass, move, come off guys, look for one-on-ones, two-on-ones, two-on-twos, three-on-threes. That's about the extent," he says. That is, in fact, about the substance of basketball, which is almost never played as a five-man game anymore but is, rather, a constant search, conducted semi-independently by five players, for smaller combinations that will produce a score. One-on-one is the basic situation of the game—one man, with the ball, trying to score against one defensive player, who is trying to stop him, with nobody else involved. Van Breda Kolff does not think that Bradley is a great one-on-one player. "A one-on-one player is a hungry player," he explains. "Bill is not hungry. At least ninety percent of the time, when he gets the ball, he is looking for a pass." Van Breda Kolff has often tried to force Bradley into being more of a one-on-one player, through gentle persuasion in practice, through restrained pleas during timeouts, and even through open clamor. During one game last year, when Princeton was losing and Bradley was still flicking passes, van Breda Kolff stood up and shouted, "Will . . . you . . . shoot . . . that . . . ball?" Bradley, obeying at once, drew his man into the vortex of a reverse pivot, and left him standing six feet behind as he made a soft, short jumper from about ten feet out.

If Bradley were more interested in his own statistics, he could score sixty or seventy-five points, maybe even a hundred, in some of his games. But this would merely be personal aggrandizement, done at the expense of the relative balance of his own team and causing unnecessary embarrassment to the opposition, for it would only happen against an opponent that was heavily outmatched anyway. Bradley's highest point totals are almost always made when the other team is strong and the situation demands his scoring ability. He has, in fact, all the mechanical faculties a great one-on-one player needs. As van Breda Kolff will point out, for example, Bradley has a "great reverse pivot," and this is an essential characteristic of a one-on-one specialist. A way of getting rid of a defensive man who is playing close, it is a spin of the body, vaguely similar to what a football halfback does when he spins away from a would-be tackler and almost exactly what a lacrosse player does when he "turns his man." Say that Bradley is dribbling hard toward the basket and the defensive man is all over him. Bradley turns, in order to put his body between his opponent and the ball; he continues his dribbling but shifts the ball from one hand to the other; if his man is still crowding in on him, he keeps on turning until he has made one full revolution and is once more headed toward the basket. This is a reverse pivot. Bradley can execute one in less than a second. The odds are that when he has completed the spin the defensive player will be behind him, for it is the nature of basketball that the odds favor the man with the ball—if he knows how to play them.

Bradley doesn't need to complete the full revolution every time. If his man steps away from him in anticipation of a reverse pivot, Bradley can stop dead and make a jump shot. If the man stays close to him but not close enough to be turned, Bradley can send up a hook shot. If the man moves over so that he will be directly in Bradley's path when Bradley comes out of the turn, Bradley can scrap the reverse pivot before he begins it, merely suggesting it with his shoulders and then continuing his original dribble to the basket, making his man look like a pedestrian who has leaped to get out of the way of a speeding car.

The metaphor of basketball is to be found in these compounding alternatives. Every time a basketball player takes a step, an entire new geometry of action is created around him. In ten seconds, with or without the ball, a good player may see perhaps a hundred alternatives and, from them, make a half a dozen choices as he goes along. A great player will see even more alternatives and will make more choices, and this multiradial way of looking at things carries over into his life. At least, it carries over into Bradley's life. The very word "alternatives" bobs in and out of his speech with noticeable frequency. Before his Rhodes Scholarship came along and eased things, he appeared to be worrying about dozens of alternatives for next year. And he still fills his days with alternatives. He apparently always needs to have eight ways to jump, not because he is excessively prudent but because that is what makes the game interesting.

The reverse pivot, of course, is just one of numerous one-on-one moves that produce a complexity of possibilities. A rocker step, for example, in which a player puts one foot forward and rocks his shoulders forward and backward, can yield a set shot if the defensive man steps back, a successful drive to the basket if the defensive man comes in too close, a jump shot if he tries to compromise. A simple crossover—shifting a dribble from one hand to the other and changing direction—can force the defensive man to overcommit himself, as anyone knows who has ever watched Oscar Robertson use it to break free and score. Van Breda Kolff says that Bradley is a "great mover," and points out that the basis of all these maneuvers is footwork. Bradley has spent hundreds of hours merely rehearsing the choreography of the game—shifting his feet in the same patterns again and again, until they have worn into his motor subconscious. "The average basketball player only likes to play basketball," van Breda Kolff says. "When he's left to himself, all he wants to do is get a two-on-two or a three-on-three going. Bradley practices techniques, making himself learn and improve instead of merely having fun."

Because of Bradley's super-serious approach to basketball, his relationship to van Breda Kolff in some respects is a reversal of the usual relationship between a player and a coach. Writing to van Breda Kolff from Tokyo in his capacity as captain-elect, Bradley advised his coach that they should prepare themselves for "the stern challenge ahead." Van Breda Kolff doesn't vibrate to that sort of tune. "Basketball is a game," he says. "It is not an ordeal. I think Bradley's happiest whenever he can deny himself pleasure." Van Breda Kolff's handling of Bradley has been, in a way, a remarkable feat of coaching. One man cannot beat five men—at least not consistently—and Princeton loses basketball games. Until this season, moreover, the other material that van Breda Kolff has had at his disposal has been for the most part below even the usual Princeton standard, so the fact that his teams have won two consecutive championships is about as much to his credit as to his star's.

Van Breda Kolff says, "I try to play it just as if he were a normal player. I don't want to overlook him, but I don't want to over-look for him, either, if you see what I'm trying to say." Bradley's teammates sometimes depend on him too much, the coach explains, or, in a kind of psychological upheaval, get self-conscious about being on the court with a superstar and, perhaps to prove their independence, bring the ball up the court five or six times without passing it to him. When this happens, van Breda Kolff calls timeout. "Hey, boys," he says. "What have we got an all-American for?" He refers to Bradley's stardom only when he has to, however. In the main, he takes Bradley with a calculated grain of salt. He is interested in Bradley's relative weaknesses rather than in his storied feats, and has helped him gain poise on the court, learn patience, improve his rebounding, and be more aggressive. He refuses on principle to say that Bradley is the best basketball player he has ever coached, and he is also careful not to echo the general feeling that Bradley is the most exemplary youth since Lochinvar, but he will go out of his way to tell about the reaction of referees to Bradley. "The refs watch Bradley like a hawk, but, because he never complains, they feel terrible if they make an error against him," he says. "They just love him because he is such a gentleman. They get upset if they call a bad one on him." I asked van Breda Kolff what he thought Bradley would be doing when he was forty. "I don't know," he said. "I guess he'll be the governor of Missouri."

JOHN MCPHEE is the Pulitzer Prize–winning author of more than twenty-five books of creative nonfiction, most recently *The Founding Fish*. He lives in Princeton, New Jersey.

Physical Education

by Francine Prose

I NEVER KNEW THAT THERE WAS SUCH A THING as a mind-body problem, let alone that I had one, until I met Miss G.

Miss G. coached all the girls' team sports and taught gym (or what was then so quaintly, and as it turned out so aptly, known as physical education) in the small, Quaker private school that I attended from the September morning when I started fourth grade until the warm June evening on which I graduated from high school. She was my nemesis, my enemy. Our relationship, such as it was, lasted longer than many marriages. Just the sight of her ruddy, humorless, equine face—a face that seemed twice as large as any I had ever known—had the power to fill me with emotion, first with a childish dread that diminished or perhaps simply degenerated into a smoldering, perpetual, adolescent irritation and resentment. Every so often, in the forty years that have passed since the last time I walked out of the gym and the locker room that were her dominion, I used to dream that I was still in her class. And I would feel the same anxious discomfort that I felt every afternoon, every week, nine months a year, for nine years.

Until that September morning, nothing could have led me to suspect that my mind and my body were not perfectly at one. Until then, both aspects of my being had seemed cheerfully cooperative, willing and able to do whatever I needed them to do. I was the oldest kid on our block. And, at least in our neighborhood, age trumped gender. I was faster and more coordinated than the boys who lived in the houses near mine, I regularly beat them at what passed among us for athletics. In early photos, I'm wearing the too-short, unflattering hairstyle that my mother imagined was stylish. But I never thought of myself as a tomboy, exactly. Tomboys liked horses and climbed trees; I did neither. I played with dolls, I wore jeans. I floated in some ether, in which I was neither girlish nor boyish, but always simply me.

The childhood world that I remember—this was in the 1950s, in a Brooklyn neighborhood populated mainly by newly upper-middle-class, mostly Jewish, doctors and lawyers and their families—was surprisingly free from the ordinary, expectably rigid divisions between girls and boys, between girls' games and boys' games. Everyone played together, everyone participated in a constantly shifting round of alliances, feuds, and reconciliations. We pelted one another with dirt clods and snowballs, we picked on the younger kids, we played punchball, stoopball, basketball, hopscotch, and jacks, the only games we knew. I wanted to win badly enough that I usually won. And if arguments broke out about scoring and what was fair and unfair, I could win those battles, too. Because (being older and being a girl) I was just a little smarter, just a little more verbal than my friends, none of whom I have seen or heard from in the many years since, one by one, we moved away from the neighborhood and into our own lives.

The physical confidence that I'd built up by emerging victorious from these gentle backyard battles carried over into my experience at the local public school, which I attended through the third grade, and where the students, by and large, were the freshly pressed, scrubbed sons and daughters of the upwardly striving families who inhabited the well-kept apartment houses and private homes near ours. Recess was a barely controlled stampede. Once a day, our minders set us free in the schoolyard and we ran around, bellowing, maddened, like little bulls turned loose from the bull pen.

And then in the fourth grade all that changed. My parents were ambitious for me and for my education. In the public school classes that were even then too large, my overworked teachers allowed me to sit quietly in a corner with a book; I'd learned to read before kindergarten and was a voracious reader. The problem was that the teachers forgot about me when the reading lesson was over, and at some point my parents (who were overworked themselves) noticed that I had somehow forgotten to learn to add or subtract.

And so they sent me to private school—and into the unforgiving, tyrannical domain of Miss G.

Everyone knew one another, but I knew no one. There were places to which we had to go, but I had no idea how to get there. There were rules that had to be followed, but I didn't have a clue. Everything was strange and confusing on my first day at the new school, and the most confusing thing of all was what should have been the simplest: recess.

Just as they had in the public school, my classmates raced out into the cement yard beside the main building. At one end was a jungle gym, at the other a chain-link fence that separated us from the court building where prisoners were held in detention while they awaited trial. But nothing was the same, nothing was recognizable; the wild free-for-all of my early school years had been replaced by an infant boot camp run by the formidable Miss G.

I had never seen an adult, let alone a grown woman, dressed like that before—in a kind of navy blue safari jumper or military outfit with short sleeves and wide, slightly flared, cuffed shorts. In other words, a gym suit. Nor had I seen adult flesh that looked anything like Miss G.'s: beefy, muscular, sunburned, displayed with no flair, no false or genuine modesty, no attempt at fashion. As I've said, I was neither a tomboy nor a princess, but like most kids I had a reasonably clear and fairly conservative sense of what was fashionable and unfashionable, acceptable and outrageous. Miss G. had short, blond, slightly curly hair that looked as if she'd cut it herself. And as far as lack of style went, Miss G. was beyond the bottom of the scale, utterly off the charts.

She blew the whistle that hung from a cord around her neck. "Let's start with capture the flag," she said. She asked me, the only new kid, if I knew the rules. Nothing seemed worse than standing there, singled out, an object of unwanted attention and perhaps even derision as she explained the game. I assumed I could figure it out as we went along, and so I began what would be the pattern of my relationship with Miss G.

I lied.

I said that I already knew how to play. I mumbled something about my old school. But in fact the rules of the game seemed impenetrable, rococo. Kids were scrambling in every direction, running circles around me, jailing and rescuing one another. All of them seemed gifted with a natural grace and sureness, a speed and confidence that was way beyond my ability to outrun the little losers on my block. Where had these girls learned to run like that? What had taught them to use their bodies in those marvelous, deft ways? Miss G., I could only assume. I felt like a ball bearing in a pinball machine, slammed around, deflected this way and that, with no volition of my own, no control, no—

Miss G. blew the whistle again. Everything stopped. She was staring straight at me. Her red face had grown redder. She waited a beat. Another. Now everyone was looking at me. She sighed and rolled her eyes back in her head. Then she said, very slowly and mockingly, "Would you like me to explay-yayn?"

And that was that. It was over. Like magic. From that day on, I was picked last each time we chose up teams. In that one in-stant, my body had changed from my brain's cheerful partner into a surly, grudging, unwilling servant. And I, in turn, passed that surliness and willfulness along to Miss G.

So much of the relationship between student and teacher is

unexpressed, understood. Or misunderstood. Could Miss G. really have despised me as much as I believed? Was she constantly stopping games to correct my mistakes, to call attention to my blunders? Did just the sight of me cause her to sigh, and her steel-blue eyes to narrow with exasperation and contempt?

From this distance, it's impossible to know. Besides, it hardly matters. What's important is that was what I believed. And that perversely, I did everything in my power to convince Miss G. that she was right about me, and at the same time to pay her back for her scorn, her slights, her injustice. So much of the teacher-student relationship is, as has been proved, a self-fulfilling prophecy. If a teacher believes you will do well, you just might possibly succeed. And if she's convinced that you will do nothing but fail, your chances are accordingly slim.

I failed. And failed again. By the end of grade school, and certainly by seventh grade, we had settled into the seasonal schedule that we would follow all through high school, and that would be reflected in the teams that traveled to other private schools to play our counterparts in Manhattan and on Long Island. I failed—I worked hard to fail—at all of it. I never made varsity anything. I got on a couple of junior varsity teams. I fouled out, I sat on the bench. I can't remember ever scoring.

Two afternoons a week, in the fall and the spring, a bus took us from our school in downtown Brooklyn to a large (it seemed to me vast) field in Flatbush. There, in the autumn, we played field hockey and soccer, and in the spring, softball and lacrosse. During the winter, we trooped down to the gym and played basketball. Girls' basketball, that is. Everything was decorous, civilized. Girls' rules applied. In our well-mannered lacrosse matches, no one got her nose broken. Looking back, I suppose I should have been grateful that we played any sports at all, thrilled that so much attention was being lavished on girls' physical education, on making girls feel confident and strong, on giving them sound bodies in which to house their sound minds. But all of it seemed to be working that way only for other girls. With every scrimmage game we played, every practice for the teams I routinely disgraced, I felt less sure, less coordinated, less brave and independent.

There were things about the whole process that I loved. I loved being out on the field, running loose amid the smell of the freshly cut grass. I loved riding out there on the bus, all of us ritualistically holding our breaths when we passed the cemetery. I loved the fact that we rode out there with the boys, for the field bus was where we had our first flirtations, and where our first crushes were born and nurtured until we reached the gates of the field and the boys ran off to practice their own more intense and serious versions of the sports we played. I loved the strangeness of the equipment. The wooden hockey sticks, the shin pads we laced on for hockey and soccer, the helmet and the mask and the armor of padding that made it nearly impossible for the goalie to walk. I loved the sweaty, leathery smell of the softball mitt and webbing of the lacrosse stick, as well as the satisfying plop that was your reward when you actually caught the lacrosse ball with that unlikely, twisting motion.

But nothing could have persuaded me to be the hockey or lacrosse goalie, with the terrifying responsibilities that those positions carried. Nor could anything have made me try hard, do my best, work hard for the team, pay attention, take it seriously. In fact I was fairly dramatic about how unserious I was. I daydreamed theatrically at second base. When I got walked from home plate to first, I took my time. My teammates didn't seem to care. We were city kids. We were cool. The only one who took it seriously was Miss G., and she was the team I was playing against.

I was a gym teacher's nightmare, I know. And now, all these years later, now that I have been a teacher myself, I can understand how maddening it must have been to have a passive-aggressive little snit like myself making her job that much harder.

But part of me thinks, as I did then, that she'd started it, she'd brought it on. She was the powerful one. The coach. She could make us win, or lose.

All the way through grade school, I still played with the kids on my block. But the fact that I could beat them at punchball meant nothing to me now, those hollow victories against those pipsqueaks were ashes in my mouth. Anyway, I was losing interest. I had more and more homework, and one day, a new kid moved onto the block and asked me out on a date. So maybe that was what was happening. I was growing breasts. There are plenty of psychologists—Carol Gilligan among them—who argue that girls, at a certain age, lose confidence, nerve, self-activation and so forth. They blame it on society, on what girls are picking up about the male-dominated world. Susan B. Anthony could be your coach, and it wouldn't make any difference.

But I don't quite believe that.

It hardly needs saying that of all the classes you take, of all the subjects you study in school, physical education is the only one that has to do with the body. Also biology, I suppose, but in a very abstracted, cerebral sort of way. To say nothing of that embarrassment known as something like "health." Only gym tends to your body, while everything else is aimed at your mind. Physical education, and especially team sports, teaches you in a visceral way about success and failure. Someone wins, someone loses, there are no pluses and minuses, no extra credit for showing up.

Over those years, in that one subject—that is, the subject of the body—my sense of self was being changed from that of a girl who won to that of a girl who lost. In my other classes, I was doing fine. In fact I was a smart kid, with the few perks and major drawbacks that went along with being a smart girl in high school and junior high. I could have been a brain on stilts, undependable stilts rapidly growing strange new body parts. Separated from my body, my mind worked overtime. My mind knew all the answers, while my body missed hockey passes and fly balls, overshot the backboard.

Eventually, we began to get grades in gym. Every year, Miss G. gave me a C minus. My parents laughed, they didn't care. I got A's in most of my subjects. And near the end of every year, there was a moment when Miss G. would stop me on my way out of class, and look into my eyes, her own eyes nearly brimming and icy at the same time. She would tell me how much she hoped that I would try harder next year. I'm sure she did hope something like that. She was being sincere. So why did it feel like a knife twist? Because she didn't have to say anything, she could have let my failure, or near failure, go unnoticed, unremarked. And she seemed to me to be reaching for another victory this time, a moral one, by taking the high ground, pretending to be a teacher who really cared. When the evidence of the past year would seem to indicate that in fact she was a woman who enjoyed the creepy, bullying battle of wits she was waging with a child.

In many ways our school was very old-fashioned. But in one notable way it was considerably ahead of its time. Years before such concerns intensified into a frenzy, my school placed a huge importance on where we got into college.

Some time near the start of the tenth grade, the college adviser took a look at my record and told my parents that it might look better, to colleges, if I were a little more "well rounded." The powers that were decided that if I couldn't make a varsity team, I could manage a team. So I managed hockey and basketball, which was a terrible mistake, since, unless I am truly interested in what I am doing, I can be forgetful, miss dates and overbook. These were not best qualities for a manager of any sort, but indeed I did try, for once, to do the best I could. Miss G. rose to the occasion—at least she didn't have to deal with me on the playing field—and became, also for the occasion, the serious, committed, brimming-eyed teacher trying to make our unlikely manager-coach partnership work out.

Somehow we got through the season. I think I even got a C. When we played the other schools, I had to learn not to be embarrassed by being associated with Miss G. as she ran back and forth along the sidelines, blowing her whistle and panting, her red face getting ever redder, looking as foolish and serious as it was possible for a grown-up to be.

The next year, my junior year, Miss G. announced a new policy. The seniors and juniors had been getting slack about essentials, like coming to class prepared, having their gym suits and socks, and so on. From now on there would be records kept, a whole system of demerits and punishments. Grade points would be taken off, dire fates would await us.

She'd said "the juniors and seniors," but she really meant me. Because, by then, I had escalated the stakes of my passive resistance. No longer the responsible manager, I became the hopeless screwup. I forgot my gym suit or socks at least once a week. Each class, I'd offer my apology for whatever I had forgotten in the bored superior tone that made it clear I'd done it on purpose.

It was a clear provocation. Miss G. failed me for the year. It must have taken some courage on her part, because the school wanted us to get into good colleges—and by now I was their best hope in my class for getting anywhere near the Ivy League—and a big red F on my record would hardly make me look well rounded. But Miss G. must have stuck to her guns. My chances for college seemed ruined. I had pushed Miss G. too far, and Miss G. had won.

Or at least that's how it would have happened now. Things were different then. Nowadays colleges can have Olympic divers with perfect College Board scores. As many as they want. But in those days colleges often leaned toward students who could do only one thing well. And there were two things I could do. I could read and write. Or maybe it was just luck that the college admissions officials who interviewed me were not themselves the sort of women who had done all that well in gym. Someone else, along the line, had taught them about the mind-body problem. They asked me about gym, the single failed course. It was something they had to do. I explained I'd habitually forgotten my gym suit. A couple of them actually laughed.

In those laughs, the Frisbee of power being tossed back and forth between Miss G. and myself once more sailed into my hands. She had no power over me. I got into the college I wanted. I was out of there. I was free.

Let me be very clear about this. I am not one of those people who blame every sin and virtue, every success and failure, on some major or minor childhood trauma. I know that anything's possible, if you want it badly enough. For example, I could have devoted myself to sports, to keeping in shape, to tennis lessons, yoga, African dance. So what if I wasn't good at it? I would have gotten better. I could have gone to dance or yoga classes without quitting after the first session, played softball on the fiction writers team without praying to get walked when it was my turn up at bat.

But it's that old mind-body problem, coming back to haunt me. Something about physical confidence. What I can and can't do. Over the years, I've ridden a couple of horses, climbed a few small local mountains, but I didn't like either activity, and will never do either again. But it's more than that, it's how I feel when I have to lift something heavy or close the back door of the van or try to fix something in the house that's broken, or run most household appliances. Or, for that matter, drive. A hesitation, an intake of breath. I think: I can't do this.

It might have happened anyway. It might be DNA-encoded. By and large the women in my family tend to be high-functioning, competent multitaskers—but not what you would call athletic. And I'm not saying that Miss G. is responsible for a change that occurred in me, for the transformation that turned the little girl who could climb fences into the older girl who couldn't. I'm just saying something happened. And Miss G. could have helped, but she didn't. In fact she let it happen, and I believe she made it worse. Most of my early teachers were helpful, but Miss G. was not. She stands out in my memory as the person at least partly responsible for the gap, the division of the self into the cerebral and corporeal. The end result of a certain sort of physical education.

FRANCINE PROSE is the author of a dozen novels, including *Blue Angel*, a National Book Award finalist. Her first nonfiction book, *Lives of the Muses*, was a national best-seller. Her most recent novel is *A Changed Man*.

Underdog

BY JOHN IRVING

THERE WAS ONE PLACE AT EXETER where I was never angry; I never lost my temper in the wrestling room—possibly because I wasn't embarrassed to be there. It is surprising that I felt so comfortable with wrestling. My athletic skills had never been significant. I had loathed Little League baseball. (By association, I hate all sports with balls.) I more mildly disliked skiing and skating. (I have a limited tolerance for cold weather.) I did have an inexplicable taste for physical contact, for the adrenal stimulation of bumping into people, but I was too small to play football; also, there was a ball involved.

When you love something, you have the capacity to bore everyone about why—it doesn't matter why. Wrestling, like boxing, is a weight-class sport; you get to bump into people your own size. You can bump into them very hard, but where you land is reasonably soft. And there are civilized aspects to the sport's combativeness: I've always admired the rule that holds you responsible, if you lift your opponent off the mat, for your opponent's "safe return." But the best answer to why I love wrestling is that it was the first thing I was any good at. And what limited success I had in the sport I owe completely to my first coach, Ted Seabrooke.

Coach Seabrooke had been a Big 10 Champion and a two-time All-America at Illinois; he was way overqualified for the job of coaching wrestling at Exeter—his teams dominated New

England prep-school and high-school wrestling for years. An NCAA runner-up at 155 pounds, Ted Seabrooke was a handsome man; he weighed upward of 200 pounds in my time at the academy. He would sit on the mat with his legs spread in front of him; his arms were bent at the elbow but reaching out to you from the level of his chest. Even in such a vulnerable position, he could completely defend himself; I never saw anyone manage to get behind him. On his rump, he could scuttle like a crab—his feet tripping you, his legs scissoring you, his hands tying up your hands or snapping your head down. He could control you by holding you in his lap (a crab ride) or by taking possession of your near leg and your far arm (a cross-body ride); he was always gentle with you, and he never seemed to expend much energy in the process of frustrating you. (Coach Seabrooke would first get diabetes and then die of cancer. At his memorial service, I couldn't speak half the eulogy I'd written for him, because I knew by heart the parts that would make me cry if I tried to say them aloud.)

Not only did Ted Seabrooke teach me how to wrestle; more important, he forewarned me that I would never be better than "halfway decent" as a wrestler—because of my limitations as an athlete. He also impressed upon me how I could compensate for my shortcomings: I had to be especially dedicated—a thorough student of the sport—if I wished to overcome my lack of any observable ability. "Talent is overrated," Ted told me. "That you're not very talented needn't be the end of it."

A high school wrestling match is six minutes long, divided into three two-minute periods—with no rest between the periods. In the first period, both wrestlers start on their feet, a neutral position with neither wrestler having an advantage. In the second period, in those days, one wrestler had the choice of taking the top or the bottom position; in the third period, the choice of positions was reversed. (Nowadays, the options of choice have been expanded to include the neutral position, and the wrestler given the choice in the second period may defer his choice until the third.)

What Coach Seabrooke taught me was that I should keep the score close through two periods—close enough so that one take-down or a reversal in the third period could win the match. And I needed to avoid "mix-ups"—free-for-all situations that were not in either wrestler's control. (The outcome of such a scramble favors the better athlete.) Controlling the pace of the match—a combination of technique, correct position, and physical conditioning—was my objective. I know it sounds boring—I was a boring wrestler. The pace that worked for me was slow. I liked a low-scoring match.

I rarely won by a fall; in five years of wrestling at Exeter, I probably pinned no more than a half-dozen opponents. I was almost never pinned—only twice, in fact.

I won 5–2 when I dominated an opponent; I won 2–1 or 3–2 when I was lucky, and lost 3–2 or 4–3 when I was less lucky. If I got the first takedown, I could usually win; if I lost the first takedown, I was hard-pressed to recover—I was not a come-from-behind man. I was, as Coach Seabrooke said, "halfway decent" as a counter-wrestler, too. But if my opponent was a superior athlete, I couldn't afford to rely on my counter-moves to his first shots; my counters weren't quick enough—my reflexes weren't quick enough. Against a superior athlete, I would take the first shot; against a superior wrestler, I would try to counter his first move. "Or vice versa, if it's not working," Coach Seabrooke used to say. He had a sense of humor. "Where the head goes, the body must follow—usually," Ted would add. And: "An underdog is in a position to take a healthy bite."

This was a concept of myself that I'd been lacking. I was an underdog; therefore, I had to control the pace—of everything. This was more than I learned in English 4W, but the concept was applicable to my Creative Writing—and to all my school-work, too. If my classmates could read our history assignment in an hour, I allowed myself two or three. If I couldn't learn to spell, I would keep a list of my most frequently misspelled words—and I kept the list with me; I had it handy even for unannounced quizzes. Most of all, I rewrote everything: first drafts were like the first time you tried a new takedown—you needed to drill it, over and over again, before you even dreamed of trying it in a match. I began to take my lack of talent seriously.

An imperious Spanish teacher was fond of abusing those of us who lacked perfection with the insensitive (not to mention elitist) remark that we would all end up at Wichita State. I didn't know that Wichita was in Kansas; I knew only that this was a slur—if we weren't talented enough for Harvard, then Wichita State would be our just reward. Fuck you, I thought: my objective would then be to do well at Wichita State. Ted Seabrooke had gone to Illinois. I didn't suppose that this Spanish teacher thought too highly of Illinois either.

I remember telling Ted that I'd had two likable Spanish teachers, and one unlikable one. "I wouldn't complain about those odds," he said.

Epilogue

And I often think about calling Ted Seabrooke, before I remember that I can't. Ted wasn't a big talker—not compared to Cliff—but Ted was insightful at interrupting me, and at contradicting me, too. I'd be saying something and he'd say, "That sounds pretty stupid to me," Or: "why would you want to do that?" And "Do what you know how to do." Or: "what's worked for you before?" Cliff used to say that Ted could clear the air.

It still seems unacceptable that both Ted and Cliff are dead, although Cliff (given normal life expectancy) would almost surely be dead by now—Cliff was born in 1897, which would make him all of 98, if he were alive today. I think it broke Cliff's heart that Ted died first—Ted died young. And Ted fooled us: after the diabetes, which he got control of, he had some healthy years; then the cancer came and killed him in the fall of 1980. He was 59.

For Coach Seabrooke's memorial service in Phillips Church, there were more wrestlers than I ever saw in the Exeter wrestling room. Bobby Thompson, one of Exeter's ex-heavy-weights and arguably the biggest-ever New England Class A Champion in the Unlimited class—sang "Amazing Grace." (Bobby is the school minister at Exeter today.)

It was an outrage to all his wrestlers that Ted was dead. He'd seemed indomitable to us. He had twice been struck by lightning, while playing golf; both times he'd survived. Both times he'd said, "It's just one of those things."

After Ted's memorial service, I remember Cliff Gallagher grabbing me with a Russian arm-tie and whispering in my ear: "it should have been me, Johnny—it should have been me." My arm was sore for days. Cliff had a nasty Russian arm-tie. At the time, Cliff was 83.

I don't lead a hectic life. It's not every night, or every week—or even every month—that I feel the need to "clear the air." Most nights, I don't even look at the telephone. Other times, the unringing phone seems to summon all the unreachable people in the past. I think of that poem of Rilke's, about the corpse: "Und einer ohne Namen / lag bar und reinlich da und gab Gesetze" ("And one without a name / lay clean and naked there, and gave commands"). That is the telephone on certain nights: it is the unreachable past—the dead demanding to give us advice. On those nights, I'm sorry I can't talk to Ted.

JOHN IRVING published his first novel at the age of twenty-six. He has received awards from the Rockefeller Foundation, the National Endowment for the Arts, and the Guggenheim Foundation; he has won an O. Henry Award, a National Book Award, and an Oscar. In 1992, Mr.

COACH

Irving was inducted into the National Wrestling Hall of Fame in Stillwater, Oklahoma. In 2001, he was elected to the American Academy of Arts and Letters. His eleventh novel, *Until I Find You*, was just published.

Something Special

BY THOMAS BELLER

IT WAS HALFTIME. I stepped out of the press room at Madison Square Garden and saw him walking toward me carrying a flimsy cardboard tray filled with hot dogs and beer. He had recognized me first, and his eyes were on me already by the time I saw him.

"Coach," I said instinctively. "I don't believe it."

"I can't believe it either," he said. "You've actually turned out to be good for something."

I was a year out of college and stringing for a wire service whose regular writers could not be bothered to watch the Knicks during the rather dismal season of 1988. The structure of the Garden in those days put even an insignificant stringer like myself at courtside, with a phone. A loose ball had bounced toward me at one point in the first half. I reached out with two hands and tried to catch it with the phone nestled against my shoulder. The ball bounced through my hands. It occurred to me later that my old coach must have spotted me at that moment. I imagined what he might have said to his friend: "He still can't catch a basketball." "Coach," I said again, slowly, as if testing to see if I could still get the word right after a long time of not pronouncing it. "What are you doing here?"

"The same thing the other ten thousand people in this building are doing, you idiot!" he said. Insults were his métier, his instrument, "idiot" in this context was a term of endearment. "Of course, I don't have seats as good as you, you big shot," he continued. "I see you're a real big shot now."

When he was part of my life, when he dominated my life, when he caused me pain both physical and emotional, not to mention posing complex philosophical questions that undercut my basic assumptions about the natural order of things, such as when he screamed at me, in response to the news that I had fractured my thumb, "Why did you see a doctor?" Coach Gallagher was someone I wanted to be away from and done with. Now I think I could use him. He might be useful on a day-to-day basis, for the purpose of motivation. Also, whatever abuse I endured would serve to make everything else in my life seem easy and leisurely in comparison.

I still remember a phrase from the first correspondence I got from him. "If you want to be part of something special . . ." It appeared in a letter I got during the summer between sophomore and junior year, before I had actually met him.

He had just been appointed head basketball coach of the Vassar Brewers men's varsity basketball team. He sent a letter to the team, the thrust of which was that we should begin training over the summer. He included a detailed workout regime. There may have been some sort of introductory pleasantry along the lines of, "Hello, I am your new coach," but I only remember the long list of push-ups, running, and sit-ups. The phrase he used to justify this shocking intrusion of winter pain into summer leisure was, "If you want to be part of something special . . ."

I do want to be part of something special, generally speaking, and Coach Gallagher would make me work for it on a day-to-day basis. How would Coach Gallagher function in my life today? Would he bark at me while I sat at my computer? Yell when my attention drifted and I checked e-mail? Would he harass me with contemptuous insults? If it was my writing he was trying to improve, perhaps he would heap scorn on all the time and energy I spend playing basketball.

He had thin lips, a small upturned nose, and dark eyes, all set in a round face topped with a fringe of short brown hair parted in the middle with a whimsical innocence. The man was all cheeks. The natural condition of his face was a kind of blank curiosity that was poised, with relatively little provocation, to ferment into amusement or aggravation, depending. When he was sufficiently upset, it would all collapse into a red tomato rage. He wasn't a sadist, he wasn't cruel, and he wasn't even a jerk (do people with these personal attributes gravitate to coaching, or does the profession pull it out of them?). He wasn't that harsh except when he was mad. He didn't get mad unless there was some sort of lack of concentration, desire, or skill. As the coach of the Vassar College Brewers, who in the two seasons previous to his arrival had won a total of about six games, he usually had something to be mad about. Regarding my own performance, suffice it to say I was familiar with that collapsed blotch of red where his face should have been. At such times, he always clenched his fist into little balls; his arms would go rigid at his sides, and at the end would be the clenched fists. He had small hands. When clenched, no bigger than cue balls, it seemed.

Once, though, he took some jump shots for a while and showed impressive skills. He couldn't have been older than thirty. We all watched in a kind of mortified amazement. The basketball skills of coaches are like the sex lives of parents— you can acknowledge their existence, but you don't want too much information.

Early in his first season, my junior year, he made us write out our course list. I listed among my credits, "Shakespear."

The purpose of this list was to allow him to monitor our academic activities and make sure we didn't screw up to the point where our eligibility was threatened. The subtext was that we were all jocks who had been recruited to play basketball and, like recruits everywhere, our academic skills were shaky. This was flattery. There was, in fact, an interesting recruiting subtext to that season, but this notion was a fallacy in the context of Vassar College, which is not, thank God, a jock school. There are no fraternities.

Vassar is a school of fantastic academic resources set on a gorgeous campus on which students gambol and roam and learn about all kinds of things. It had been a girls' school, one of the Seven Sisters schools (Yale's sister), with a reputation for primness and white gloves at tea time, which Jane Fonda was alleged to have attended, in protest against the dress code, wearing nothing but white gloves. It had been a girls' school until 1969. By the time I arrived in the mid-eighties the mix between boys and girls was approaching even. But the balance seemed a bit strained. I think the girls were, on the whole, smarter than the boys; they came from a more competitive pool of applicants.

There wasn't much sports culture. There were sports teams, and the intramural football league I played in got rather intense at times, but the emphasis at Vassar was on other things. The campus was so verdant. So was the student body. There was just so much stuff to think about and do, it was as though the sheer loopy plentitude of the place worked against the martial atmosphere that surrounds organized team sports.

Still, at the time of my arrival the school was trying to emphasize sports. They were trying to emphasize science, as well. They were trying to build up the facilities and programs where you often find concentrations of heterosexual males. They had recently built a huge field house up near the golf course, and it looked lonely up there.

"There's an E at the end of Shakespeare, for Christ sakes!" Gallagher had yelled upon seeing my list of classes. But he was smiling. "You're an English major and you don't know how to spell 'Shakespeare'? What do they teach you here?"

I felt a tiny pang of camaraderie. He taught second grade English at a public school somewhere. He was an English major, too. This turned out to be our warmest moment for some time to come.

What is it with the put-upon, exasperated demeanor of basketball coaches? Football coaches have the field-marshal grandeur; baseball managers sit there like yogis, calculating how many relief pitchers can fit on the head of a pin. (They've transcended the word "coach" altogether.) But basketball coaches, my God, they look as though they have for years been trying to whittle down a giant tree with a penknife while a clock counts down to zero. The ones who aren't former players are often small, downright runty figures with a physical energy made frantic from being packed into too small a package. The Van Gundy Brothers, Stan and Jeff, are the current embodiment, but the legacy seems to go way back to Red Holtzman, Red Auerbach, and beyond. At the college level the equation is a little different, the players are younger, the balance of power shifts drastically to the coaches, but I think the basic principle applies. It applies to coaches at every level of the game assuming they care about winning, which, being coaches, they usually do. This is because basketball coaches deal most directly with the elements. Most people's sense of the planet is embodied by spinning globes that sit on their desks. Spin it and close your eyes, put your finger down, and see where you land. This globe is usually the size of a basketball, give or take. Basketball embodies the world on both a physical and a metaphysical level. If this sounds suspiciously abstract, consider the synonym for "elements," a word basketball coaches everywhere have made into a mantra of the sport: "Fundamentals."

George Gervin, famous for his smooth game and finger rolls in the seventies, once offered a journalist the following non sequitur. The journalist asked about the mechanics of a last-second game winner that Gervin had produced. Gervin's answer, which admittedly could also be described simply as "stoned," got at a basic truth about the game. "The earth is round," he said.

Basketball is the world, in all its chaos; its players are, among all the sports, except soccer, which it resembles, most physically free; basketball coaches have to bring it all into a scheme, make sense of it, and try to control it. No wonder they so often seem to be in a bad mood.

Walker Field House looked like a series of medieval huts, the roof rising to sharply pitched points in several places like waves slapping together. The floor was a thin layer of tapioca-colored rubber laid over concrete. The ceiling was lined with wood panels, and for four years I lay on my back during pregame stretches and stared at the knots in the wood. The bleachers were modest. During my freshman year, home games often were witnessed by a smattering of people, among whom a single figure stands out. His name was Sal Lobreglio, the father of one of my teammates. He was an ex-cop who wore a jacket and tie over his substantial and rather round frame. He attended every game, even road games. He drove a Cadillac Seville.

Sal Lobreglio was an enthusiastic clapper and yeller, especially when his son John did something good. John Lobreglio was one of our stars. He was a gentle kid with a very nice jump shot and a level of Bronx-bred street toughness that never failed to emerge when necessary. John was also a very spiritual, academic-minded religion major who was to play an important role in the recruiting intrigues of later years.

The coach for my first two years was a man named Sam Adams. He had put in time as an assistant at Army, against whose JV we always had a preseason scrimmage, and he had some connection to Bobby Knight at Indiana, who every year sent Adams an Indiana team poster. All this might suggest a fiery figure who motivated by intensity and screaming (or perhaps, like Bobby Knight himself, the occasional Sprewell-esque episode of neck throttling), but that was not the case. Coach Adams's most intense feature was his fine, bright blond hair, which he had in a side part, as smooth as silk. He was neat and fastidious. He rarely raised his voice. He was so mild that he rarely even inflected his voice.

Coach Adams was working with limited resources—his players. There was an exhausted feeling of doom around his tenure as coach, a kind of Wonder Bread fatalism that was devoid of rage or other spices. Adams was a team player, and a bit of a bureaucrat. He felt—correctly—that basketball, and team sports in general, were a low priority at Vassar, and that he had little in the way of resources to build a better team. Things were the way they were.

There was the team revolt my sophomore year. Complaints were made to the athletic director. We wanted a new coach. The athletic director, in an unusually confiding moment, said firing Adams would be difficult because he always had his paperwork in on time and it was flawless. The secret life of a coach as bureaucrat and politician was revealed to us momentarily, and it was depressing. We wanted someone with some fire. With all due respect to Coach Adams, I don't really recall very much of his coaching. I don't recall pain and suffering and humiliation. I don't recall him screaming and yelling at me or anyone. Is this what makes a coach? No, but it sets a tone. I mostly recall being part of a small enterprise, a budget line at the school, an activity, and all the shouts and cries from those first two years are drowned in the huge tapioca interior of Walker Field House, and are encapsulated by the almost spiritually lonely sound of Sal Lobreglio, the ex-cop, clapping and calling out encouragements.

John had told me that at Christmastime his father was always a prodigious giver of gifts. Piles of them. With no regard to personal finances. "Now the credit cards are going to be after me," Sal would say to John and his brother after they were all open. "I have to run for the hills!"

Looking back on it, Sal Lobreglio was Coach Adams's alter ego—loud, dark, a little dangerous, ferociously optimistic, sticking up for us on one side of the court, while across the court our mild and slightly disgusted coach stood in his bright blondness observing our demise. The idea that Sal Lobreglio was a doppelganger coach came to a bizarre realization during a road game when Coach Adams somehow got lost on the way to the game.

I say this hesitantly because it's been a long time and maybe this happened during Coach Gallagher's first year—Adams was very organized. At any rate the team was there, but no coach. Lobreglio, either on his initiative or at our request, came down from his perch and took over. One of his executive decisions, which of course deeply endeared him to me for life, was to insert me, the underachiever, into the starting lineup. The fact of the matter was that I got to see a lot of Sal in the stands because I was spending a lot of time on the bench. I missed his turn as coach. I was playing.

The arrival of Coach Gallagher coincided with the arrival of our second savior. Gallagher did more than send us a letter that first summer of his appointment. He recruited. He had been in touch with the Lobreglios of the Bronx. They had led him to a special case in the neighborhood. The special case's name was Seamus Carey.

I'm tempted to say that Seamus Carey's arrival swept through the campus like a rumor of salvation, but that is not true. It swept through the little basketball community whose congregation met at Walker Field House for pickup games in the off-season, and we were suspicious.

There had been a savior the previous year. Coach Adams had landed a prized recruit. His name was Pete Tombs and he had done the very serious-sounding basketball thing of taking an extra year after high school at one of those super-competitive basketball prep schools. He was a little over six feet and played point guard. My guess, now, is that Pete was the sort of talented player who can keep things under control enough to facilitate the more talented players on his team. When necessary, he could hit an open jump shot. He wasn't the sort of player who could carry a team on his back, which at any rate seemed to be going to hell from almost the moment he arrived. Pete was good, but he was no savior. He seemed sincerely happy to be getting a good education at a plush spot like Vassar. Like a pro player who puts up great numbers in a contract year, Pete hit his peak the year before we met him. The contract was now signed, he was in, probably with a good aid package, and his best game was in the rearview mirror.

Seamus Carey was even smaller than Pete Tombs, black Irish, a stocky five eight or so with eyes that looked like they had seen wars and famines. My heart sank when I first saw him, but during our first pickup game he demonstrated speed and toughness that was clearly on an entirely different level from anything we had dealt with. He drove to the basket like a cannonball being shot through a field of wheat. I count myself as one of the wheat.

There was a problem, however. Seamus had a bad reaction to Vassar College. It did not help that he had been put in Ferry House, an interesting, anomalous piece of modern architecture that sat amidst Vassar's many nineteenth-century buildings in squat Bauhaus splendor, a kind of stylish one-building shantytown that may as well have had a neon sign above it blinking the word "Vegan!"

There was a kitchen, the duties of the house were communal, the politics were anarchist, etc. Ten days into the year Lobreglio approached me, ashen-faced, with the news that Carey had deserted. A note of apology, though not explanation, had been tacked to his door at Ferry House.

He was convinced to come back. Different housing. But there were other problems. One of the seniors on the team was supplying him with old papers for his philosophy class. Like many of the players on the team (other than Lobreglio, the religion major) Carey's emphasis was on the jock standby—economics. But he had taken a philosophy class, and a guy whose nickname was "Spanky" had been plying him with his old papers, because Seamus was a jock and a savior, an actual bona fide recruit to this fey, enlightened institution, and Spanky was thrilled to play a role in coddling and corrupting him, thereby impersonating the dramas of big-time athletics. What happened was that Carey decided, halfway through the semester, to try and write his own paper. He was promptly called onto the carpet and accused of cheating. The paper was too good.

What does a coach do when he inherits a poor team and tries to improve it? He tries to get better players. And he tries to make his players better. The latter is an arduous process. Gallagher arrived with his round and, I thought even then, somewhat innocent face and it was immediately clear that he was ambitious. We were to be the vehicle of his ambition. This was a responsibility and a compliment. I was filled with gratitude and excitement, until those sensations were replaced by pain.

These days one hears a lot about the importance of work in the weight room. I wish—with an occasional flare of passion that is probably unseemly—that all the amazing machines, all the faith in weights and strength conditioning, had existed back in the eighties when I played college ball and was a long gangly concoction of arms and legs. As it was, the weight room was usually occupied to capacity by the Orangutang Gang known as the rugby team, who were in the process of rapidly evolving into muscle-bound beef packages about twice the size of their former selves.

The emphasis in basketball training was on running and conditioning, not strength. Weights were viewed with suspicion, because they might screw up the extremely mystical, unexplainable, and delicate mechanical process by which the ball, having left your fingertips, flies through the air and falls into the hoop. Gallagher encouraged us in the weight room. But it was optional, whereas the running was unavoidable. Running is not a word that does justice to what takes place in basketball practice. Soccer players run, and run. Football players sprint. But for basketball there is a special drill whose name explains a lot: Suicides.

Let's contemplate the title, a dramatic plural of an unpleasant word. If it were singular it would be, in practice, less morbid. "Now it's time for the suicide," coaches across the land would say. And one awful thing would occur and then it would be over.

But it is not singular. It is plural, like the rings of Saturn or the gates of hell.

Here is a suicide: you run to the foul line, touch it with your hand, then run back to the baseline from which you started, touch that with your hand, then run to the half-court line, touch that, then back to the baseline (touch it, or risk having to do it all over), then the far foul line, then back to the baseline (touch!), then the far baseline, then all the way back in a sprint that is accompanied by a countdown. The countdown, called out by Coach, started at an arbitrary moment. He always looked at his watch but I never believed it was a scientific thing. He would wait until the last, slowest person on the team would get into finishing range, and start counting down from ten. Then this last hapless person, who was invariably, with a scientific precision much greater than any faux watch glancing, me, would reach down deep to try and get to the end before the countdown. If you did not, the whole team had to run an extra suicide. We did ten of these after every practice, sometimes more, with thirty-second breaks in between.

Sam Adams had made us run the same drill. The difference, besides the diabolical countdown, was that Gallagher had us run more. And yet if that was the only difference, it would mean the big difference was more of the same. More suicides, more discipline, and an extra practice day (Saturday morning at eight!). But that was not the case. Coach Gallagher brought intensity to the program, a need. He needed it to be successful. He needed basketball to be the most important thing in our lives. And though he didn't go out of his way to communicate this, we got the strong impression it was the most important thing in his life. His previous coaching position had been as an assistant at Manhattanville, a school that we played and who regularly trounced us. However, his actual job did not change when he came to Vassar. Now, as before, he taught second grade English somewhere far away, perhaps Long Island or Westchester, I wasn't sure. He lived far away, too. He had a wife and young daughter.

His car was a somewhat disheveled gray Toyota. I remember seeing him pull out of the parking lot once, when I had stayed extra late working on my shot and he too had stayed late. It was a cold, wintry night and I saw his face in profile under the parking lot lights. My thought then, seeing him in that little car, an hourlong drive ahead of him, was to marvel at how strange it was that my coach was now a citizen, only that, and would have to obey traffic laws just like everyone else. And somewhere beneath that, unarticulated but felt: Wow, he must really like being a coach to come all this way.

Our first year was a moderate success. We won more games than we had, though we didn't break .500. Against Manhattanville, his old team, we played tough until the final seconds. Down by one point, I grabbed an offensive rebound directly under our basket and spastically flung it off the backboard. We lost. Already I was in the unhealthy but inevitable habit of looking over at Coach whenever something good or bad happened on the court. I looked over helplessly, but for a change there was no red tomato rage, only the man's slumped back as he walked down the length of the bench with his pigeon-toed stride, away from me, his fists balled to the size of marbles.

I was, and continue to be, a player for whom the point-blank layup is more difficult than the spinning fallaway in traffic. I had played team ball since junior high school, yet my game was primarily formed on summer playgrounds. In order to thrive I needed flow, improvisation, unconsciousness, and the ball—all the habits coaches will try to erase from their players. When we were walked through the various offensive sets, I responded like an automobile driver who has stopped to ask for directions and promptly zones out, returning to consciousness only when the litany is over, just in time to say thank you. I wasn't without talent, but one of the difficult-to-communicate things about organized basketball is the invisible talent, separate from physical talent, or basketball talent, that is required to integrate your talents into the team system. Every year of my career I had at least one breakout game. I was in the starting rotation for part of every season, only to get benched again, even my senior year.

"You could do that every night if you wanted to," said Coach Gallagher after one of my big games. And it strikes me now that the other half of that question is, "What's holding you back?"

The mysterious alchemy of overcoming personal limits is something Gallagher approached bluntly, with force. You were to be bludgeoned by the force of his personality, the precision of his schemes, the wisdom of his drills. There was something else, too—his commitment. I don't know when it first dawned on us, but at a certain point the team became aware that our coach was working extremely hard. Every opposing team was scouted at length. The man was driving to games on whatever free time he had and returning with detailed diagrams of our opponents' plays, their star players' strengths.

His emphasis was on passing and motion, a banal observation for anyone who follows basketball, and yet at a certain point, the sheer meticulousness with which a plan is presented to you begins to carry its own moral authority. Were we the most scrupulous students of the Gallagher system? Not really. There was a play called "Power," which was signaled by his raising a fist. He would call it from the sidelines in the spirit of a sneak attack or a secret weapon. We went into a bit of assigned choreography, and the result was that one of our big men (myself included) was supposed to get the ball in the low post.

Big deal! Every basketball coach in the world has some equivalent play. And yet I can still feel the conviction with which he explained its design, the triumphant raising of the fist on the sidelines, where he prowled in his disheveled suits, the unquenchable hope with which he yelled it out, small white fist in the air held in what now strikes me as a kind of Black Panther revolutionary-style salute: "Power!"

For all this, I don't think it would be fair to measure Coach Gallagher on his success with the team. And yet I report with pride that his first season we managed a substantial improvement, and his second season, my senior year, we finished with a winning record, ending the season with a winning streak to get that exalted statistic, something that had either never ever happened at Vassar before, or not for a long time, no one was sure. Lobreglio, father and son, were now gone, but their legacy lived on in the form of Seamus Carey and another recruit, Seamus's little brother. There was also a very interesting figure named Karl Butler, formerly of the Irish Olympic team, who materialized from the mists of the Irish basketball mafia to which Gallagher was obviously connected. Like Carey before him, Butler was somehow placed in Ferry House, but he was a basketball nomad, kind of homeless, and extremely merry wherever his game should take him. Butler integrated the bulgur, barley, kale, spinach, and whatever other wholesome ingredients that prevailed at the Ferry kitchen with his usual diet of Guinness. The political discussions at Ferry took an interesting twist when he brought out the photographs he had snapped of his native Belfast, children cavorting among burning cars and so forth.

I used one of those flaming pictures on the cover of a magazine I was editing. I lived mostly in the arty, boozy margin of Vassar life; I hated jock culture in general even as I loved basketball; at Vassar you could have it both ways. Gallagher did not see it that way, really, though in a way he understood.

"Fucking poet," he muttered once when I showed up at the van for the two-hour drive to an away game dressed in whatever outfit I thought cool at the time. Gallagher was aware of my pretensions and ambitions in the literary field, and though he feigned impatience I always thought that deep down he approved. He had a winking, conspiratorial humor and a kind of warmth that he displayed in tiny measured doses, on the sly, when no one was looking. He murmured that comment about my outfit with a smile. I was a hopeless case, though promising. I existed in the harsh galaxy of Coach Gallagher's basketball cosmology. I was part of something special.

THOMAS BELLER is the author of *Seduction Theory: Stories*, *The Sleep-Over Artist: a Novel*, and *How to be a Man: Essays*, all from W. W. Norton. His short fiction has appeared in the *New Yorker*, *Ploughshares*, *Elle*, *Southwest Review*, and *Best American Short Stories*. He is a founding editor of *Open City* magazine and *Books* and Mrbellersneighborhood.com. He has played basketball in places as far-flung as Montana and Phnom Penh, but mostly goes to the court near his apartment in New York.

Ironing

BY CHARLES MCGRATH

MY MOTHER, NOT MY FATHER, was the sports fan in our family. We lived outside of Boston, and so naturally she followed the Red Sox. She listened to the games in the kitchen while smoking Old Golds and doing the ironing, and we could tell if the Sox were doing badly by how heavily the iron thumped on the board. My mother also followed Boston College football, sometimes humming the fight song to herself, and because my brother and I both played hockey, she paid a certain amount of attention to the Bruins, though she took a dim view of hockey players as role models. All retired hockey players, she once told me, would end up living alone in rented rooms and eating soup out of cans. My mother's idea of the proper sport for her sons was golf. It was she (over my father's financial objections) who insisted that we join a little nine-hole club near our summer cabin and that we take a couple of lessons from the leathery, whiskey-breathed local pro.

My mother, as far as I know, never played golf herself. She was mysterious about her past athletic accomplishments and, by the time she was ironing for us, was mostly retired from vigorous physical activity. But we were clearly given the message that she could have been good at golf. She had two sisters, my aunts Libby and Gert, who were both excellent golfers, and in her view, that was proof enough that she had the gift. This may well have been true, it turns out, except that the gift must re-side in the females' mitochondria; it was my sister who inherited all the golfing talent, not my brother and me. Lessons didn't really help. The aforementioned pro and I did not hit it off, and I was mostly (and disastrously) self-taught until late into my teenage years, when my Aunt Gert decided to intervene. We used to play at the local muni, where she was also a ranger, and by patience and example she tried to teach me etiquette and self-control. Some of the lessons took a while to sink in. Gert not only knew the rules (which I regarded much as I did the speed limit back then—as more or less optional), but she played by them and expected others to do likewise.

She accepted "gimmes" the way she would accept a second helping of dessert—graciously but very seldom, and with the clear implication that too much of this could not be good for you. It drove me crazy that Gert didn't hit her driver a whole lot longer than her five-iron; all her shots went more or less the same distance, in fact, a hundred and fifty, a hundred and sixty yards, and straight as a string. Her game was, to my testosterone-engorged mind, boring and—well, womanish. Three shots and on, three shots and on; and did I mention that she was a wizard with the putter? She turned a lot of certain bogeys into pars. But where was the thrill in that? Where was the adventure? My idol in those days was Arnold Palmer, and I didn't in the least mind hitting my approach shots from two fairways over—as long as I was out there. The more I tried to impress Gert, however, the more erratic I became; my scores rocketed and displays of bad temper quickly followed. I would now happily settle for her strategy of three-on and in—except that it's much harder to bring off than I ever imagined back then. Gert and I have a date to play next spring, and I hope to pick up another tip or two from her. Gert is eighty-one, I should add, and still plays almost every day. That's her most inspiring lesson of all.

Years after the sessions with Gert, my sister Mary came along. My parents had given up the country club membership, and Mary, fifteen years younger than me, picked up the game on her own—if picking it up is what happened. I sometimes think that her swing was just there waiting for her to notice it, and it's a swing to die for. She has a big, sweeping turn, is high starting down and long coming through the ball, and finishes high again and in perfect balance. Since Mary is five foot two, and on a rainy day weighs a hundred pounds, the effect is a little disconcerting. She's like a Volkswagen Beetle with a nitro-breathing dragster engine under the hood. She'll smoke you. She even plays off the men's tees sometimes, and invariably elicits wondering head-shakes from the big, beefy guys waiting their turn. That's my sister! I sometimes feel like crowing—except that they would then expect something similar from me.

If Mary has a weakness, it's her short game, and a few lessons from Aunt Gert wouldn't do her any harm either. She has a little of my impatience, my temper, and my distractibility. I can sometimes beat her—not on skill, but by resorting to little fraternal tricks: the jingled change, the well-timed adjustment of my golf-glove Velcro. What are families for if not to teach us how to get under one another's skin? And to teach us some surprising lessons about men and women, our potentials and our limitations.

I won't say that having my aunt and sister as role models has put me in closer touch, exactly, with my softer, feminine side. But it has made me a better golfer, and, who knows, possibly a better guy—though that's not for me to say. Mary and Gert would probably have other ideas. But on one score, at least, my mother would be reassured. My great personal failing, she always felt, was a lack of humility, and my years of golf have long since cured that.

———————————————

CHARLES MCGRATH, the former deputy editor of the *New Yorker* and the former editor of the *New York Times Book Review*, is a writer at large at the *Times*.

The Coach Who Wasn't There

BY DAVID MARANISS

AFTER SPENDING FOUR YEARS GRIPPED in the biographical obsession of Vince Lombardi, whose gap-toothed smile surely would be carved into a Mount Rushmore of American coaches, I inevitably had to ask myself: Could I have played for him? No question could be more theoretical, since my sport was baseball, not football, and I bailed out on a curveball. Still, the question seemed intriguing. I imagined that Lombardi's first words upon catching sight of me would be some variation of, "Son, get your goddamn hair cut!" If he bothered to talk to me at all, that is. As I had learned from interviewing his Green Bay Packer disciples, the old man only barked at you if he saw some promise. Lombardi chewed out Dave Robinson nonstop for five seasons, most memorably after the talented linebacker flushed out Don Meredith near the goal line and forced an interception that clinched the 1966 league championship against the Cowboys in Dallas. "You were out of position," Lombardi instructed Robby before embracing him during the postgame locker room celebration. Far worse if he ignored your imperfections; that meant you were a goner.

Lombardi was not an entirely foreign personality. In some respects, he reminded me of my father, Elliott Maraniss, a quintessential city editor, imposing and intelligent, with a boyish enthusiasm for his occupation and a loving touch beneath a brusque exterior. Never was my father more Lombardiesque than one summer when my brother Jim, on break from Harvard and hired as a temporary fill-in reporter at the *Madison Capital Times*, was told to interview a mother whose toddler had been killed by Winky the elephant at the Henry Vilas Zoo.

"Dad, I can't do that," Jim said, finding the assignment mawkish and unseemly.

"Then you're fired," came the reply, echoing through the newsroom.

Pause. "And don't call me Dad!"

Maybe the kinship had something to do with Brooklyn, where both Lombardi and my dad grew up (Lombardi in Sheepshead Bay, my father in Coney Island), or the fact that they both wore trench coats and chain-smoked and struggled early in their careers until finally, deep into middle age and almost out of options, they found their way to Wisconsin near the end of the 1950s and were able to shine at last.

If Lombardi in that sense was familiar, I still found it strange to think about whether I could have played for him, and it struck me that the reason had less to do with him than with the very notion of coaches. I've had several powerful mentors coaching me in my life and career, none greater than my own father, who shaped how I view the world and how I write, and I'd even include Lombardi high on the list of people who gave me perspective, though the lessons he taught me came decades after he died. But the reality of my childhood, the dominant theme of my youth, in fact, is that my friends and I grew up with the coach who wasn't there. We were almost utterly free from adult pressure or influence, good or bad. It wasn't the anarchy of *Lord of the Flies*, and there was nothing whimsically fantastical about it like *Peter Pan*, it was just, for better and worse, the way we lived in Madison during our baby boom youths of the late fifties to mid-sixties. Time let us play and be golden then, as Dylan Thomas wrote—or maybe our parents did.

When my dad moved our family to Madison in the summer of 1957, the sweet-sweat aroma of baseball scented my life. The Milwaukee Braves of Aaron, Adcock, Bruton, Burdette, Crandall, Covington, Logan, Matthews, and Spahn were resplendent, on their way to winning the National League pennant and conquering the evil Yankee empire in the World Series. In my mind's eye, those pros pose forever in freeze-frame positions: hammering, toting lumber, bunting, squatting, scooping, high-kicking, flinging, all framed in dark green; not the verdant field of County Stadium, but the painted background green that signified you got a beloved Brave during that first heart-thumping thumb through a pack of baseball cards.

I was eight years old that summer, a bony, bucktoothed, asthmatic shortstop whose black high-top gym shoes were perpetually untied. It was my inaugural season, the first of many, in what was the Madison recreation department's equivalent of organized baseball. It was organized only to the degree that our teams had names, our games had an umpire, our leagues had standings, and we wore uniforms—two-toned pullover jerseys with zippered fronts and the lettering of a local sponsor on the back: K & N Water Softener, Bowman's All-Star Dairy, Kippert Construction, Pertzborn Plumbing, Southside Optimists, Karstens, the Hub, Octopus Car Wash, Iowa National, Coca-Cola, Padgham Paint, Findorff Construction, Klein-Dickert, Frautschi's, H & R Variety (inevitably, we called it Hock and Run). Sometimes a boy had a father who worked at the sponsoring business, but more often there was absolutely no connection, and we never heard from them, win or lose.

In our childhood idyll, there were two home fields, one at Vilas Park, the other at Wingra Park. From our homes in the old University Heights neighborhood near Camp Randall Stadium, we rode to the games like a posse on our bikes, one speed, fat tires, gloves flapping on the handlebars. I can't remember a single time that I or any of my teammates got a ride to a game from our parents. This was before the era of minivans and SUVs, but it was also before the era of soccer moms and dads. (Soccer! We never played soccer, barely even heard of it. On the cement playground of Randall School, we did play soccer kickball, which seems to be making a coed young-adult comeback now, four decades after its heyday, and which is really more like baseball, only played with a large boingy rubber ball that you kick instead of a hardball that you bat.)

Parents, in any case, were not part of our summer world. I have a shadowy recollection of an early evening game in the season after seventh grade when our third baseman, Mike O'Meara, raised his glove to cover his mouth, the way big leaguers do when they are telling each other what the next pitch is going to be, and calling out to me at shortstop, "Hey, Dave, is that your dad standing over there behind that tree?"

That scene just about said it all. A parent sighting was so outlandish that it would be called out, and so out of the ordinary that it required a hiding place. I was very close to my dad, and one of the enduring threads of our relationship was baseball. I could listen forever to his story about the time he took my older brother and sister to Briggs Stadium in Detroit and they sat out in the centerfield bleachers, and the Tigers were beating the Red Sox by three runs with the bases loaded and Ted Williams at the plate, and my dad was yelling, "Walk him! Walk him!" and the words were barely out his mouth when the ball rocketed off that distant bat in a monstrous mortar arc and clanged off the seats a few rows away. I also loved nothing more than spending a few hours with my dad on a summer's night listening to a Braves game on the transistor radio. Dad would be down to his boxer shorts and T-shirt, managing the game from our side porch. Yet all of that was apart from my own young sporting life, which I never wanted him to watch, never expected him to watch.

There was an official Little League on the far west side of town, a distant universe, with its modern split-level homes and newly planted greenery in clean boulevard strips. Once, in the summer after sixth grade, a few of us went out to watch a game, and we viewed it with equal parts envy and horror. They had full cloth uniforms, not our synthetic pullover jerseys, and bright white bases, and dugouts, and outfield fences—wow! But they also had adult coaches ordering the boys around and a group of loudmouthed parents in the stands, including one particularly obnoxious mother who was merciless with the umpires. We saw an adult-run system out there that seemed important and alluring, yet also frightening and repellent. The ambivalence I took away from that experience was one that would stay with me for many years.

In the city league, we held our own tryouts and practices, we decided on our own batteries and lineups. Our boys' subculture was certainly haphazard, and not entirely democratic. There were no votes to determine the player-coaches. When we approached adolescence and the brave new world of sex, there was a period when there seemed to be a direct correlation between puberty and influence. But with us it wasn't really a macho thing. It was just that the early developers tended to have deeper voices and more adolescent confidence. At that age, it even had to do with birth dates. I was born in August, and the kids born in February and May seemed so much more worldly.

One might assume that a team run by and for kids would be lax in fundamentals, but that is not how I remember it. Our teams enjoyed taking infield as much as playing the games themselves. Taking infield, to us, was an art form, and we practiced it hour upon hour, day after day. A residual thrill still runs through my body when I think about a perfectly executed infield practice play: a sharp grounder is hit to me at short, I pick it cleanly and rifle a throw to first, then bound over to the second base bag as the first baseman, Dave Foster, heaves one home to the catcher, Steve Marvin, who turns and flings it back to me, my glove slapping the bag as I take his perfect peg. We couldn't hit that well, especially when we faced Iowa National and Dave Jevne's overhand curveball, but no one could beat us at infield practice.

In retrospect, I think here is a place where an adult coach could have made a difference. We couldn't hit that well because we had no one to teach us technique. At the big league level, pure hitters are born, not made, but in the earlier years that isn't so much the case. I've seen entire teams of teenage players who've learned essentially the same method, using their legs to time and control the swing, and at that level, against most pitching, the rote hitting technique learned through repetition can be amazingly effective. We were completely on our own, each of us with our own peculiar stance and swing, which tended to grow more exaggerated year by year. I had a habit of opening up too soon and pulling everything foul. It was just my signature hit, a hard grounder left of third, and no one ever helped me get over it.

Great coaches, of course, do more than teach technique; they impart on their young charges invaluable lessons of life. Or so it is said. I can speak to that only indirectly because I never had a great athletic coach.

Our baseball coach at Madison West High, Russ Paugh, the father of one of my close friends, Jim Paugh, had been a great player himself in his day, but that was long before he reached us. He was a grandfather by then, in the final years of his career. His southern Indiana drawl sounded alien in Madison, and his outdated vocabulary overflowed with clichés that seem endearing now, when I look back on it, but at the time served only as material for behind-the-back mocking, supercilious wise guys that we could be. "Jeeeem," he would say exasperatedly to his son, a pitcher and left fielder, who was no more adaptable to adult coaching than the rest of us, "show a little gumption, Jeeem!" As Coach Paugh led us through calisthenics every day, including jumping jacks, we could be sure to hear him urge us on with the words "No pain, no gain." He was just the wrong coach in the wrong place at the wrong time.

Our final semester in high school, and our last baseball season, came in the spring of 1967. The Summer of Love was approaching, the world was clanging and changing around us. Our natural inclination toward independence, now combined with our earliest tastes of the free-spirited sixties counterculture, created a combustible mix. Perhaps no coach could have controlled us that season. We lived on the edge of the University of Wisconsin, and although much that was going on there was beyond our imaginations, we could not help but notice the more exotic public events. Along with various sit-ins and protests against the war in Vietnam, there was also a "Be-In" that spring, held out on Picnic Point, featuring the poet Allen Ginsberg and various campus hippies and activists, chanting, dancing, reciting poetry, smoking dope, and doing whatever else they felt like doing. There was a buzz on our yellow school bus the following Monday afternoon as we headed from West High out to Franklin Field for the next practice. As I recall it, Lee Higbie, a utility outfielder, who had already established his unconventional credentials by driving a beat-up old red-and-white hearse, concocted the idea of staging our own varsity baseball "Be-In."

While Coach Paugh was on the mound, tossing batting practice, the rest of the team sprinted out to center field and congregated around Higbie, who was leading us in a rendition of Martha and the Vandellas' "Dancing in the Streets" . . . Philadelphia, Pee-A. Don't forget the Motor City . . . On cue we fell onto our backs and started doing the bicycle, pumping our legs in the air, then jumped to our feet and began dancing and doing jumping jacks and pretending we were airplanes and shouting and laughing that we were part of a happening. At some point, the batter broke up and pointed out to the field. Coach Paugh spun around and gazed toward center, a blank look, nothing coming out of his mouth, then turned back and resumed pitching. Soon enough we ran out of gas and went back to our positions. Maybe he understood us after all. With all that, West had a pretty fair baseball team that year, led by Bobby

Freed, my childhood chum, and Tom Seybold, a southpaw who was recruited to pitch at Florida, a college baseball powerhouse. We won our division and lost in the tournament to Janesville Craig.

That was the end of my hardball career. After that, I played fast-pitch softball for many years on a team sponsored by the *Capital Times* and coached by my father. Here, finally, when I was no longer a kid, I didn't mind having my dad watch me play—and I began to appreciate what an amazing coach he was. Elliott knew baseball, he had gone to the University of Michigan on a partial baseball scholarship and had been a bird dog scout for the Baltimore Orioles, but that is not what set him apart. He was cool in his appraisal of talent, understanding precisely what you could do and what you couldn't do, yet he always made his players feel that they were better than they really were. If I turned my back to the infield and ran from my shortstop position out into foul ground deep in left to bring in a fly, he could tell me with bubbly enthusiasm that I'd made a major league play, and though I knew the difference, I sort of believed him, and went after the next long foul even harder.

It was an expression of that same optimism by my father, a few months earlier, that had marked what I consider the single most decisive event in shaping my career as a writer. I had grown up in the intellectual shadows of my older brother Jim and sister Jean. Family members tend to fall into roles, and in our family they were the scholars and I was the jock. In truth, they were far brighter academically than I was athletically, but that was all I had going for me, or so I thought. One day when I was sixteen I accompanied my dad into the newsroom at the *Cap Times*, and he introduced me to one of his reporters by saying, "This is my younger son, Dave. He's going to be the best writer of all of us." I had no idea that he thought I could write, and I certainly wasn't sure that I could, but that assertion moved me in a way that nothing had before, and awakened me to another world of possibilities. Many times after that, whenever I

doubted myself, that unexpected prediction from the tough old
city editor—the same guy who'd almost fired my brother for refusing to interview a grieving mother—kept me going. I wanted
to prove him right.

I believe deeply that those long-ago summers that my friends
and I lived in an adult-free world were largely positive. They
taught me how to survive on my own wits, and they encouraged
my slightly nonconformist nature, an important attribute for a
writer. In recent years, as a mentor to younger people in the
newspaper business, I've given a speech that I call "How to
Stay One Step Ahead of Your Editors," in which I try to help reporters think through their beats and coverage in a way that allows them to both satisfy their editors and their own interests at
the same time. Now I realize the origins of that journalistic instinct—it comes from the coach who wasn't there. But I also realize that without that push from my dad, I would not have such
fond and positive memories of my childhood. In the yin and
yang of life, I needed some way to channel the freedom of my
youth into a discipline as an adult. My father got me started,
and, in an odd way, Vince Lombardi pushed me further, again,
a few decades later.

Lombardi died in 1970, when I was twenty-one and in college. As I was researching my biography of him in the late
1990s, I came to realize that he was a largely misunderstood
myth, misappropriated by the right and left for different purposes. The right loved him as a symbol of the old way, of un-
bending discipline; God, family, and the Green Bay Packers.
The left detested him as a symbol of a win-at-all-costs pathol-
ogy. Both sides had him wrong. He was far more flexible than
many believed, a master psychologist who treated each of his
players differently. His obsession with football distorted his pri-
orities, despite his best intentions. It was God and football tied
for first, family a distant third. But he was not obsessed with
winning so much as with excellence. He was always harder on
his teams when they played poorly but won than when they lost

but gave their all. The phrase most often attributed to him—
"Winning isn't everything, it's the only thing"—wasn't even
coined by Lombardi, but rather was first uttered by a young actress in the John Wayne movie *Trouble Along the Way*, and she was
talking to a social worker played by Donna Reed.

Lombardi was a contradictory man inside a simple exterior;
an imperfect figure driving for perfection in others. I disagreed
with him on many things, but on one large philosophical idea I
found that I learned more from him than I ever expected. It is
the idea of freedom through discipline. That is, the only way
truly to be free is to discipline yourself to master the world
around you. With Lombardi, his players were disciplined to
learn the Packer sweep, one running play, over and over, every
practice, day after day, but they practiced it so often and learned
all of the possible variations of it and defensive responses to it
so thoroughly that it became not a matter of rote but of intu-
ition. They could see everything more clearly, as if in slow motion, so that once a game started, they had tremendous freedom
to react. That philosophy of freedom through discipline kept
them one step ahead of their opponents. What is true for football players also holds for other professions, even ones that on
the surface might seem so different. A jazz musician becomes
free through the discipline of knowing the music; it is only then
that his improvisations become great. And so it is with a writer.
Just as his old players were different people when they finished
playing for him, I felt I was a different person when I finished
writing about Lombardi. In that sense, I put him up there with
my father, the two men I needed most, and finally knew what
to do with, after the sweet ease of my coachless youth.

Pulitzer Prize winner DAVID MARANISS, who grew up in Wisconsin during the glory years of the Packers, is an associate editor at the *Washing-*

ton Post and author of several critically acclaimed and best-selling books about Vietnam and the sixties, Bill Clinton, and Vince Lombardi. He dedicates this essay to his father, Elliott Maraniss, who died in 2004.

The Depression Baby

BY FRANK DEFORD

IN AL MCGUIRE'S OFFICE AT MARQUETTE, images of sad clowns abound. Pictures, all over the place, of sad clowns. Everybody must ask him about them. McGuire is touted to be a con, so the sad clowns have got to be a setup. Right away, commit yourself to those sad clowns, you're coming down his street. *Hey, buddy, why do you have a banana in your ear? Because I couldn't find a carrot.* Zap, like that. And yet, how strange an affectation: sad clowns. Obviously, they must mean something. It cannot be the sadness, though. Of all the things this fascinating man is—and clown is one—he is not sad.

Another thing he is, is street smart. McGuire has grown up and left the pavement for the boardrooms, so now when he spots this quality in others, he calls it "credit-card-wise." One time in a nightclub, when the band played "Unchained Melody," all the 40-year-olds in the place suddenly got up and packed the floor, cheek to cheek. Nostalgia ran rampant. Right away, Al said, "Summer song. This was a summer song when it came out. Always more memories with summer songs."

Perfect. He got it. Right on the button. Of course, this is a small thing. A completely insignificant thing. But the point is, he got it just right. And this is a gift. It is McGuire's seminal gift, for all his success flows from it. The best ballplayers see things on the court. McGuire lacked this ability as an athlete, but he owns it in life. Most people play defense in life, others "token it" (as Al says), but there are few scorers, and even fewer play-makers, guys who see things about to open up and can take ad-vantage. McGuire is one of life's playmakers. He perceives. He should be locked in a bicentennial time capsule so that genera-tions yet unborn will understand what this time was really like. There will be all the computers and radar ovens and Instamat-ics, and McGuire will pop out from among them in 2176 and say, "If the waitress has dirty ankles, the chili will be good." And, "Every obnoxious fan has a wife at home who dominates him." And, "If a guy takes off his wristwatch before he fights, he means business." And, "Blacks will have arrived only when we start seeing black receptionists who aren't good-looking."

Words tumble from his mouth. He's a lyrical Marshall McLuhan. Often as not, thoughts are bracketed by the name of the person he is addressing, giving a sense of urgency to even mundane observations: "Tommy, you're going to make the turn here, Tommy." "Howie, how many of these go out, Howie?" And likewise, suddenly, late at night, apropos of nothing, un-prompted, spoken in some awe and much gratitude: "Frank, what a great life I've had, Frank."

This starts to get us back to the sad clowns. The key to un-derstanding McGuire is to appreciate his unqualified love of life, of what's going on around him. e.e. cummings: "I was mar-velously lucky to touch and seize a rising and striving world; a reckless world, filled with the curiosity of life herself; a vivid and violent world welcoming every challenge; a world hating and adoring and fighting and forgiving; in brief, a world which was a world." Al McGuire: "Welcome to my world." With him everything is naturally vivid and nearly everything is naturally contradictory, the way it must be in crowded, excited worlds.

So with the clowns. It is not the sadness that matters, or even the clownishness. It is the *sad clown*, a contradiction. By defini-tion, can there be such a thing as a sad clown? Or a wise coach? "Sports is a coffee break," McGuire says. And Eugene McCarthy once observed, "Coaching is like politics. You have to be smart enough to know how to do it, but dumb enough to think it is important."

Now, if all of the foregoing has tumbled and twisted and gone in fits and spurts, that's what it is like being around Al McGuire. His business, making money (it includes coaching as a necessary evil), comes ordered and neat, hermetic—to use his word, *calculated*—but everything else veers off in different directions, at changing speeds, ricocheting. Actually, all of that is calculated, too, only we cannot always fathom to what purpose. For example, later on here McGuire is going to expound at length on how he is not only sick of coaching but how he no longer applies himself to the task, and how Marquette could be virtually unbeatable if he just worked harder. Now, these remarks were made thoughtfully and have been repeated and embellished on other occasions. Obviously, they are going to come back to haunt him. Other recruiters are going to repeat them to prospects. If Marquette loses a couple of games back-to-back, the press and the alumni and the students and even those warm and wonderful fans who don't have shrews for wives are going to throw this admission back in his face. And he knows this, knew it when he spoke. So maybe you can figure out why he said what he did. Probably it has something to do with tar babies. Somehow he figures that other people who slug it out with him in his world are going to get stuck.

People are dazzled by McGuire, by his colorful language and by the colorful things he does—riding motorcycles at his age, which is 48, or going off on solitary trips to the four corners of the globe. That stuff is all out front, hanging out there with the clown pictures, so people seize upon it and dwell on this "character." They miss the man. First off, he is a clever entrepreneur, a promoter, a shrewd businessman, an active executive of a large sports equipment company (vice president of Medalist Industries). This interests him much more than the baskets. "And I have an advantage," he says, "because people have a false impression from reading about me. They expect one thing and suddenly find themselves dealing with a very calculating person. I scare them. I want to skip the French pastry and get right down to the numbers."

The fans and the press think of McGuire as the berserk hothead who drew two technicals in an NCAA championship game, or the uncommonly handsome, dapper sharpie, pacing, spitting, playing to the crowd, cursing his players, themselves attired in madcap uniforms resembling the chorus line in *The Wiz*. The fans and the press overlook the fact that McGuire's Marquette teams have made the NCAA or the NIT ten years in a row, averaging twenty-five wins a season the last nine, and they got there by concentrating on defense, ice-picking out victories by a few points a game. As a coach, you can't much control an offense: *They just weren't going in for us tonight.* A defense is a constant, seldom fluctuating, always commanding. Just because people see Al McGuire's body on the bench, they assume that is he, carrying on. You want to see Al McGuire, look out on the court, look at the way his team plays, calculating. McGuire will play gin rummy against anybody; he won't play the horses or a wheel in Vegas; he won't play the house. You play him, his game, his world. "People say it's all an act, and maybe it is," he says. "Not all of it—but I don't know myself anymore whether I'm acting. Not anymore. I don't know. I just know it pleases me."

The motorcycle, for example, gets involved here. McGuire adores motorcycling. Most mornings at home in Milwaukee, he rises at seven and tools around for a couple of hours on his Kawasaki. Before the regionals in Louisiana last year, he rented a bike and went to a leper hospital. So the motorcycle business is for real. Also, it is French pastry. Let us look at McGuire vis-à-vis more important things; for example, cars and women.

Now, most coaches adore automobiles and have no rapport with women. That is not to say that they don't like sex; it is to say that they tolerate women because women provide sex. But they don't enjoy the company of women. They don't like them *around.* This is what upsets them about women's athletics, not the money it's going to take from men's sports. Just that they're going to be around. On the other hand, American coaches are nuts about cars. Cars count. The most important thing to coaches is to get a courtesy car to drive around town in. This is the sign of being a successful coach. Almost any American coach will sign for $10,000 less if you give him the use of a $6,500 car.

Naturally, being one of the most famous and successful basketball coaches in the land, Al McGuire has a courtesy car. It is a Thunderbird. He gets a fresh one every two years. But, unlike other coaches, he has no relationship with his car. It doesn't mean anything to him. Last February, after a whole winter of driving the thing, 3,200 miles' worth, he still didn't have any idea how to turn on the heat. He had to be shown. And while he can whip around on his motorcycle, he is nearly incompetent as an automobile driver. Sometimes he hunches over the wheel, sort of embracing it, and lets the car carry him and his country music along. Other times he takes both hands off the wheel to properly gesticulate. As a rule, he stops at all stop signs, including those that face down the other road of an intersection. This leads to some confusion in the cars behind the courtesy Thunderbird. Or sometimes, when a topic especially involves him, the car will sort of drift to a halt as he is talking. Just kind of peter out by the side of the road.

But as he does not fraternize with cars, so is he the rare coach who enjoys and appreciates women. This is not telling tales out of school. This has nothing to do with his marriage, which is going on twenty-seven years. This has to do with women generically. "I get along with women better than I do with men," Al says, simply enough. Whenever he talks to a woman he knows, he takes her hands gently in his and confides in her. But understand, the consummate calculator doesn't flash those green eyes just to be friendly. There are many ways to be credit-card-wise. "I've always believed that if you get women involved in anything, it will be a success," McGuire says. "Frank, most men in America are dominated by women, Frank."

He is not. He and Pat McGuire share a marriage that is not unlike the way he coaches. They do not crowd one another. In the twenty-six years he has been married, he has never used a house key. When he comes home, Pat must let him in. When it is late, which it often is, she is inclined to say, "Where have you been?" He replies, "Pat, were there any calls for me, Pat?" When Marquette is on the road, McGuire never sits in the game bus waiting for it to leave. He waits in a bar for the manager to come in and tell him everyone is aboard. Then, if someone was late, he doesn't know. "A lot of coaching is what you choose *not* to do, *not* to see," McGuire says. "This is hypocritical, of course, but it is also true."

This, however, is not to suggest that Pat McGuire puts up with him completely. Like her husband, she is not crazy about all kinds of surprises. This leads to the Al McGuire First Rule of Marriage: when you have something unsettling to tell your wife, advise her thereof just before you go into the bathroom. Thus, when Al decides to take off for Greece or the Yukon or any place where "I can get away from credit cards and free tickets," he announces the trip to Pat as he walks down the hall. "Yes?" she answers. "I'm going to Greece tomorrow for two weeks," he calls out. "What?" she says, afraid she had heard him correctly again. She has. Then he repeats the message and closes the bathroom door. This has worked, more or less, for twenty-six years. Is it at all surprising that his unorthodoxy has succeeded so well at Marquette for a mere twelve?

Now that you are more than somewhat confused, let us go back to his beginning. Al McGuire is influenced by his family and his heritage. He was born on September 7, 1928, in the Bronx but grew up in the Rockaway Beach section of Queens, where his family ran a workingman's bar. It was a club, a phone, a bank; they cashed paychecks. There were fifty-six saloons in seven blocks, meaning a) the McGuires had a lot of competition, but b) they were in the right business for that particular constituency. Al was named for Al Smith, then running as the first major Catholic presidential candidate. Al Smith was the quintessential New Yorker. He was fervently opposed to Prohibition, he wore a derby hat and said such strange words as "raddio" for what brought us *Amos 'n' Andy.* The namesake McGuire, removed from New York for two decades now, first in North Carolina, then in Milwaukee, still honors the other Al by talking Noo Yawkese. The *r*'s in the middle of many words evaporate. Thus, the fowuds play in the conner, whence they participate in pattuns. And there is the occasional awreddy and youse and den (for then), and the missing prepositions so reminiscent of that disappearing subway culture: down Miami; graduated high school.

McGuire also claims to have enriched the language. It was his interest in the stock market, he says, that brought the term "blue chip" into sports ("But I wasn't famous enough at the time to get credit for it"). Likewise, "uptick," for when a stock/team advances. Gambling, a familiar pursuit of his father's, an illness for his legendary older brother John, provided "the minus pool" (for losers), "a push" (a standoff), and "numbers," the word McGuire invariably uses for dollars. "What are the numbers?" is a common McGuire expression. Then, from the old sod, there are the adages: "Never undress until you die" (always save something, or, "Squirrel some nuts away"). "Congratulate the temporary" (live for the moment, or, "Go barefoot in the wet grass"). He has recently developed an interest in antiques, which he hunts down on his motorcycle forays, and promises us new terms from antiquing soon.

But it is his imagery, original and borrowed, that is the most vivid McGuire. Seashells and balloons: happiness, victory. Yellow ribbons and medals: success in recruiting. Memos and pipes: academia. Hot bread and gay waiters: guaranteed, a top restaurant. A straw hat in a blizzard: what some people, like the NCAA, will provide you with. Even a whale comes up for a blow sometimes: advice to players who can't get their minds off women. Hot lunch for orphans: a giveaway, some sort of PR venture. French pastry: anything showy or extraneous, such as small talk or white players. Keepers: good-looking broads (you don't throw them back). Closers: people who get by the French pastry and complete a deal, e.g., yours truly, Al McGuire. Guys who charge up the hill into a machine gun: most X-and-O coaches; see also "Brooks Brothers types" and "First Communion guys." Welcome to my world: come uptown with me.

Moreover, McGuire has begun more and more to turn nouns into verbs. Thus, to "rumor it out" is what a smart executive does when he keeps his ear to the ground. And: "Guys like Chones and Meminger magnet kids for us." Or: "You've got to break up cliques or you'll find players husband-and-wifing it out on the court." Or: "If you haven't broken your nose in basketball, you haven't really played. You've just tokened it."

It is the custom at Marquette to let teammates fight, to encourage fights, for that matter, until the day the season opens. McGuire lets them go a minute. One day he stood there, biting his lip for the required time while an older player beat his son Allie, a pretty fair guard, all to hell. This policy is calculated to let frustrations out, draw the team together. Calculated. For he has no stomach for it. McGuire has seen all he would ever want of fighting.

It was an old Irish thing. His father, John Sr., delighted in it. What more could a man want than to sip a beer and watch his boys mix it up? If not large for a basketball player—6′ 3″— McGuire was a big kid in a saloon, and he worked behind the bar from an early age. It was the bartender's job to break up fights. If you hired a bouncer, the trouble was he was liable to start fights himself; otherwise, he couldn't justify his job. So, fight started, the barkeep had to come over the bar. Feet first. Always come feet first. Or, if the action was slack, a slow Tuesday or whatnot, old John McGuire might drum up a fight for one of his own boys, and they would "go outside" to settle things.

Al McGuire played ball the same way. His older brother Dick, now a Knick scout, was the consummate Noo Yawk player for St. John's and the Knicks—a slick ball handler and passer. Al was what he himself calls a dance-hall player. He was good enough to star as a college player, at St. John's, but as a pro could only hang on as an enforcer for three seasons with the Knicks. Once he grabbed Sid Borgia, the famous official, in what was described by horrified observers as "a boa constrictor grip." Counting two technicals, he got eight fouls in less than a quarter in one game. He boasted that he could "stop" Bob Cousy in his heyday, which he could, after a fashion, halting the action by fouling Cousy or the guy who sets picks for him. It was McGuire's big mouth that first sold out the Boston Garden for the Celtics. They paid to see the brash Irishman try to stop their Celtics. In the off-season McGuire would go back to Rockaway, tend bar, and go outside when his father asked for such divertissement.

"We all thought it was so romantic," he says, "so exciting, but, Frank, looking back, it wasn't, Frank." Not long ago McGuire was in a joint in Greenwich Village. A few tables over, there was an argument. The guy took off his watch. It took six, seven guys to subdue him. McGuire turned to the businessman he was with. "He'll be back," he said. He had seen it so many times. Sure enough, in a little while the guy was back, and there was another mess. The next morning, at breakfast, McGuire began thinking about the previous night's incident, and just like that, he threw up. "Maybe it was the orange juice," he says, "but I don't think so. It was what that fight made me remember. It scared me. I don't want those memories."

One time, when he was about 24 or 25, his father got him to go outside with a guy. "I was handling him, but I couldn't put him away," McGuire says, "and I knew I couldn't get away with this." He was very relieved when the cops came and broke it up. Al went back into the bar and told his father, "Dad, that's it, Dad. I'm never gonna go outside again." And he never did. His father sulked for a month or more. It was not long after that that Al decided all of a sudden he could be very successful in life at large.

But money, or the lack of it, has influenced Al McGuire more than taking guys outside. Some people who grew up in the Depression are that way. The McGuires had food on the table; they weren't on the dole. Still, money was a concern. Of the sons, John, now 52, was considered the clever one. And he was, except for the gambling. He has adapted well; he runs a gay bar now. Dick, 50, was considered the bright one. At an early age he could do the *New York Times* crossword. Al, the youngest, would become an Irish cop, an FBI man if he got lucky. He was scheduled to take an FBI physical one day but played golf instead. He thought he had blown a great chance in life and, remorseful, on his way home he stopped his car on the Cross Bay Bridge, got out, and chucked his clubs, the cart, the whole business, in the water. It was a little while later, when he was an assistant coach at Dartmouth, that he decided he could be a success, he could make money.

You see, even when nobody figured Al for anything, the family let him handle the books. The kid was at home with the numbers. And then one day at Dartmouth, where it snowed a lot, he was alone, and had time to think, and he figured out he had more talent with the numbers than with the baskets. "Since then I've never had any trouble making money," he says. "All I have to do is sit down and think. I believe I can do anything in that area."

Since then, while he has coached every year, while it is his profession, coaching has never been the ultimate. As a consequence, he is not vulnerable there. McGuire often says (indeed, he doth protest too much), "I've never blown a whistle, looked at a film, worked at a blackboard or organized a practice in my life." Which is true, and which drives other coaches up the wall. But McGuire, the anti-coach, regularly discusses land mortgages, Medalist shoulder-pad marketing, and his theories on the

short-range future of municipal bonds. Intellectually, tempera-
mentally, what is the difference between a fascination with a
high-post back door and a short-term bond yield?

And yet, McGuire is only hung up on the numbers in the abstract. *The numbers:* It is a euphemism, like the Victorians using
"limbs" for legs. Real money doesn't mean anything to him. He
carries it all scrunched up in his pocket: bills, credit cards, notes,
gum wrappers, identification cards, all loose together. He takes
out the whole mess and plops it on the counter. "Take what you
want," he says. A credit card? Two dollars and sixty-three cents
for breakfast? My driver's license? Take whatever you want.
The Depression baby just wants to know that the money in the
bank is solid and permanent. *Never undress until you die.*

"I must be the highest-paid coach in the country," he says. "I
wanted it. I thought it would be a goose for basketball. I don't
mean just what I get from Marquette. I mean all the numbers.
If anybody put all the numbers together it would amaze people.
But understand: It hasn't changed me. I've always lived the
same. My friends are still hit-and-run types. I eat the same as
ever, drink the same, clown around the same. My wife still
wears Treasure Island dresses."

He is not friendly with many coaches. Hank Raymonds has
been beside him on the bench all twelve years at Marquette and
has never had a meal at the McGuires'. Raymonds and young
Rick Majerus do the Xs and Os, the trench work. McGuire believes in "complementary" coaches, as he does in complementary players, units that support each other's efforts, not
duplicate them. "I can drink enough cocktails for the whole
staff," McGuire says. "I don't need another me."

His assistants (McGuire, out of respect and guilt, has taken to
calling them "co-coaches") understand his soft-shoe. One asks
Majerus: What is it above all about McGuire? We are so used to
hearing about the originality, the insouciance, the motorcycle
flake, the ability to get along with black players—what is it really with McGuire? "The one main thing," Majerus answers, "is

this insecurity Al has about money. Still. I guess he'll always be that way."

There was a group with McGuire a couple of winters ago after a road game. As always, he wouldn't countenance any talk about basketball, but soon enough he brought up the subject of the numbers. Typically, it was the woman in the gathering that he turned to, confided in. Speaking softly, as he does on these occasions, he told her he thought he had things worked out OK for his three kids, for Pat. They were going to have enough. For a Depression baby this made him feel good, he said. But what if he accumulated more money, the woman asked him, what would he do with that?

McGuire was not prepared for the question. He thought for a moment. "A park," he said then. "With what's left, I'd like to see them build a park for poor people."

To most everybody in the business, McGuire is a nagging aberration. Listening to him lecture 500 coaches at a Medalist clinic, Chuck Daly of Penn whispers, "If the rest of us operated his way, we'd be out of business." That is the conventional wisdom. But before he said that, Daly made another observation: "Al's logic is on a different level, above everybody else's." And that is the conventional wisdom, too. So wait a minute. If McGuire wins twenty-five a year and he has the logic, he obviously has the right way. That is logical. Nonetheless, he remains the only coach who waits in the bar, and he stays frustrated that coaches have such low esteem and little security.

"Coaches are so scared," he says. "Every day, practice starts: gimme three lines, gimme three lines. You come out and say gimme two lines, everybody will look at you like you just split the atom. Me, whether it's business or coaching, I'm so pleased when I look like a fool. When I don't do foolish things, make foolish new suggestions, I'm not doing my job. I'm just another shiny-pants bookkeeper.

"The trouble with coaching, the prevailing image, is that coaching is like what you had in high school, because that is the last place where most people were involved with coaching. But coaching college is not pizza parties and getting the team together down at the A and W stand. People can't understand my players screaming back at me, but it's healthy. Also, I notice that the screaming always comes when we're fifteen, twenty ahead. When it's tied, then they're all listening very carefully to what I have to say."

Many adult coaches demand unquestioning loyalty from 20-year-old kids. As McGuire points out, some of the most successful coaches even refuse to accept kids with different philosophies, conflicting egos. "Dealing with problems, with differences—that is what coaching is," he says. "Running pattuns is not coaching." He does not believe that character can be "built" with haircuts and Marine routines and by coaches so insecure that their players can never challenge them.

Off the court, McGuire sees his players only when they come to him in distress. He would be suspicious of any college kid who wanted to be buddy-buddy with a middle-aged man, and vice versa. "I don't pamper," he says. "These guys are celebrities in their own sphere of influence—top shelf, top liquor. Everybody around them touches them with clammy hands. That's the only word: clammy. Well, they don't get that from me." Often, he doesn't even bother to learn their names. For much of last season the starting center, Jerome Whitehead, was called Chapman. Sometimes McGuire has stood up to scream at a player and then had to sink back down because he couldn't remember the kid's name.

"Look, if you're into coaching heavy, into the blackboard, if you're gonna charge up the hill into the machine guns, then you might as well stay at St. Ann's in the fifth grade," he says. "Because coaching up here is something else. You're gonna have to deal with the fifth column, the memos and pipes. And you're gonna get fired. The trouble is, every coach thinks he has the new wrinkle and is gonna last forever. Coaching is a mistress, is what it is. If a job opened up in Alaska tomorrow, two hundred fifty guys from Florida would apply, and they wouldn't even ask about the numbers, and they wouldn't ask their wife, either, like they wouldn't about any mistress.

"But to the players you ain't a love affair. You're just a passing fancy to them. It's pitiful, too, because about every coach who leaves makes better numbers on the outside."

Everyone assumes McGuire gets along with his players—especially the inner-city blacks—because of his unique personality. It counts, to be sure, every charmer is an overlay. But look past the French pastry and his calculation surfaces again—just as he promises. No con works unless the conned party figures he is the one really getting the edge. McGuire settles for a push. "They get and I get," he says. While the players don't get an uncle-coach, they get, as McGuire calls it, "a post-recruiter." He virtually forces them to get a diploma, and he hustles them up the richest pro contracts or good jobs in business. It is surely not just a coincidence that McGuire has thrived during the years when the big-money pro war was on. He has been a cash coach in a cash-and-carry era. On one occasion the Marquette provost had to personally intercede to stop McGuire from pressuring the sports PR man about withholding unfavorable statistics that might harm a player's pro chances.

Shamelessly, McGuire promotes his seniors, a ploy that keeps a kid hustling, playing defense, giving up the ball for his first three seasons, so he will get the ball and the shots (and maybe then the big numbers) his final year. Already, in anticipation of this season, McGuire has begun to protest that Butch Lee, a junior guard, got too much publicity as the star of the Puerto Rico Olympic team. Bo Ellis, a senior, is scheduled to get the ink this time around.

The McGuire Arrangement is, basically, us against them— "The only two things blacks have ever dominated are basketball and poverty"—and it works because he tends bar for everybody. Nobody ever fussed with McGuire more than last year's ball handler, Lloyd Walton. "Sit down!" he would scream at his coach all through games. Says Walton, "He figures your problems are his problems. Hey, I've had a black coach in summer ball, but I never had the rapport with him I had with Al."

When McGuire learned one November night back in 1968 that revolutionaries on campus were pressuring the black players to quit because they were being "exploited," he met with the players in a motel room sometime after 2 a.m. He didn't go long on philosophy. He told them he would support their decision if they left and gave up their scholarships, but he also reminded them that there were more where they came from—maybe not so good, but they weren't Marquette basketball. He was.

Then he faced down the radicals. The smooth-talking theorists he screamed at. The tough guys he ridiculed. He suggested to an idealistic white coed that she should take one of the black players home to her suburb for Thanksgiving. To a priest, he snarled, "Don't come after these kids from the Jesuit house. You never bought a pound of butter in your life, and you're asking them to be kamikaze pilots." By 4:30 a.m. when Pat came to the doorbell to let him in, the revolution was dead.

The relationship between Marquette and McGuire is a curious one and, it seems, a push. Marquette is one of the few Catholic schools left that compete, year after year, with the huge state institutions. For that matter, Marquette is the only private school of any stripe that is always right there at the top. The Warriors not only sell out for the season, they do it head to head, in the same building, against the Milwaukee Bucks, a first-class pro team.

Never mind the ratings: Basketball pays a lot of bills at Marquette. It retired the oppressive old football debt. And McGuire must be reckoned with; for several years now he has been athletic director as well as coach. Of course, there are certain Marquette elements leery of the image of the school being filtered through the McGuire prism.

What the nation sees of Marquette University is a self-proclaimed hustler, ranting and raving at the establishment, running a team of ghetto blacks dressed in wild uniforms. What is this, some kind of desperado vocational school? In fact, Marquette is a relatively subdued place, Jesuit, stocked for the most part by white middle-class midwestern Catholics who end up as schoolteachers. Typically, McGuire—who sent all three of his children there—guarantees that it must be good academically or it couldn't get by charging such high tuition numbers.

While the coach and the school do share the same religion, McGuire does not get faith confused with the pattuns or the players who execute them. His only public concession to Catholicism, such as it is, is his pregame exhortation, which went like this last season, all in one breath: "All-right-let's-show-them-we're-the-number-two-team-in-the-country-and-beat-the-shit-out-of-them-Queen-of-Victory-pray-for-us."

Mostly the Jesuit fathers confine themselves to second-guessing the coach's substitutions rather than the morality of his antics. Says Father William Kelly, an associate professor of theology, "Al does use a few cultural expressions that some might find flippant—'Hail Mary shot,' that sort of thing—but he is not sacrilegious in the traditional faith context. He has just found congeniality in colloquialism. In fact, in terms of his ideals and his faith, he is very much a man of the Church. He is really a very conservative Catholic, if not necessarily a very good one. But Al is loyal and deep in his faith. He is competitive, but when he loses there is no blame. And he always points toward other, more important things."

Ay, there's the rub. The man has never really relished coaching, and with each succeeding season has cared for it less. When the call came, out of the blue, to interview for the Marquette opening ("They were desperate, obviously; otherwise they would have taken a First Communion guy"), he was drifting into real estate and other ventures, coaching with his left hand at little Belmont Abbey College in North Carolina. He went

6–19 and 6–18 his last two years there and was preparing to leave coaching altogether.

He appears to be approaching that estate again. In many ways, as he is the first to admit, Marquette basketball survives on his reputation and the hard work of Raymonds and Majerus. McGuire deigns to make only one recruiting visit a year ("The kids know more about me now than I know about them, but even though I don't work at it, I'm the best recruiter in the world"), and, invariably—eleven years out of thirteen—he gets his ace with his one-shot road show. He is often late for practice; sometimes he doesn't even know where the team is practicing. He gets older and smarter, but for a coach time stands still. The kids area always 19 going on 20, and most coaches and fans are one-track zombies; the Germans have the best word for them: *Fachidioten*—specialty idiots. McGuire would rather talk about how his new uniforms will televise than about his player prospects. When he gets to the Arena floor, the first things he checks are the four most distant corner seats—the worst ones in the house. If they are sold, he figures he has done it again. Then, only then, does he come to life as a coach. For two hours.

"I hate everything about this job except the games," McGuire says. "Everything. I don't even get affected anymore by the winning, by the ratings, those things. The trouble is, it will sound like an excuse because we've never won the national championship, but winning just isn't all that important to me. I don't know why exactly. Maybe it's the fear, the fear of then having to repeat. You win once, then they expect you to win again. On the other hand, I found out when I got those two technicals in the NCAA finals that people sympathized with me for making an ass out of myself. I get thirty-five million people looking at me, I can't help it, I immediately become an ass. People relate to that.

"But, Frank, I'm not doing the job anymore, Frank. I never liked coaching, but at least I should be available more. I should be more courteous to my staff. I should have a more orderly process with the university. Maybe it's the repetition. You take the clinics we do for Medalist. They're almost a success, but now, just when they're getting to be that, I don't have no thrill anymore. I wonder about myself. Can I be a success in anything permanently? Anything permanent?

"I figure I'm wrong eighty percent of the time, but it takes too much time to be right. I won't pay that price with my life. I'm jealous of guys like Dean Smith, Bobby Knight. I'm jealous of their dedication. I wish I had it. I admire the way their teams are dressed, the way their kids handle themselves. At the regionals last year one of our kids came down to lunch barefoot. But I just don't like coaching that much to put the time in on a thing like that. It's not my world. I run my team the only way I can run it and still keep my life.

"I'm ready to get out. It's just the numbers. So many of my numbers depend on me coaching. I'm scared to get out. Fear there, too. So maybe it's time I concentrated on coaching just for one year. It's been long enough I haven't concentrated. Frank, we could have a destructive machine if I worked at it. A destructive machine, Frank."

Is he acting now? It certainly doesn't seem so. The green eyes are neither twinkling nor blazing theatrically, the way they do when they signal routines. By happenstance, McGuire has been momentarily distracted. He came to an out-of-town place under the impression it was a greasy-spoon Mexican joint, but it has turned out, instead, to be a fancy-Dan supper club. With floor show. With table linen, yet. McGuire, in his sneakers and sport shirt, wasn't figuring on this—and place, setting the stage, is very important to him.

He wants to recruit around the kitchen table. Depression babies are kitchen guys, not parlor people. When a player comes to talk to him, get him out of the office, out of Marquette; get him down into some back-alley saloon. Welcome to my world. Visitors are escorted to an oil-cloth-covered dining-room table in the back of a rundown Mexican bodega for a home-cooked

meal. Or he just walks with people. Nobody anymore walks
along and talks except for Al McGuire. Right away, the other
guy is off stride, in the minus pool. You know what it must come
from?" From the going outside to fight guys. The meanness is
out of it, but it's the same principle, same game. OK, let's you
and me go outside. Let's go in here. Let's drive out to this lake
I know. Let's go to this guy's apartment. Let's go to this little
Chinese place. Let's take a walk.

Everybody makes such a to-do about Al McGuire's exotic
travels. Big deal: New Zealand. What is that? Anybody can go to
New Zealand. That is the diversion, his escape, the smoke
screen. Look at his world. That is the truly exotic one. How
could a guy so Noo Yawk fit in so well in Milwaukee, or in Carolina before that? It's easy. Wherever McGuire is, he constructs
a whole universe out of selected bars and restaurants, places to
walk, acquaintances, teddy bears and zanies, places to drive,
back rooms and penthouses, motorcycles and country music
jukeboxes. Tall guys with broken noses are also a part of this
community. There is a cast and there are sets—everything but
a zip code.

Nobody else is permitted to see it all. He tells his secretaries
when he hires them: two years. After two years, no matter how
good you are—especially if you're good—out. *It's 3 a.m., where
have you been? Pat, any calls for me, Pat?* The only person who
lives in Al McGuireland is Al McGuire. Cynics and the jealous
take a look at the characters who pass through, and they check
out his con and whisper that he is really an ice-cold man who
surrounds himself with bootlickers and sycophants. But that is
not true. On the contrary. Sure, they all play up to McGuire—
remember now, charmers are an overlay—but he has a need for
them, too. Not just the players and the coaches, but all the people and places in Al McGuireland are complementary. Like his
players, all retain their individuality and integrity. That's the
whole point: Otherwise they're no good to him. Lloyd Walton
screaming back is the Lloyd Walton that McGuire wants, in the

same way that sometimes he selects a fleabag hotel precisely because he wants a fleabag hotel.

The one permanent thing is the numbers. They are distant and bland, to be sure, but they provide permanency. The other things—the people and the places and the basketball games—are vivid and dear, but they consume too much of him to be sustained. And critics say it is all an act. McGuire wonders himself. But, no, he is not acting. He is directing all the time. Al, you're a director, Al. You're always running pattuns.

FRANK DEFORD's work has appeared in virtually every medium. In magazines, he is the senior writer at *Sports Illustrated*. On radio, he may be heard as a commentator every Wednesday on *Morning Edition* on National Public Radio, and on television he is a regular correspondent on the HBO show *Real Sports with Bryant Gumbel*. Moreover, Deford is the author of fourteen books, two of which—the novel *Everybody's All-American*, and *Alex: The Life of a Child*, his memoir about his daughter who died of cystic fibrosis—have been made into movies. His latest book is *The Old Ball Game*, about Christy Mathewson and John McGraw and baseball at the turn of the century. As a journalist, Deford was most recently presented with the National Magazine Award for profiles for his story on Bill Russell. He has been elected to the Hall of Fame of the National Association of Sportscasters and Sportswriters. Six times Deford was voted by his peers as U.S. Sportswriter of the Year. *American Journalism Review* has likewise cited him as the nation's finest sportswriter, and twice he was voted Magazine Writer of the Year by the *Washington Journalism Review*. *Sporting News* has described Deford as "the most influential sports voice among members of the print media," and the magazine *GQ* has called him, simply, "the world's greatest sportswriter." In broadcasting, Deford has won both an Emmy and a George Foster Peabody Award. For sixteen years, Deford served as national chairman of the Cystic Fibrosis Foundation, and he remains chairman emeritus. He resides in Westport, Connecticut, with his wife, Carol. They have two children—a son, Christian, and a daughter, Scarlet. A native of Baltimore, Deford is a graduate of Princeton University, where he has taught in American Studies.

Long Island Shaolin

BY DARIN STRAUSS

THE TOUGHEST MAN I EVER MET, the strongest, quickest, the most immovable, was a middle-aged guy who stood about five foot three. His name was Tony Lau. One day, a kung fu expert kicked Tony Lau in the balls and Lau didn't react—he didn't give a shudder, he didn't even grimace.

But Tony Lau taking it in the nuts is not the way I want to begin this story.

As a kid I was thin as soup-kitchen consommé, not very athletic, given to homesickness. In the fifth grade a little girl called two of my friends and me "the Shrimp, the Blimp, and the Wimp"—the name stuck. (I had one short friend and one chubby friend, but you probably guessed that.) My skinniness kept me in internal precincts of unease. Though I knew Batman comics were more exciting and had better artwork, it was Superman in his immeasurable power who was an obsession of mine. Maybe most of all, I loved karate movies.

I actually went to a few karate classes when I was five, and I got my father to come with me. Though he was a grown man with no interest in martial arts, he chopped and kicked and howled "hii-ya!" by my side, which shows what a good father he was. He only took three or four lessons, which shows that even the best parents are only human. I quit karate soon after my father did—I was better suited to dreaming of heroics than to participating in real, mundane violence—but my acquaintance with such words as "roundhouse kick" and "sensei" earned me some crumbs of playground credibility.

Years surged and passed without my having entered another martial arts school. All my karate talk, however, came to infect my friend Frank, the chubby one—the Blimp, to use elementary school vernacular—and by the ninth grade Frank had started taking classes himself.

Hadn't the Blimp known I was halfway bullshitting about my desire to take up karate again? It was so bittersweet for me to ponder how good a fighter I'd have been if only I'd stuck with it—why would I have bothered actually to go to classes again?

The Blimp was my best friend but we were radically different. When I'd first met Frank Santoro Jr. he'd been a genial, floppy-haired fourth grader who liked *The Benny Hill Show* and whose parents had already begun to scream their way toward a divorce. By the ninth grade, Frank Jr. was quite strong, and so he had different reasons than I did for liking karate. His father, on rare occasions, would hit him.

It'd always been an advantage to have a bigger friend around. Once, in elementary school, another friend of ours—not fat, nor a shrimp, and not particularly skinny, just an asshole named Tony Battista—used the term "dirty Jew" in front of me, though he knew I was Jewish. The scandal this caused seethed for days, and eventually it boiled over into a schoolyard brawl, a ten-on-ten fistfight. Bedlam—I'm not sure how that happened. But in the center of the chaos, the suburban air teeming with little fists, a kid named Ryan Woodman held my hands behind my back, while the assholic Tony Battista kept punching me in the face.

My pal Frank materialized at my side—or so it seemed to me—and as I remember it, Frank threw Ryan Woodman out of frame and then managed to grab hold of Tony Battista himself. Frank held Tony's hands behind him, restraining him in just the way I had been restrained a moment before.

"Hit him!" Frank said.

I made a fist and readied to use it; Tony Battista was looking at me with sad, humid eyes and a trembling pout against which neither anger nor retributive justice had a chance.

"Are we not kind people?" Tony Battista seemed to be saying. "Don't you think I know exactly how wrong I was to have punched you when you'd been defenseless, the way I am now?" said his pout.

I unfisted my hand. Tony Battista broke free and decked me in the jaw, and—like some dark lesson to pierce Robert Fulghum's heart—this taught me all I really needed to learn in elementary school about human nature.

Anyhow.

By ninth grade Frank had a lovely girlfriend by the unfortunate name of Katy Sukoff, and as he bicycled to meet her for a night of third-base near-sex, Frank caught sight of a leaflet for a karate school—or rather, for the Ying Yee Kwoon Asian Martial Arts Center. Sifu Tony Lau, the leaflet read, was offering classes in southern Chinese–style Shaolin tiger-crane Hung Gar kung fu. This was a more intense, more pure, martial art than the karate I had studied.

Shaolin: the word had an incantatory power for Frank and for me, and for millions of other kids our age. Every Saturday afternoon in the New York area, where we lived, the pre-Fox-era TV station Channel 5 would broadcast Chinese-language martial arts films as part of its three o'clock "Drive-in Movie." The best of the films was *The 36th Chamber of Shaolin* (also known as *The Master Killer*)—but almost all the films on "Drive-in Movie" involved one of the two celebrated Shaolin temples. According to legend, the temples were the birthplace of Asian martial arts, and a training ground for many who fought the unpopular, powerful Manchu invaders. ("Drive-in Movie" often aired a second film, *Shaolin and Wu Tang*, which inspired nine other New York–area kids to form the Wu-Tang Clan and record the 1993 hip-hop album *Enter the Wu-Tang: 36 Chambers*.)

Frank came back from his first lesson bruised along his arms and wrists. "They have these blocking exercises," he said, his speech quickened by joy. "You have to whack your wrist into somebody else's wrist, and then—here, wham!, like this—you slam your forearm into the other guy's forearm. I go against this really bony guy. It fucking kills!"

I was jealous.

(I was also lazy, fearful of pain, and of change. Because I thought I wouldn't have been able to hack it, I didn't sign up.)

After Frank had been there a few months, I got enthralled by his stories about Tony Lau, the teacher.

"Uh, he's not called 'Teacher,' dude—he's called Sifu," Frank said. (Sifu is a way of saying teacher in Chinese.)

Sifu could, by bending his pointer finger at the first pha-langeal joint, punch a hole in a can of soup using only his knuckle. Sifu would challenge five of his best students at once to touch his body—and, because of Sifu's bobbing and block-ing, no one came close, not even the students in back of him. Best of all, Sifu, according to Frank, had the power to concen-trate his entire body's life force, or "chi," into one spot—thereby bringing a measure of invulnerability to his hands, say, or his head, or his balls—at least for a moment.

"His balls?" I pictured "Iron Balls" McGinty, from Steve Martin's *The Jerk*.

"That's what I heard, yeah," Frank said, nodding. "His balls can be invulnerable."

I went to sign up.

Sifu Lau's training regime was said to be one extended cry of agony; he considered women unable to handle it and for that reason he refused to teach them. And even I, as a fourteen-year-old boy, wasn't guaranteed a spot in his class; Sifu Lau didn't like to accept any students who were under eighteen. I had to meet him and prove I'd be able to manage it.

"You want take kung fu?" Sifu asked me. His voice was surprisingly high-pitched, but not shrill—it had a thick quality like a flute that has been out in the rain.

I told him I did want to take kung fu.

We were talking in the office in the back of the Ying Yee Kwoon Asian Martial Arts Center—really, it was a rented-out dance studio. Sifu only had the place on Tuesday and Thursday nights, from 7 to 9:30. If I'm remembering correctly, the tiny office where he and I stood had one chair, a cluttered desk, and a photo on the wall of a male dancer in mid-pliet, his groin conspicuous in ballet pants.

Sifu said, "You think everyone who want to know kung fu should be allow to know kung fu?"

"Well, I understand that it's not easy," I said. "But I want to be good at it, sir. I'll work hard."

"But you think everyone who want should be allow?"

"Allowed?" I said. I was confused. "I've never thought of that," I said.

Sifu had—after having taught on Long Island for about five years—slackened his eighteen-and-over policy; he accepted me on the spot.

Counting me, there were around fifteen students, four of whom were fourteen or fifteen. The other youngsters were: my friend Frank Santoro, of course, who was already very good by the time I started; Bob Martin, a gaunt, serious guy who approached kung fu with a scholar's diligence, and whose every feature and action gave the impression of a body moving relentlessly forward—his long, craneish nose, his meticulous straight punch; big, goofy Kenny Dubicki, ever smiling, ever busting someone's chops, who had tried a few times to be a bully but didn't really have the heart for it; and Bill Groupe, a social outcast living by the occasional, glancing acquaintanceship.

Bob Martin I didn't know, but all the others went to my high school, and, once Sifu let me start studying at Ying Yee Kwoon, I was afraid Bill Groupe would take my having joined the class as a green light to embarrass me in the lunchroom by acting as if we were friends. I am not proud remembering this.

Sifu's workouts were extreme unto torture. They varied, but on the hardest days—after some informal stretching, during which each kung fu student would place his leg on the ballet bar—you had to do: (1) organized stretching; (2) twenty "jump-knuckle brick push-ups," which meant you'd perform a push-up with each of your hands fisted atop a brick. After the first push-up, you'd heave yourself off the bricks and land, knuckles down, on the floor. And then, after doing a knuckle push-up there, you'd hop, fist first, back up onto the bricks—which was sort of like punching the bricks with all your weight; (3) twenty fingertip push-ups; (4) ten "superman" push-ups—the name of which was a particular favorite of mine. These are push-ups performed with your hands at your solar plexus; (5) a lot of sit-ups; (6) those blocking exercises that had bruised up Frank's arms; (7) leg raises using the bricks as leg weights; (8) you had to run around the room for five minutes; (9) run for another five minutes carrying someone who weighs approximately what you do on your back; (10) you had to do a duck walk around the room for a few laps; (11) get in a squat and hop for a while, like a Russian folk dancer; (12) stand in "horse stance" until your legs feel like fire ants were eating away at your thigh muscles. Horse stance is done by pointing your feet straight ahead, about two shoulder widths apart, gripping the floor with the toes, keeping your back straight, and lowering your hips by bending your knees forward over the ankles, until your thighs are parallel to the floor. Sometimes—not often, thankfully—you'd do horse stance with someone standing on your thighs.

I got to know Sifu very little in the beginning. He was short, unassuming; he didn't seem explicitly muscled. He walked with a limp, and had a very sparse chin beard that looked like a few iron filings stuck there by magnetism. When he punched or kicked in front of us—a rarity—he would make a sound like "hup," a great pressure of breath getting checked, and his high voice didn't so much deepen as sound sharper at those moments, like something broken off and splintering.

"A straight punch is the most important thing," he told me. "Straight punch and straight kick—plain, basic, and the best, most important thing."

I didn't believe him; I already knew how to do a straight-ahead punch and a straight-ahead kick. Everyone in the world did. You didn't need lessons for that.

But then I found out something remarkable about Sifu Tony Lau.

He had emigrated from Hong Kong after spending his life studying Hung Gar kung fu under teachers who could trace their lineage back to the Shaolin monk named Hung Hei Geun, the father of Hung Gar; and then, when Sifu got here, he spent another twenty years learning Goju—a Japanese style of martial arts, a karate style; and after all that—after becoming a world-famous master of two different martial arts—he made the straight punch and the straight kick his expertise. After learning thousands of techniques, in other words, he had settled on the most basic moves, the ones you learn the first day of any class.

(Later in my life, I'd think about this a lot. Especially when I encountered the works of great artists who shrugged off intricacy as they aged, distilling their technique until only the essential remained.)

"Sifu would use just that punch or that one kick if he ever had to defend himself now," Ying Yee Kwoon's best student and assistant instructor, Paul, told me.

"And he would win."

Paul had been responsible for bringing Sifu to Long Island. A self-described "lower-middle-class kid, very lower," Paul—when he'd been sixteen—had read a story about Sifu in *Inside Kung-Fu* magazine. The article called Tony Lau "America's greatest master of Hung Gar kung fu," and it'd had pictures of Sifu in his school in New York's Chinatown. After reading the article, Paul traveled into Manhattan, found Sifu, and pestered him for lessons. Though Sifu at this time had had no non-Asian students, and though Paul wasn't yet eighteen, he did allow the kid to study with him in Chinatown. Eventually, Paul convinced Sifu that he could organize a second school in Long Island, and so that's how the greatest practitioner of Hung Gar kung fu West of Hong Kong ended up teaching in a rented dance hall in Glen Head.

Paul often hit me. He hit all the young guys, especially on Tuesdays, when Sifu didn't make the trip out from Chinatown and instead let Paul run the show.

Twenty-one, burly-built, of a dashing handsomeness with an Errol Flynn goatee and thick wavy hair, Paul radiated malice down to his protuberant, brick-hardened knuckles and his cheeks that often excited to a frightening pallor, like the rage of a prison guard after his charges have gone missing. His body had stormed right through the last evidences of puberty—he was a man, strong and packed tight everywhere—and he imposed his will on those of us who were not yet grown men.

"How do you do a leopard punch?" I asked him once.

"Like this," and, lunging to close the distance between us quicker than fear, twisting his hips, stomping the ground and steeling all the muscles of his body at the very second of impact, he jabbed me in the temple, certainly not a hundredth as hard as he could have, but still prodding his knuckles into me with remarkable focus. The blow that shot into my head was one of the most exact human movements ever thought up, and I had to struggle to keep tears from my eyes. Not only because it hurt—although that was a huge part of it—but also, I wasn't used to being hit, least of all by an adult, a teacher.

How would Sifu have reacted if he knew how often Paul hit us? Hard to say; I was always unwilling to be a stoolpigeon. Plus, the truth is, Sifu would often give hands-on demonstrations on us, too, and sometimes quite painful demonstrations—but Paul's blows contained so much violence, and happened so recurrently, that his punches and kicks had a darker character than Sifu's did.

Usually, if it had been you who asked the question, it was you who got hit, but occasionally—if you positioned yourself far enough from Paul—you might avoid the blow yourself, because Paul would demonstrate on someone closer to him. And so Kenny Dubicki would often try to get me whacked by pestering Paul about one move or other when I was standing between them. It rarely worked; Dubicki got hit more than anybody else, except maybe me.

Once, I used getting hit to my advantage. After I had been studying a few months, another friend of mine—"the Shrimp" from fourth grade, as it turned out—was interested in taking lessons with Frank and me. The Shrimp and I were on our way to losing touch, and—this is embarrassing to admit—I wanted the Shrimp neither to become good at kung fu nor to horn in on my friendship with Frank (the Blimp). And so, when the Shrimp came to observe the class, I asked Paul: How do you do a tiger claw again?

"You know how," he said, and grabbed me by the shirt. This wasn't vicious enough for my purposes; I was hoping that the sight of me getting hit would scare off the Shrimp.

"Paul, wait—one more thing. How do you do the crane move to block a punch?"

"Punch."

I did, and he blocked it and walked off.

"Wait, Paul—"

On my fifth or sixth question, Paul, with the Shrimp watching, kicked me in the chest, sending me careering across the room. If Frank and Kenny Dubicki hadn't caught me in their arms, I would have fallen to the floor. As it was, I was more than half dazed, and, when I came to, I noticed that the Shrimp had left, never to return. This, I believe, is known as a pyrrhic victory.

I got woozy in class other times, too. Once, running around

the room with Bill Groupe on my back, I felt faint; black splotches like those you see in decaying film appeared in the air; for some reason I still can't explain, my kung fu pants fell down to my ankles as I started to pass out. I was not Sifu's heartiest student.

Why did I stay with the studies, then? Mainly for Sifu. He rarely talked to me, we had almost no rapport, and yet I loved knowing someone like him. He gave us written tests on the history of kung fu—and I would love imagining myself back in olden China with the Shaolin monks, with men like Sifu. "Best defense is to run away," he liked to say. Still, older students would whisper in the dressing room: "He once fought ten men." "But he hates fighting." "Oh, he'll fight if he has to."

Sifu scoffed at Bruce Lee—"Sloppy," he would say. "No forms; movie stuff"—and yet, as a young man, he had starred in an early Hong Kong kung fu movie called *Wu Ze Tian*.

When Sifu had sneered at what Bruce Lee lacked, he'd been referring to the primary element of Shaolin kung fu: the Form. Here's how it works: a student, at the beginning of his study, learns a few moves; eventually, he's taught to group those moves together into a set; then he links the sets together into forms—long, choreographed arrangements, each like a solo dance routine. To move up the ranks, a student has to do his forms perfectly—not just executing the moves well, but in the correct order. (Bruce Lee did away with forms when he invented a style called Jeet Kune Do).

Rising in the ranks was important, but our class had no belt system. "Belts are for karate," Paul would say derisively. "Yellow belt, red belt, brown belt, green belt—enough with karate and its belts, you know? We don't need that. Fucking belts, man."

We did, however, have belt-like sashes.

Three sashes: yellow, red, and black. You started out with a yellow sash, on which you could earn up to three stripes by proving that you'd mastered certain moves, and then by taking a written exam on Shaolin history; after three stripes, you moved up to red sash; and so on, until you earned black sash. Paul had a red sash with two stripes. It was said to take about fifteen years for one to earn the highest sash.

As for me, after learning four forms in eight months, I was a yellow sash with two stripes.

"You would do better," Sifu told me, "if you learn how to breathe and stand." That was the thing about kung fu: you found out you really knew nothing at all.

I liked learning the forms, because in performing them I found it easier to imagine using the moves against villains. But to my surprise I also liked sparring, which often got brutal. Sparring: the class would watch two students square off in a simulated fight. Punches were to be thrown open-handed, and, more, they had to be stopped before hard contact was made. Kicks, too, were supposed to be pulled. Kicks and punches are hard to control, though.

Once Kenny Dubicki and I were good enough for it, Sifu allowed us to go at each other—though Kenny was much bigger than I. Sifu would laugh because we were so competitive. Kicks and punches got progressively more vicious.

"Okay—these two crazy," Sifu said.

During sparring my heart would clamber up to my throat, it all happened too fast to register, a punch would come, I'd block it and start on a punch of my own, and I wanted so badly to hit Kenny in the face, though I liked him quite a bit. That was part of kung fu, I guessed. Like Paul (like most of the class, actually), Kenny Dubicki described himself as "lower middle class"—"I ain't no fortunate son," he liked to say—and though my own parents were far from rich, Kenny used to tease me about my comparative wealth and about my future at a "real college," which he knew I would have. After class, or the next day in high school, Kenny, Frank, and I would laugh about the peculiarities of Ying Yee Kwoon—Bill Groupe's convulsive punches, the time my pants fell down, the profound and silly noise Sifu would make when he'd throw a punch.

Once I had to spar against Frank, and, of course, he beat the shit out of me. This made me very sad—not because I lost (he had seven months of training on me and was clearly better and bigger than I was) but because he was so forceful in his assault. But what had he been supposed to do? Go easy on me? That wasn't Shaolin.

After about a year, Sifu and Paul took Frank, Kenny, and me to participate in a kung fu tournament in Chinatown. It was like the competition in the movie *The Karate Kid*. I fought a big guy, scary in demeanor, with slicked hair. We circled in the little ring, this kid and I; about five people watched us; the kid held his mouth open as we orbited each other. Then he lunged at me, kicking ferociously, shrieking. One roundhouse kick to my face, slap against my cheek. One point to Mr. Slick Hair. It only took two points to win this fight, and so I was in a big hole already. My cheek tingled as if freezing air were blowing on it. And the kid was back at me—he punched, but I used the crane move, a placid circular motion to fend off his blow, and I tapped him lightly on the head. Point for me. One to one. Next point would win. The kid jabbed, I backed away and—as he missed—I noticed he'd left his head unguarded.

I sprang at him, hit him full strength in the face.

I was disqualified for full contact, and I felt guilty as hell. But also good about myself. I had been disqualified, for being too rough. Fuck Tony Battista.

I felt most connected to Sifu and his lessons at that point. I worked out at home all the time—now I was getting pretty limber, and I'd never been this strong in my life. Was Sifu pleased with me? I'm sure he didn't notice. He was a laissez-faire instructor. I realized I knew nothing about what kind of a person he was. Was this well of arcane knowledge a nice guy? Was he nasty? I couldn't say—he was neither nice nor nasty, really. He showed no personality.

And then he was kicked in the balls.

It was Chinese New Year, for which Sifu took the best students from his Long Island and Manhattan schools to participate in a lion dance street performance; three students had been picked to manipulate a huge red-and-yellow paper lion—one student wore a giant head that had moving eyelids, mouth and ears, the other two students stood under a long, red tail. The tiger danced the streets of Chinatown, accompanied by the loud music of a large drum, a gong, cymbals, and firecrackers. (Evil is afraid of loud noise.)

Sifu and his lion turned the corner of some small Chinatown street and came face-to-face with another lion.

The chief rule of a lion dance is that if two lions meet, they have to fight. I guess that Sifu, being the head of the school, was the lion personified—which meant that he personally had to square off against the other lion.

Our sifu and the second lion's sifu met in the middle of the street and—according to all the witnesses (I wasn't there)—the other sifu kicked our sifu in the nuts.

Most kung fu, of course, is based on techniques, or "moves"—punches, leg sweeps, etc. Everyone knows the phrase "a good kung fu move." But beyond even mythic moves like the "No shadow kick," which only a sifu is supposed to know, there exists a form in Hung Gar kung fu that transcends any notion of "moves" at all; it's the highest and most difficult form, the mastery of which marks the end of one's training. Called the Tit Sin Kuen form, or the "Iron Thread," it is the quintessence of all Chinese martial art, an internal training begun at the end of one's physical study. According to the great book of Hung Gar kung fu, written by Lam Sai Wing (1860–1943), if you master the Iron Thread, you "can withstand, with no consequences, the strongest of blows, including ones with heavy objects or cold steel; can bend thick iron rods with [your] hands, and [your] power to root [yourself] to one spot is so strong that [you] cannot be displaced by a group of people. In addition, this wonderful method strengthens all internal organs, bones, muscles and sinews. The entire body thrives and rejuvenates." Based on control of breathing and the emission of loud sonorous noises—every sound being aimed at a specific organ—it allows one to marshal all of one's life energy, to move it internally. Sifu Tony Lau didn't feel the kick to the balls for the reason that his balls were infused with the vital force believed in Taoism to be inherent in all things.

Once the other sifu witnessed Tony Lau's mastery of the iron wire, the man just bowed, turned, and left.

This seems unrealistic, but many eyewitnesses told me it was true. What I had more trouble believing was that grown men would engage in this behavior in a public street—that, even in 1986, "if two lions meet, they have to fight."

I recently saw again *The 36 Chambers of Shaolin*, the film that first got me excited about Chinese martial arts twenty years ago. More than most kung fu movies, *The 36 Chambers* emphasizes the hero's training. The film spends more than an hour and a half going into great detail about a man named San Te's metamorphosis from novice into master. What strikes me now about the film—in which San Te, as part of his training, has to attach sharp blades to his elbows before carrying pails of water, so that he'll pierce his own sides whenever his energy flags— what strikes me now is the way that the film makes a fetish of persecution and of self-persecution. San Te spends years butting his head against hard-packed sand bags to develop a strong skull; he places his face between two flames as he tries, unsuccessfully at first, to follow the movements of a beam of light without turning his face into the fire. And on it goes.

To the students and to the teacher of Ying Yee Kwoon, there was no mythology in *The 36 Chambers of Shaolin*; it was the truth, and it was a model. The character depicted, San Te, was a real man, and in fact the real San Te was Sifu Tony Lau's teacher's teacher's teacher. In Ying Yee Kwoon Asian Martial

Arts Center in Glen Head, Long Island, the rigors of the temple were to be followed as closely as possible.

"We're Shaolin, dude," Paul once said. He'd been talking to this guy Mark—one of the older, better students—after Sifu had found out that Mark had used his kung fu to beat up some people in his neighborhood. "We have to be serious about being like monks and shit," Paul said. No matter that Paul, too, had been known to use his kung fu for mischief outside the confines of the dance studio. He saw himself, at least after getting a talking-to from Sifu, as a monk. Seriously. It was becoming clear to me—even at sixteen, and even though I was so eager to buy into the whole fantasy—that Ying Yee Kwoon suffered from the ridiculousness of the anachronistic. Real Shaolin monks had trained in the eighteenth century, in the shadow of death. You couldn't have a Shaolin Temple West in 1986, at least not in the American suburbs—where, thank goodness, many such dark shadows had been scrubbed away.

In other words, if two lions meet, they don't have to fight. Not always, and not anymore.

I didn't quit the Ying Yee Kwoon Asian Martial Arts Center, not officially; I just stopped going.

Frank eventually stopped, too. He's now a lawyer, a prosecutor in California, and—because he likes to "go after bad guys"—he spends his free time as a volunteer police officer, patrolling the toughest neighborhoods in Los Angeles in a squad car.

I saw Kenny Dubicki a couple times after high school, and we'd always joke about our time together in kung fu; we'd pretend to spar, two adults in a bar squaring off, or else we'd make fun of someone from the class. Kenny fought in the first Gulf War, came back, went on to become the New York State Grand Prix Overall Bodybuilding Champion, and then, on December 3, 1995, Kenny Dubicki lost his life in a car accident at the age of twenty-five.

As for me, I actually tried to take up kung fu again when I was thirty-one, attending a different school, with a different teacher, but I only lasted for two months.

I never saw Sifu Tony Lau again.

DARIN STRAUSS is the author of *Chang & Eng* and *The Real McCoy*, as well as the forthcoming novel *What Is Crooked Cannot Be Made Straight*. He lives in Brooklyn and teaches at NYU.

Golf Lessons

BY GEORGE PLIMPTON

LAST YEAR I HAD A CHANCE TO DO SOMETHING about the wretched state of my golf game. I was invited out to the Callaway Test Center in Carlsbad, California, to spend a few days with their top instructors and write about the experience. Frankly, I was skeptical about their chances. My handicap lurks somewhere in the twenties. The last round I'd played had been a lost afternoon of bogeys and double bogeys, not a par among them, and that had been some years before.

But of course I jumped at the chance. After all, one leaves one's car with its inexplicable engine chatter, one headlight malfunctioning, a brake problem, in the corner garage for the mechanics to fuss over, and a day or so later it emerges in fine working order. Why not such a transformation in my golf game?

My main problem is what I carry in my mind during the process of hitting a ball. I have been told great golfers have an image of where the ball is going to land . . . a distant green, a spot on the fairway favorable for an approach to the green, a knoll on the other side of a pond, and so on. On the putting surface the track of the ball to the hole is in their mind's eye as exact as the lines on a graph.

I have tried this, of course. What is quite visible in my mind's eye when I get ready to hit the shot is the flag on the green, not the base of an equipment shed wall where my ball ends up. My main problems in imaging are bedeviling mental quirks . . . that a bug, for example, or a bumblebee is suddenly, like an apparition, going to materialize on the ball just as I start my downswing. Moreover my body doesn't seem to do what it is called on to do. Those of great athletes, as often described in metaphor, are like well-oiled machines. Not in my case. I once described mine as a colossal, slightly wobbly edifice, like the superstructure of a Japanese battleship, its control tower manned by admirals who hold ancient voice tubes into which they yell the familiar orders, "Eye on the ball! Chin steady! Left arm stiff! Swing from the inside out!" Down below, at the command centers situated at the joints, are a dispirited, eccentric group of dissolutes with drinking problems. At the commands, floating eerily down to them through the voice tubes, they reach sulkily for various levers, sometimes pulling the right one, sometimes the wrong. So that, in sum, the whole apparatus, bent on hitting a golf ball, tips and convolutes and veers, the Japanese admirals clutching for each other as the control tower sways back and forth, and when they look out the windows what they see is a shank. "A shank! Another shank!"

I wrote this in a book called *The Bogey Man*. It disturbed some of my golfing friends who had read the book, good golfers who in some cases blamed the temporary deterioration of their games on what I had written. One of them came up to me at a cocktail party on Long Island and said, "Those damned Japanese admirals of yours," and turned away.

What most good golfers do is wash such errant thoughts from their minds. "Take dead aim, drive all thoughts out of your head" is Harvey Penick's famous advice from his best-selling volume, *The Little Red Book*. But there's the rub. The problem of driving foreign matter out of one's brain is easier said than done.

A solution occurred to me . . . that if you can't drive the images out of your mind, then find the right one. Perhaps the Callaway instructors could provide me with a mental image that would work . . .

On the place out to California I read a self-help book entitled

What to Say When You Talk to Yourself by one Shad Helmstetter. Helmstetter's rather alarming idea is that 77 percent of what you tell yourself may be working against you. He writes of the brain being a complex computer into which are fed negative impulses as a child—don't do this, don't do that—until finally the brain accepts these commands and acts accordingly. This results in negative self-talk—such as "I can't remember names," "I'm just no good at math," "I can't take it anymore," or in golf terms, "I can't reach the green," "I can't sink this putt."

Helmstetter offers a solution to this: "conscious positives." He gives an extraordinary example of how this works. A smoker trying to quit is urged to say in the course of lighting up a cigarette: "I never smoke." This is to be stated in the presence of other people—standing around at a cocktail party, for instance. Helmstetter does admit that the procedure can be discomfiting. He writes, "Your friends are going to think you're a little strange." I'll say!

I tried to imagine how the principle of conscious positives works on a golf course. Let's say you're on the third hole of the Piping Rock Club, playing with the club president and two business associates. You've had a strange lunch at which you have had a chocolate mousse for dessert. You're trying to give up chocolate, so you announce loudly to the table: "I never eat chocolate mousse." Then you pull out a cigar. "I never smoke cigars," you say as you apply a match to its tip.

Perhaps by the time your partners have reached the third hole they will have forgotten this strange behavior pattern. But then after pushing the ball ten feet past the flag you announce with great authority, "I never miss a putt." Or just before hitting a ball into a pond, "I never hit a ball into a hazard." Even if you miss the pond, the effect of such an alarmingly self-congratulatory posture is bound to grate on the others in the foursome . . . to the point of having your membership looked at by the club president and probable cancellation of deals with the business associates, especially when in the clubhouse barroom—naturally called the Nineteenth Hole—you order a gin and tonic and flatly proclaim, "I don't drink alcoholic beverages."

I put Mr. Helmstetter's book aside. I couldn't imagine looking a Callaway instructor in the eye after saying to him, "I never shank the ball!" and then promptly doing so.

Oddly enough, I discovered on my arrival that the Test Center at the Callaway complex where I was to take my lessons is named after Richard C. Helmstetter, no kin to Shad of the "conscious positives," but in fact a golf club designer, most noted for his famous driver known as Big Bertha.

The RCH Test Center is one of a dozen or so buildings that make up the complex in Carlsbad. I was buzzed in through a security gate and greeted by John Redman, one of golf's most noted teachers, respectfully referred to, of course, as a guru. His prize pupil is Paul Azinger, turned by Redman from a mediocre golfer into a star player on the Tour.

I was shown around. The practice fairway, as groomed as a putting green, fans out towards a distant hummocky hill and trees far beyond. The Test Center is used by tour golfers to sharpen up their games. Two or three players were belting balls into the distance. The range was unique in that every golf range I've ever been to has golf balls lying around within a dozen feet or so of the practice tees—mute evidence of the ineptitude of those whaling away. I have seen a ball five feet from the tee, still very clear in my mind because I had flubbed it there myself, barely topping it with a six-iron.

But the nearest balls on the Test Center range were all a respectful wedge shot away. I told Redman that I was sure to mar the purity of his practice range and hoped he wouldn't mind.

He grinned and said, "Well, let's see what we've got here."

He took me into a net-hung room in the annex called the Evaluation Bay where my golf swing was subjected to a photo image machine called the Greenway and then analyzed. Redman said they would compare the findings with another test at the end of my instruction.

On the way out we paused in a large room that fronts the practice range. A pair of robotic devices were at work whacking golf balls against padded walls. I was told the tensile strength of club shafts was being measured . . . Technicians sat in front of screens looking at rows of numbers and graphs. The robots were referred to as "Iron Byrons." I was fascinated by them. Each reminded me vaguely of the Terminator at the end of his career—nothing left of Arnold Schwarzenegger but a skeleton of thin steel pipes. The contraption's steel arm holds the club and when the machine is in operation, the arm slowly comes back, pauses ever so briefly at the top, and then descends in the perfect arc of a powerful golf swing. If really cranked up, an Iron Byron can generate a club-head speed of around 155 mph and can hit a ball 370 yards on the carry. Sometimes the sides of the building swing up like garage doors and the Iron Byrons hit balls out onto the practice fairway. I wish I'd seen that—one of those souped-up drives clearing the tips of the trees three hundred yards away. The technician working one of the robots told me rather solemnly that his machine had hit over two million balls and not one of them had been an errant shot. I sat and watched the machines cranking out these perfect swings, never a deviation or a fault, and I wondered if I kept staring at them whether the swing could somehow become entrenched in my own mental process.

Not so. Out on the range with Redman I began the instruction. He made some radical changes with my swing. I was edged much closer to the ball. He changed my grip. In theory, what I was being told made perfect sense, but it was difficult to readjust. I hit some miserable shots. I got under a ball and it rose almost straight up. As he looked up, Redman grinned and said, "That's a giraffe shot. It's high and it stinks."

At the end of the lesson I jotted down a few of the things John had instructed me. Some of them he learned from Tommy Armour who taught sitting under a big umbrella to keep out of the sun and drank martinis as he watched his pupils: Hit it off the side of your body, not the front. Kick that right knee in. Get that bag of sugar off your shoulders. (An image for me!) Nerves are like wild animals. I have never seen a good golfer with a weak little finger on his left hand. Very hard to hit a good shot unless your left shoulder is up under your chin. Pull the club with the motion of your hips. Imagine you're swinging a rope with a rock tied to the end. (Hey, another image!) Let your arms and hands feel as if they were hanging off your shoulders. Pretend you're turning in a barrel. (Ah, yet another!!) Don't unload early. Redman's law—keep the hands passive. The hands equals less consistency and power. Slow back. Toll the bell (another!!!). Swing rather than hit.

At one point Redman said, "Let the little finger and the ring finger of the left hand do all the work. Try it."

It seemed odd to be hitting a golf ball using the power generated by just two fingers, but I tried it and the ball sailed out much further than I would have guessed.

But it had been a discouraging outing. Too many flubs. Too many changes suggested. I remembered the adage of Ernest Jones, a one-legged English golf professional who popularized golf in New York City in the twenties by giving lessons for $5.00. "If you dissect a cat you'll have blood and guts and bones all over the place, but you won't have a cat."

But the next day I was better. I had some images to work with—turning in a barrel. Swinging a rope with a rock at the end. Getting rid of the bag of sugar on my shoulders. I was introduced to my next instructor—Mike Donaway, known in the golf world as one of the truly long hitters, if not the longest. John Daly, the PGA champion known for the prodigious length of his driving game, has admitted that Donaway is one of the very few capable of outdriving him. Mike was a club tester at Callaway and indeed was the first to hit a golf ball with the famous Big Bertha driver. Among his statistics is a 318-yard drive in a Long-Drive Contest in 1990. He told me he had once hit a ball 518 yards but that was with a following wind of 45 miles per hour.

I have done research on lengthy drives. The record in tournament play would appear to be one hit by a 31-year-old PGA tour veteran named Carl Cooper, who at the time was 190th on the tour money list. The shot was hit during the 1992 Texas Open held at San Antonio's Oak Hill Country Club. Cooper stepped up at the third hole, a par four, 456 yards, and over-drove the green by 331 yards! Anyone who has pushed or hooked a ball onto a cart path and marveled at the grand rabbity leap that the ball takes would well guess what happened. Cooper's ball, knocked onto an asphalt cart path, kept bouncing downhill alongside three fairways until it ended up against a chain-link fence. Cooper's caddie measured the distance as 787 yards. I mentioned it to Mike.

"Well, that would have it," he admitted.

On the practice range he had some more tips to add, including an image or two. "The golf swing is like a gate," he said. "The left leg is the post." He demonstrated.

"I'm very anxious to have more of those," I said. "I keep thinking the key to my game may be something like that—a 'swinging gate' could make all the difference."

Mike offered a startling image. One of his early teachers had suggested for getting the right side into the swing, he should imagine a midget standing a foot in front of the tee.

"Yes."

". . . and then smack that midget in the ass."

The slight form of the midget formed in my mind almost instantly.

"With the club."

"Of course."

"Just in front of the tee, eh?"

"Right," Mike said.

"Hit him in the ass with my five-iron."

"Whatever," Mike said.

"Well, that's a hell of an image," I said in admiration.

I hit four or five fine shots by my standards, and I thought, My God, I've been given the "key"—a midget! I'll be able to carry him around in my head, as important as the sand wedge in my golf bag.

"I liked that one," I said. "Do you have any more?"

"Do you know the one about being a puker or a lover?"

"A puker or a lover?"

"It's a little picture in your mind to keep your head back and to keep from going over the top."

"Yes?"

"Well, the puker always has his head forward, right, that's the typical position."

"You mean . . . ?"

"Yes, when he's puking into a bowl or the sink, right?"

"Right," I said. "And the lover?"

"His stomach is always out in front, right?"

I must have looked puzzled.

"That little picture will take care of your center of gravity."

I thought for a moment and told him I thought I'd stick with the midget.

On the morning of my last day we spent an hour or so in the Evaluation Bay hitting balls into a netting and being checked over by the Greenway machine.

At noon I took a putting and chipping lesson from Paul Runyan, the former PGA champion (1934, 1938), who is 91 years old, a small, peppery gent who disapproved of almost everything I was doing. "No, no, no, get your grip right." He tugged at my hands, twisting them until they were to his exact satisfaction. I walked around the green with the club fixed in my hands, not daring to relax my grip. His voice was sometimes smothered by the noise of jets taking off from nearby Palomar Airport, and I would bend down to hear him saying, "No, no, no, the arms are out at an angle 45 and 45," and he would wrench at my arms. I walked around that way. He liked numbers. "Numbers don't lie," he said. "The fairway on the putting green is four and a half inches wide." He was speaking. I bent down again. "The top of the club head should be at your belly button." He pushed the putter into my stomach. It was midday and hot and I was relieved when without a word he walked away across the practice fairway, the lesson over, his work done.

That afternoon word came from the Evaluation Bay that the speed of my club head hitting the ball was 62 mph and the ball-speed off the club-head was 93 mph—the ball hit twenty yards longer than I'd hit it when I arrived. Hmmm. And how did this measure up to, say, John Daly's statistics? I was told he generates 125 mph at club-head speed; the ball coming off the club head whisks out there at 188 mph to roll dead around 250 yards out. Still an improvement for me. I told Mike that every time I hit the ball into the netting I had his midget out there in front of me.

"Golf is turning me into a sadist," I said.

Later that afternoon Mike and I went out to a neighboring golf club called Aviana to play a few holes. Aviana looks as though it had been fashioned by a landscape architect, the fairways threaded through a botanical garden. Each tee was bordered with flowerbeds. Very fancy. The club superintendent said the course was crowded—everyone out in the sun. We would have to start at the tenth. That was fine by us. We followed the superintendent in our golf cart. He wheeled up to the tenth tee. Two men were getting ready to hit their shots. They were apparently halfway through a round of play, a young man, natty in blue golfing slacks, who turned out to be a professional at a nearby golf course, and his partner, a fine golfer who apparently—though we never asked—was taking a playing lesson. When we arrived, the superintendent asked if they would mind our joining them—the course was crowded to capacity, and so on—and making up a foursome. They complied, but they looked sort of grumpy about it. I couldn't blame them. I was wearing sneakers, a frayed pair of khaki trousers, and a beachwear striped shirt. Mike's shirt, a brown polyester, was sweat-stained. In those fancy surroundings, the groomed fairways, and the flowerbeds banked around the tees, we could well have been taken as refugees from a public course, two duffers certainly from the look of it, and hardly good company for a round of golf on a fine sun-drenched afternoon.

The tenth hole at Aviana is a par four. A pond runs along the left side of the fairway with a tall grove of trees at the far end. The fairway dog-legs to the left behind the trees with the green, of course, out of sight.

Our hosts drove first. The older gentleman hit a crisp, efficient drive down the center of the fairway. The pro stepped up and aimed a bit more left. His ball carried over the corner of the pond and a few trees at the end. He would have an easy approach to the green.

"Nice ball," Mike said, with just that suavity of tone to suggest it wasn't that much out of the ordinary.

My turn. The usual Finnegans Wake stream of words murmured in my head . . . chin steady, no puking, swing like a gate, get the sugar bag off your shoulders, turn in the barrel. I set the midget down in front of the ball.

I topped the drive and the ball hopped frantically down the fairway, at least in play. I didn't hear any reaction from our hosts but I knew that inwardly they were thinking, "Oh my God, we're going to have to deal with this . . ."

Then Mike stepped up. "Which way's the green?" he asked.

"Dog-leg around to the left."

"No, I mean what's the line to the green."

The two looked at each other. One of them pointed with his club. "Well, it's out over the pond to the left, out over those trees . . . but . . ."

Mike squared around, twenty degrees or so off the plumbline down the fairway. It was evident he was going for the green over the pond and the trees beyond. It seemed incongruously absurd, like driving a ball off the stern of an ocean liner or into the wastes of the Grand Canyon. I could hear the whisper of his slacks as he swung into the ball. I wanted to watch the expressions on the faces of our friends—a sagging of the jaw. I suspect—but I watched the ball until it was just the barest speck in the sky before it began to drop beyond the trees and plopped down, we determined later, at the edge of the green. I fumbled briefly for something to say. It seemed an important moment in what I'd been going through, something to reflect that I was a changed golfer now, worthy of playing with a crack golfer as a partner. It came to mind.

"Nice ball," I said evenly.

GEORGE PLIMPTON (1927–2003) was the legendary founding editor of the *Paris Review*—where he tirelessly promoted, for more than fifty years, new writers and the craft of writing. He was also a humorist, and sometimes an actor, who referred to himself as the "Prince of Cameos". His books include *Paper Lion* (named by *Sports Illustrated* as one of the top ten sports books of the past hundred years), *The Bogey Man, Open Net, Out of My League, Shadow Box,* and *Mad Ducks and Bears.*

Tripp Lake

BY LAUREN SLATER

AT THE AGE OF NINE YEARS I went to my first and only camp, located in Poland, Maine, way up off 95, by a kidney-shaped lake where, across the shore, we could see the serrated lines of red roofs, and on sunny days, white sails walking along the water. The camp was called Tripp Lake and it was for girls, or so my parents said, who were especially competitive, girls like me, not yet pubescent, packed with all the power of a life that has yet to really unfold, bringing with it the hard parts, the shames, the sadnesses, none of that yet. I wore my hair in what was called a "pixie cut," which was a nice way of saying it was short as a boy's, crew cut really, and, at that age, white-blond so the stubble glittered silver in the summer sun. I spent my evenings playing capture the flag, an exhilarating game that requires fast feet, and a bit of cunning.

Understandably, my parents thought it best to send me to a place where my energies could be shaped and expanded. I agreed. I thought I might be Olympic quality, like those skaters I'd seen, or the skiers hunched over their poles, ricocheting down mountains where ice hung from all the trees.

I remember the first night at the camp, but no, let me begin before then, at the bus stop, about to leave, and feeling, for the first time, a shudder of intense grief. My mother, an aloof woman whom I nonetheless adored, looked pale, her eyes foggy and distant. My father was a small man in the bakery business;

lately they'd been fighting. She wanted something grand out of life, something more than a muffin, whereas he was content to nozzle whipped cream on top of tarts. I loved my father but I loved my mother more, more problematically is what I mean, in the crooked hooked way only a daughter can.

I hugged my parents good-bye and when I hugged my mother I could feel a circle of sadness in her. By leaving I felt as if I were betraying her. I had heard their voices at night, his quiet, hers shrill, you and you and you, and I'd seen my mother sometimes sitting on the porch looking out at nothing. She was a severe and brittle woman, but even at that age I knew brittle was breakable. Sometimes, driving in the car, she crushed the accelerator to the floor, just for the feeling of speed, and other times she cried with her mouth closed. I had the feeling, there at the bus stop, that she wished she were me, about to board a bus heading for the horizon, a green-striped bus with Peter Pan dancing on its flank and girls unabashedly eating apples. And because I felt her longing, inchoate, certainly unspoken, my chest seemed to split with sadness, and also guilt. This was a new emotion, an emotion that sits in the throat, an emotion that is maybe more imagistic than all the others; guilt made me imagine that while I was away, my mother would come undone; her arm would fall off; her hair drift from her head. Guilt made me imagine that she would sit in the nights and cry, and what could I do about that? I wanted to say I'm sorry, but I didn't really know what for. I couldn't have said it then, what I've since felt my whole life, that separation is a sword, painful, to be avoided at all costs.

My first night, at camp. I could hear the flagpole rope banging against its post; I could hear the cry of what were maybe coyotes in the woods, and the susurration of thousands of tree frogs. I couldn't sleep, so I stepped outside, onto the damp dirt that surrounded the cabin, and in the single spotlight that shone down I found a tiny toad, no bigger than a dime, with still tinier bumps on its taupe back. I lifted the amphibian up. I could not believe God or whoever could make an animal so small, an animal that would have, if I cut it open, all the same organs as me, in miniature, the locket-sized heart, bones like white wisps. How easy it is to break an animal; I could have crushed that frog with my fist, and part of me wanted to, while another part of me wanted to protect it, while still a third part of me wanted to let it go.

Before camp I'd been a more or less happy girl, but that first night I couldn't sleep and by morning a wild sadness had settled in me. Where was I? Where was she? Someday I would die. Someone somewhere was sick. It was as if a curtain had been pulled back to reveal the true nature of the world, which was terror, through and through.

I became, for the first time in my life, truly afraid that summer, and the fears took forms that were not good, that did not augur well for my later life, although I didn't know it then. That first day, sitting on the green lawn, watching a girl do a cartwheel and another girl mount the parallel bars, I developed an irrational fear that is still hard to explain; I became hyper-aware of my own body, the swoosh of my blood and the paddling of my heart and the huh-huh-huhs of my breath, and it seemed amazing and tenuous to me, that my body did all of this without any effort on my part. As soon as I became aware of this fact—almost as though I'd discovered my lower brain stem and how it hitched to the spinal cord—as soon as I came to consciousness about this, I thought, "I can't breathe." And truly, it felt like I couldn't breathe. I thought, "I am thinking about my breathing and if I think too hard about my breathing, which you're not supposed to think about, I will concentrate it right away," and I swallowed hard, and then I became aware of all the minute mechanisms that comprise a swallow, and so I suddenly felt I couldn't swallow anymore. It was like the lights were going out in my body, while meanwhile, in front of me, girls did cartwheels on the green lawn, completely unaware that I was dying.

After that, the fears came fast and furious. I was afraid to think about walking, because then I would fall. Breathing because then I would suffocate. Swallowing was the worst one of all, to suddenly feel you have no way of bringing the world down into your throat, of taking it in, no way. I then became afraid of the dining hall, with its vicious swordfish mounted on one wall, and its huge bear head with eyes like my mother's, dull, distant eyes, eyes at once wild and flat. I became afraid of pancakes, of toothbrushes, of cutlery, of water, the counselors urging me into the lake, where fronds fingered through the murk and scads of fish darted by, making a current cool against my legs. That first week at camp, I fished a dime out of my uniform pocket (we wore only blue-and-white standard-issue uniforms) and called my mother. From far far away I heard her voice. When had her sadness started? With my father, or before that, with her mother, who insisted she, the oldest of three girls, do endless tasks and childcare, so she was never able to shoot marbles, too busy shining the silver. My mother, I knew, had been a good girl, exceedingly good, and because of that, she hated my grandmother. She called her "Francis" and all holidays were barbed affairs, my mother sniping at her mother, making faces at the food, because she, if only given the chance, she could have done better.

My mother did not go to college despite the fact that she's bright. In my imagination, when I construct her history for her because she's so closed about her own, she wants to be a singer on a lit stage, or she wants to be a painter with her canvas at a quiet lakeside. She wants something larger than her own life, larger than her husband's life, larger than the house and kids, where what she does all day is clean. Much much later on, when I was near grown, after she and my father divorced, my mother would develop a passion for Israel, its military might; she became fiercely ragefully Zionistic, and, totally bursting the caul of her confinement, she smuggled Bibles into the USSR. But this was later, when she found an outlet for her energies, and if only I'd known that was going to happen, that she was going to get something good, if only I'd known maybe my fears would have been a little less.

From far away my mother answered the phone and I said, "I want to come home," and she said, "Don't be a quitter, Lauren." She wanted for me a larger life, a life where girls stand on stages, take charge of a team, swim the length of a lake, and back, in a Speedo suit. But as long as she didn't have these things, I felt much too guilty to take them for myself. None of this did I say.

At camp, we were divided into teams and every activity, from drama to Newcomb, was cast as a competition. It was a summer of color war. I watched the older girls run with their lacrosse sticks, cradling them close to their sides, the ball in the gut string pocket a soft blur. I watched as we, the younger girls, were taught to dribble and to shoot. Part of me wanted fiercely to win these games, while a still larger part of me could not even allow myself to participate, for somehow I would be betraying her if I did.

I was put on the Tigers Team. Every morning after breakfast, standing at attention beneath that mounted swordfish we would sing:

> Shielded by orange and black
> Tigers will attack
> Catching every cue
> Always coming through

I remember, in particular, a game called bombardment, which we played in the gym on rainy days, Tigers versus Bears. In this game, each side is given a whole raft of basketballs, and the purpose is simply to hurl them at each other as hard as you can, and whoever gets hit, is out. Before I'd left home, maybe I could have played this game, but certainly not now. Brown basketballs came whizzing through the air, smacked against the lacquered floor of the gym, ricocheted off a face or a flank, and one by one each girl got hit and so would sit out on the sidelines. I was so scared of bombardment that whenever we played it I hung way in the back of the court, where the other teams' balls could not reach me. And then one day, because of this, I lasted throughout the whole game; everyone on my team had been hit except me, everyone on the other team had been hit except a senior girl named Nancy, a fourteen-year-old who had one leg longer than the other. Because of this, she had custom-made shoes, her left heel stacked high enough to bring her up even, so she didn't tilt. I'd watched Nancy walk out of the corners of my eyes; even with her shoes she was strangely clumsy, gangly, always giggling nervously just at the rim of a group of girls, her desire to be taken in palpable.

And now Nancy and I were the last two left in the game. Everyone on the sidelines was screaming go go go. Nancy's skin was as pale as milk, the strands of veins visible in her neck. Her gimp foot, supported by the huge rubber heel of her sneaker, seemed to wobble. Go go go, but I couldn't do it; I couldn't hurl that ball at her; it seemed existentially horrible that we were called to do this sort of thing in the world, to live in a way so someone had to lose. I stood there, locked in place, mesmerized by her skin and her foot, while Nancy lifted the basketball high above her head, and hurled it toward me with as much muster as she could muster, and I just stood there, and let the ball hit me on the hip. Nancy won. That was the only outcome I could tolerate.

It didn't take long for the counselors to realize something was wrong with me. I cried all the time. During free swim I retreated into the fringe of woods. The woods were next to a red barn where horses hung their heads over stall doors, and there were golden squares of hay. Somehow, being near the horses calmed me. I liked their huge velvety lips, their thoughtful mastications. I liked the way they almost seemed to slurp up hay. I liked their rounded backsides, their plumed tails; I even liked their scat, flecked with grain and sweet smelling. Still today whenever I enter a barn and smell that smell, I do a Proustian plunge back to that first barn, and the chestnut ponies.

Riding was a camp activity reserved for the older girls. I began to watch those girls cantering around the ring, the horses seeping dark sweat on their muscular chests. The riding coach's name was Kim. She was a wisp of a woman in tan jodhpurs with suede patches at the knees. Once, when I was alone in the barn, I found her riding clothes hung up on a hook, near the tack room. I tried on her green hunt jacket. It hung huge on me, but it felt cozy, and on its lapel there was a tiny brooch in the shape of a dragonfly.

"Would you like to try?" Kim asked me one day. "I'm only ten," I said. "Well," she said, "I have a horse who's only ten too; maybe you would make a good match."

"What's his name?" I asked.

"What's yours?" she said.

"Lauren," I said.

"Smokey Raindrops," she said. "But we call him Rain."

Rain, rain, what a beautiful name. It was more a sound than a designation. "Yes," I said.

In fact, I didn't get to ride Rain that day; first all the counselors, along with Auntie Ruth, the camp director, had to discuss it. Should I have lessons even though that was not a part of my camp curriculum? Would that make me happy? They thought it might.

Riding is a sport that, like any other, requires more than just the circumscribed activity. There is the ritualistic preparation, the waxing of skis or the oiling of strings or, in my case, the grooming before the tack. A few days later Kim showed me how to do it, use a currying comb, pick a hoof, leaning down and cupping the hairy fetlock, lifting the leg, the shine of the silver shoe with six nail heads in it. Time passed. Days passed. I found caring for the horses soothing, and I found when I was at the stable, by these big breathing animals, I could forget about my own breath and just breathe.

All through the summer Kim taught me how to ride, alone, no other girl there. She taught me how to post, how to do dressage, how to jump. I learned to hoist myself up, foot in one stirrup, other leg flung over the broad rank back. "When you post," she said, "watch the left leg. As it extends, you rise." The trot of a horse is like a metronome. It synchronizes you. It hypnotizes you. Left foot rise. Left foot rise. Your whole mind funnels down into this foot, the flash of hoof in the summer sun. And I'll never forget the day Kim taught me to canter, how she said, "Trot out, give him a kick with your inside foot," and suddenly the horse's tight trot broke into the rocking run, around and around the ring we went, so fast it seemed, the world blurring by in a beautiful way.

Riding is largely a singular sport; although there are shows and red ribbons, first places and sixth places, it can still be done, nevertheless, with no attention to that. You cannot really play lacrosse, or soccer, unless you are playing against someone, and this against-ness requires that you see yourself as separate, with all that that implies. But horseback riding you may do alone in the woods, or in a dusty riding rink, or even in your mind, which can canter too. Riding is not about separation. It is not about dominance. The only person you might hurt is you. You are, at long last, without guilt.

Riding. It is about becoming one with the animal that bears you along. It is about learning to give and take, give the horse his head, take the rein and bring him up. It is about tack, the glorious leather saddles, and the foam-stained bits, which fascinated me, how Kim would roll them in sugar and slide them into the animal's mouth, its thick tongue clamped. It is, more than anything else, about relationship and balance, and as Kim taught me how to do these things, walk trot canter, a sort of peace settled in me, a working through my mother and me, a way of excelling at no one's cost.

And so the summer progressed. The only thing I could not do well was jump. Each time we approached the fence the horse seemed to sense my primordial fear, fear of the fence and fear of everything it contained, and it would bunch to a scuttering halt, or, more humiliating, the horse would stop, and then, with me kicking and kicking uselessly, it would simply walk over the bar. I watched Kim jump; she was amazing, fluid, holding on to his hair as she entered the air, her face a mixture of terror and exhilaration, the balanced combination of which means only one thing: mastery.

One month into the camp season was visiting day. My parents arrived, carrying leather fruit rolls and a new canteen. They seemed as separate as ever, not even looking at each other. My mother was appalled at the condition of my wardrobe. My clothes stank of sweat and fur. The soles of my boots were crammed with flaking manure. That was the summer, also, when I started to smell. "What's this?" she said, flicking through my steamer trunk. "Do you ever do your laundry?" She pulled out a white shirt with black spatters of mud on it, and stains beneath the armpit, slight stains, their rims barely visible.

"Lauren," she said.

"What?" I said.

She pursed her lips together and shook her head. She held the shirt out, as though to study it. And, once again, I saw that look of longing cross her face, but this time it was mixed with something else. I saw the briefest flicker of disgust.

A few minutes later, she went into our cabin bathroom, which we called the Greenie. She closed the door. I stalked up to it, pressed my ear against its wood. What did I do with my body? What did she do with hers? I heard the gush of water from the tap, the scrunch of something papery. The bathroom had a lock, on my side only. Quietly, and for a reason I still cannot quite explain, I turned the lever and the lock slid quietly into its socket.

A few minutes later, when she tried to get out, she could not. She rattled the knob. We were alone in the cabin. I stood back and watched. "Lauren?" she said. "Lauren?" Her voice hurt me. It was curved into a question, and when I didn't answer, the question took on a kind of keening. "Lauren, are you there? Open the door." I stood absolutely still. I was mesmerized, horrified, by the vulnerability in her voice, how small she suddenly seemed, and how I was growing in girth by the minute. For some reason I suddenly pictured her trapped in a tiny glass bottle. I held the bottle in my hands. I could let her out, or leave her.

I let her out.

"What are you doing?" she said. She stared at me. I stared back at her. I could see her sweat now; it ran in a trickle down the side of her brow. I wanted to wipe it away.

They left in the evening, when colored clouds were streaming across the sky. I stood in the parking lot and watched their station wagon rattle over the dirt road, raising clouds of dust. The next few days, I backslid. My fears returned. There was the problem with my breathing, but also, accompanying this obsession was now the need to walk backwards while counting. I saw for sure that I was growing while she shrank. I saw for sure that I was growing because she shrank. I also saw something pointed in me, some real desire to win. Hearing that lock sink into its socket, there had been glee and power.

I stopped riding then. I stopped going to the stables. I stayed in my bunk. I wrote letters and letters to my mother, the act somehow soothing my conscience. Love Lauren XXX. Kisses and hugs. I love you.

At last, after four days had passed, Kim came to my cabin to get me. "You disappeared," she said.

"I'm sick," I said.

"You know," she said, "I never much liked my mother."

I stared at her. How had she known?

"What will you do?" she said.

"I don't know," I said.

"Are you going to sit on a cot for the rest of your life?"

"Maybe," I said.

"Just sit there and cry?" she said, and there was, suddenly, a slight sneer to her voice.

I looked away.

"I once knew a girl," said Kim, "who spent her whole life going from hospital to hospital, because she loved being sick. She was too scared to face the world. Is that you?"

I have thought of her words often; a premonition, an augur, a warning, a simple perception.

I followed her back to the barn. It was noontime. The sun was high and hot. She brought Rain out into the middle of the ring, tightened up his saddle strap, and tapped on the deep seat. "All aboard," she said.

Sitting high on the horse, I could smell the leaves. I could smell my own sweat, and all it contained, so many contradictions.

"We're going to jump today," she said.

She went into the center of the ring, and this time, she set the fence at four feet high. "Now," she said, "cross your stirrups and knot your reins. A rider has to depend on her inner balance only."

I cantered toward the jump, hands on my hips, legs grasping. But each time, at the crucial moment of departure, Rain would screech to a halt and I'd topple into his mane.

"He senses your fear," Kim said.

At last, on the third or fourth try, she went into the barn and came back out with a long black crop. Standing in the center of the ring, right next to the jump, she swizzled the crop in the air, a snapping sound. The horse's ears flashed forward. "You have to get over it," she said. I centered myself in the saddle. I cantered twice around the ring and then turned in tight toward the bar. Kim cracked the whip, a crack I still hear today whenever I feel my fears and I do, I often do, but I rose up, arms akimbo, in this leap merged with the mammal, its heart my heart, its hooves my feet, we sailed into the excellent air, I did it. I found a way to move forward.

LAUREN SLATER is the author of *Opening Skinner's Box: Great Psychological Experiments of the 20th Century* and, most recently, *Blue Beyond Blue: Extraordinary Tales for Ordinary Dilemmas* (Norton, 2005).

The Last of the
Great Dreamers

BY TOURÉ

LET ME TELL YOU about the last of the great dreamers. The last of this century's Jackie Robinson revolutionaries, who dreamed out loud, broke down doors, and opened the gates wide. There was Alvin Ailey and Arthur Mitchell in dance, Spike Lee in film, Jean-Michel Basquiat in painting, and in tennis, there was Mister Smith. A man with a belly as large, round, and solid as Santa's, a wisdom as encyclopedic and a face as ageless as Yoda's, and a fire-snorting mien as gruff as Sonny Liston's. Like the others he knew it would take Puritan-style blue-collar hard work to get where he wanted—"Spit in one hand and wish in the other," he loved to say, "and see which one fills up faster." But like those others he never looked at what is in the world and asked why, he saw what is not in the world and asked, why not?

In the early '70s Mister Smith built four indoor courts on Blue Hill Avenue in Dorchester, Massachusetts, chased dona-tions, sold an hour of court time for $8 to bring in as much busi-ness as possible—hence the motto "adults pay so kids can play"—and created Sportsmen's Tennis Club, aka Franklin Field Tennis Center: a not-for-profit tennis mecca in the mid-dle of the ghetto. When I tell you it was a Black club, I don't mean just that damn-near everyone in there was Black (but not

everyone, a few Irish families and an Indian one were part of
The Club family). I mean the fabric of the place was Black, the
rhythm was Black, the fucking air felt Black if you can believe
that. And not white-sweater-vest Black. Not So-nice-to-see-
you-again-General-Powell Black. The place was ghetto. It was a
place where Conway, Julius, and Bootsy could feel at home.
Where there were cracks in the courts and holes in the nets and
no one cared because the place had the kinetic, propulsive energy and high theater of the Mississippi juke joint, the Watts
backyard BBQ, the late night Harlem street corner. It was a
place where they played tennis Blackly.

In time Mister Smith added three outdoor courts, three more
indoor, and two red clay, but the upkeep quickly killed those
two. And he attracted street kids from Dorchester, Roxbury, and
Mattapan—Boston's little Vietnams—by charging $5 for an en-
tire winter of twice-a-week after-school lessons, another $5 for
the spring, and less than $100 for an entire summer of all-day
camp. He was a genius at turning a beginner into a top regional
player and he trained us to be little tennis assassins, pro-
grammed to win junior tournaments, possibly go on to major
college tennis, and maybe, with hard, hard work, make it to the
tour. It was like a tennis program in a third world country—
threadbare in materials, heavy with the dreams of a nation.

We arrived at New England junior tournaments as if they
were racialized Davis Cup ties, infused with a healthy disdain of
white people. We were at war with tradition, class, privilege, ex-
pectation, and all those little white kids whose strokes seemed
so crisp and coached you could hear a cash register cha-ching
when they swung. And when we beat them we learned we
didn't need the advantages they had. We learned that the white
man's ice is no colder.

In that pre-Venus, pre-Zina world, African-American tennis
meant Arthur Ashe and Althea Gibson. Ashe came to The Club
once and gave an inspiring clinic (as did Billie Jean King), but

mostly the only serious players we ever saw were each other. Until the ATA Nationals.

The ATAs were a festival of blackness and tennis where long-distance friendships were rekindled, life lessons were learned, and Big Fun was had. Every summer The Club's elite juniors went off to San Diego or D.C. or Atlanta for an all-expense-paid week of tennis, parties, and no parents. One year, the gang drove to Detroit, spending 20 hours on the road, switching radio stations every hour, screaming each time Rick James's new hit came on—"Supafreak! Supafreak! She's supa freeee-kay, Yow!" In San Diego, after lights-out, Drew, Karl junior, Patrick Perry, and Glen Lloyd snuck out, climbed the fence, and went wild on the university's football field until campus security arrived and they had to sprint and hide their way back. In New Orleans, it was rumored, one of us conspired with an old friend to ensure a good show in the finals: they would trade the first two sets, get to 5-all, then play it out. The other boy took the third 6–4 and all hell broke loose. One year Karl junior got pushed into a pool and, even though he couldn't swim, remained too cool to call for help. We stood there and watched him struggle and splash for two full minutes. Every year the girls from Houston mesmerized. Most for their hourglass shapes, two for their knockout playing: Lori McNeil and Zina something or other. On the final night in Detroit, Drew, Karl junior, Steve Perry, and Malcolm had a pillow fight so wild that Malcolm's brand-new trophy for winning the 10-and-unders was broken in three. He cried all 20 hours home. All of the The Club's top players scrapped all winter and spring for that moment in early summer when Mister Smith convened us on the side of Court One and announced which eight or nine of us would make the long trip, stay in the cheap motel, and have the Big Fun.

But for Mister Smith, the trip was yet another motivational ploy. He'd do anything to make us better because each time one of us got better it got him one step closer to his big dream: creating a professional tennis player, or in his words, a player. He wanted just one who would make it to the Big Dance. To him we were little pawns he could push through the ranks and maybe turn into a queen who would win big, prove what a great coach he was, and bring more attention and thus money and thus power to The Club. Mister Smith dreamed of college scholarships, full or partial, for most of us. But every time he looked over his crop of juniors he was like an 1849 California prospector, carefully sifting his pan, searching for one bright glimmer of gold.

You were six or seven when your moms took you to that place your brothers and sisters had been going, with the two light green warehouse-like buildings on Blue Hill Avenue. You walked inside the doors, past the front desk and Sandy the cranky receptionist, past the life-size photo of The Club's first nine juniors, past the bathrooms that were really little clubhouses where girls made up new dances or practiced the Smurf and gossiped and boys listened to cassettes of a new rap group called Run-DMC and complained about scrub teachers. As a beginner you went to court seven, way in the back, waiting until a teacher came and unlocked a giant black chest that held all the little wooden rackets. You grabbed one, got in line, had a ball or two tossed to you, tried to make contact, then took your place at the back of the line behind 20 or so other children. Once, while waiting in line, I asked a boy where he lived.

"I live in a project," he said.

"You can't live in a project." Of course not. A smart first grader like me knew better than that. "A project is something you make."

Eventually, you learned enough to make it onto the Intermediate courts where you had fun teachers like long, tall Paul White who oozed charisma even as he fed balls with a Connors T2000 and created a mystique by never, ever taking off his sweatpants, even on July's hottest days. You did the Buddy System—tossing balls to a partner to hit into the backdrop until it was your turn. And you played games like Around the World, where everyone forms a single-file line on each baseline, hits one ball, then runs to the back of the line on the far side of the court. Miss a stroke and you're out. When there were four or three kids left you had to hit a moonball just to have the time to sprint from one baseline to the other.

After a few years, and Mister Smith pointing out a few kids who had learned faster than you and already moved up, you ascended to the tournament caste, playing and drilling on Court One in front of the large glass window. Now you rubbed elbows with The Club's living legends. There was Patrick Perry who had the backhand slice of life: the ball floated off his Wilander Rossignol, crossed the net in slow motion, landed inches from the baseline, and just skipped like a perfectly thrown rock across water. There was Velina Rhodes, an Energizer bunny who made you hit twenty strokes per point. She had perfect brown skin, a smooth, deep voice, a slim, shapely figure, high, almond-shaped cheekbones, and was probably your first crush. There was Benny Sims, the beloved drill sergeant head pro with crisp strokes and military-starched clothes—he was so clean he could sweat and not get dirty. And there was Lars: the tall, thin, red-faced blond with a serve as fast as Roscoe Tanner's. He gave the ball a few tense bounces, tossed it an inch above his head, let it hang there for a heartbeat, then slashed his little wooden Jack Kramer Wilson through the air and did violence to that ball. His violence often landed near the baseline, but we were still impressed.

He cemented his legend one year in a club tournament by hitting a backspinning backhand drop shot that crossed the net then came back to his side for an unbelievable winner. And more, he'd been telling us he could hit that shot for years.

Come summer you lived at The Club, hitting on the rickety wooden backboard, jogging on the abandoned clay courts, lunching on McDonald's or a 50-cent so-called pizza defrosted in a toaster oven, and, in every free moment, playing mini-tennis, a game of touch using just a single service box. There were constant trials by fire. Like a Roman emperor with Christians and lions to spare, Mister Smith looked for a matchup that intrigued him—two kids of similar ability or age, or, best of all, two who had talked smack to each other, saying, maybe, "I'll beat you a donut and a french fry!" (meaning love and one), or, "I'll beat you double donuts!" (love and love). The two would be snatched by their collars and thrown into a public steel-cage match (after Mister Smith, like a kid egging others on to fight, had told them things like, "He's gonna hit the ball so hard it'll make your head swim.") (Weird thing, he was always talking about making your head swim.) More than once I suffered through a tense set against my sister, a year younger and, during the first half of our teens, taller and stronger. Everyone watched while I played, terrified that one early misstep would give her a slight lead and multiply my fear of losing to my so-called little sister and paralyze me into further errors that would end in a defeat I would never, ever hear the end of. I never lost, but never felt like a winner. Still, after that crucible, no one could make me fear losing. (This system didn't always work: after Kyla beat her big sister Crystal in front of a crowd, the older girl quit the game.)

And there were annual trips to the pro tournament at the Longwood Cricket Club in upper-crusty Brookline. We'd mull around the courts for a while, then one of us would distract the guard while another snuck by and went into the clubhouse and the players' lounge. We were assumed to be Ashe's cousin or Yannick Noah's little brother, so no one complained as we walked through the locker room and sat in the clubhouse and watched Ion Tiriac chomp through a sandwich, or Jose-Louis Clerc towel off, or Guillermo Vilas strut, South American machismo style. These were men with an inner calm, a deep seriousness, a minisculely apertured concentration, and an unshakable confidence. Men who knew they were baaad. These were not normal people. Climbing Everest seemed easier than entering their club. We would not tell Mister Smith that.

Every summer morning began with all the juniors assembled on the side of Court One for yet another of Mister Smith's unscripted lectures delivered in the barking tone of a hellish lieutenant and the dramatic timing of a Baptist preacher. He waddled out, his giant belly somehow supported by two bow legs so thin and spindly it looked like spider's legs steadying a beer keg, and invariably began, "If you wanna be a player..." and then meandered for up to forty-five long minutes through mental toughness, cutting off angles, and thinking two shots ahead. He would always work in one or all of his mantras—"You're no good until you beat somebody better than you," and "A player will win with a frying pan," and "When I say jump, you don't say, 'How high?!'" (you were supposed to just jump as high as you could)—and in his never-ending crusade to omit needless movement from our strokes: "K-I-S-S! Keep it simple, stupid!" To him the worst things we could ever do were choke or push—he hated the words so much he spat them from his mouth like dirty gum. And not a day went by that he failed to speak of poise—that quality which the great ones used to make the difficult appear easy, the final gloss needed to be a player.

There are about sixty weekday mornings in a summer and no more than four stock lectures in Mister Smith's repertoire, so even though he improvised somewhat, sprinkling in new anecdotes, pasting in patches of other lectures, your attention would float as he rumbled on, thinking, I've never seen him play, I wonder when we'll get to play, I've never even seen a photograph of him playing, Keisha Mac looks good in that skirt, I can't even imagine him playing, Isn't this the same lecture he gave three days ago? Still, you had to listen because he might ask a question—"When I say jump, what do you say?"—and you feared getting it wrong. You feared Mister Smith more than your father, or the school principal, or maybe even God. God was far away. Mister Smith was up in your face, wagging his short, stubby finger, calling you a turkey when you blew an easy shot.

Even though he stayed cloaked in humble, frugal clothes—tan Members Only jackets, cotton Izod shirts, plain polyester pants, cheap, padded shoes, all from Filene's Basement or Marshall's—Mister Smith always appeared to be draped in full general's regalia as he strutted about The Club like a European dictator, espousing his unyielding dogma on how strokes should be hit, beheading teachers who crossed him, keeping all the juniors in fear by playing shameless favorites. He would anoint one member of the tournament caste and lavish them with extra-intensive teaching and attention—Maybe, you could hear him thinking, she'll be the one. But that weight was too great to bear and after a few months he lost faith in his favorite and chose another. We all stood in the corner grumbling, Why does Courtney deserve all that?, secretly hoping to be next.

If you were black you probably had a father or uncle like Mister Smith, whose meanness was his way of expressing love, so some of his abuse and belligerence rolled off your back. But also, you knew that he alone was responsible for bringing The Club to Dorchester, that he alone had schemed and networked and somehow made tennis affordable for kids with food stamps. But he also made tennis available to us on a cultural level. The same way Alvin Ailey came along and breathed Black into those old white dance moves, Mister Smith breathed Black into this white game. I'll never forget how he taught us that when you hit the backhand slice approach shot, "you got to crossover step like you're dancin'," and as he showed us he would do what seemed like a little soft-shoe.

Very, very few of us would've had the opportunity to play without the door he alone opened. And to play for Mister Smith was to learn how to deal with strategy, human nature, pressure, and the white, white world. He brought this beautiful game to us. And for that we loved him.

He loved us, too, I think, but not well. Despite his genius, there were levels of this game above his head. If tennis were math, he got us to understand geometry and algebra and trigonometry, but not the advanced calculus of national junior tennis or the quantum physics of the tour. But in his mind taking outside private lessons was the ultimate betrayal. It meant you felt the white man's ice was colder than his. In the tiny Boston tennis community it was impossible to have a long-term relationship with a coach without Mister Smith eventually hearing of it. So the better Mister Smith made you, the more you had to choose between paralyzing Club loyalty and self-destructive advancement. He was a jealous lover and it doomed him: only two of the many talented kids of my generation ever made it anywhere near the Big Dance. Those two, twin girls who took lessons at The Club and with private coaches and endured Mister Smith's griping—it may have been easier for them being white—are currently in the top 750.

My last summer at The Club, before I went off to college, there was a men's tournament. At the last moment I entered the doubles with Charles Hardison, a dark brown 16-year-old with twinkling eyes, a warm smile, and a smooth manner that let him get along with everyone in The Club, no small achievement in that cuckoo's nest. I was small for my age and he was smaller than me. He was lightning-bug quick, but a risk-taking shotmaker who either has a great day or an awful one. I expected only to play hard and have fun.

We won two matches against much older, but far less well-schooled men, and then, thanks to Charles's eye for the perfect sharp angles, pulled out a tough three-set semifinal, as Mister Smith watched with glee. We were the longest long shots to ever make a final, a full head shorter than our opponents. We succumbed quickly, but just being there was victory enough. At the summer's end, we decided we would try some local men's tournaments when I returned from my freshman year. I don't remember our good-bye. I knew for sure that I'd see him again.

The next spring, on a late Sunday night, after a long raucous weekend at Mardi Gras in New Orleans, I called my father. His voice was cold. He asked if I was sitting down. "On Friday afternoon," he said, "Charles was found dead in his mother's house."

She had come home late Thursday night and found his keys still in the front door, assumed he was in his bed, and went to sleep. The next morning she found his bed still made. He was in the basement, lying face up. Her ex-boyfriend, who Charles had never liked, had shot him with a silencer, while Charles's grandmother sat upstairs, unaware.

I wanted desperately to phone his father and ask for one of Charles's rackets as one last thing to remember him by. I couldn't. I quit tennis instead.

That was ten years ago. Patrick Perry took his beautiful slice to Dartmouth and has become a lawyer. Drew, inspired by years of playing the ATA sectionals on Yale's courts, went to school there, and is now a financial consultant at Merrill Lynch. Benny Sims is on the pro tour coaching Chanda Rubin. We've become a producer for Oprah, a fashion model in Paris, a doctor in Brooklyn, and a computer programmer. We've started a power-washing company, a casting agency, joined the navy, and done time. After years of trying, Lars finally gave up his dream of playing on the tour and now drives a limo.

The cost of court time at The Club soared to $18 an hour, but chronic financial problems continued. In time a new board of directors developed, one that did not remember The Club's old days. Tired of Mister Smith's histrionics and power games and ceaseless dreams that became more and more fanciful as he grew older, they kicked him off the board. Like an old powerless dictator, he was exiled. He was almost 80 then. A year or two later his wife, Gloria, always his partner in The Club, succumbed to cancer. Mister Smith died just over a year later. I never asked how. With no Gloria, no Club, and none of his juniors to watch play on television, he must've been quite alone.

There are no Jackie Robinson dreamers anymore. Those days are over. Now most Blacks know any Antartica that won't have us ain't worth going to. That the white man's ice ain't worth a damn.

But I think Mister Smith is still here.

After nine years away from the game I picked it up again and found him still in my muscles and my mind. Now I'm playing tournaments again. Maybe I'm still enamored with striking balls. Maybe I'm trying to see how far I can get without Mister Smith breathing down my neck. Maybe I'm looking for the respect I missed as a child. A few weeks back I pulled out three tough three-setters and found myself in the quarterfinals of a big tournament in Manhattan's Central Park. Up a break in the deciding set of a rough match I heard a voice in my head say, "Wish Mister Smith was here." The next point I got a short ball on my backhand side and, with him in my blood, danced through it, nailed it down the line, and knocked off the weak return for a volley winner. Then I knew he was there.

TOURÉ is the author of *Soul City*, a novel, and the pop culture correspondent at CNN's *American Morning*. He's also a contributing editor at *Rolling Stone*, the host of MTV2's *Spoke 'N' Heard*, and the author of the *Portable Promised Land*, a collection of short stories. He lives in Fort Greene, Brooklyn, and still plays tennis as often as possible.

The Boy They Cut

BY BENJAMIN CHEEVER

"LOT OF SMOKE, NO FIRE, CHEEVER." That's what the wrestling coach used to shout, when I was groaning noisily in an attempt to escape from the opponent who was powering me around the mat. This was in high school and it's when I first learned that time stops if you're anxious enough and in pain. I could look up at the clock three times during a 45-second drill.

I was supposed to escape, but I was supposed to escape carefully. It was also possible—all during a 45-second eternity—that I'd be flipped like a tortoise and pinned. (If you've never been pinned, never heard the slap, slap, slap of the ref's hand on the mat, then you can look it up in dictionary under "M" for mortification.)

So I struggled cautiously, and when I moved, I groaned. Apparently, my groans were more convincing than my struggles were; hence the coach's comments. And yet I liked the wrestling coach. I went out for wrestling. Most sports I didn't go out for, or not on purpose. Most coaches I didn't like.

I can still summon their hoarse masculine voices today: "Heads up, Cheever! Step into the batting box. I said into the batting box. Keep your eye on the pill, son. Dig it out. Hustle! Hustle! Hustle!"

There are men out who had their lives saved by the attentions of a rough-hewn coach. Not me. I know boys who when they came home from college or the war, they'd stop for pie and coffee with Coach, before they stopped for pie and coffee with Ma. Not me.

I hated coaches. And they hated me right back.

I thought them heartless. They thought I didn't have any heart.

It just so happened that I hit the playing fields at the dawn of that era when coaches—until then perfect autocrats—were first compelled by social mores to give every boy a chance. I was a boy, but I was not an asset.

I began my athletic career at Scarborough Country Day School, in Scarborough, New York. This institution, since defunct, was built by Frank A. Vanderlip, a business titan who wanted his children to be able to go to school without having to leave the property.

The campus was life-sized, but somehow also miniature. We had an auditorium modeled after the Little Theatre in London. The inscriptions above its two doorways were: "Life Is for Service" and "Manners Maketh Man."

The school song included the lines: "Fight oh fight for Scarborough/Fight with pep and vim." Vim was meant to rhyme with "win." We almost never von.

I'm not sure today if the school was small because it was elite, or if it was small because so few people wanted to go there. There were, just for instance, six of us in the sixth grade. With a student body so limited, every pupil expected to get a chance on the playing field.

Poor old Coach. I was fat, I was slow, I was uncoordinated, but it was worse than that. I was easily frightened.

Take baseball, for instance, the national pastime. There's a reason they call it hardball. The ball, or pill, it's hard. Like a stone. I didn't want to be hit by one of those. I'd as soon have jumped into a wading pool full of hammerhead sharks as step into the batter's box. I was supposed to stand there, all tender parts exposed, while another boy hurled stones down at me from a hill or mound. If I'd had any chance of hitting the wretched thing, I might have mustered a little courage. There was no chance. Legendary Red Sox batter Ted Williams is supposed to have been able to see the stitching on a ball screaming across the plate. I rarely saw the ball at all. I wasn't even certain it had been thrown until I heard it thunk into the catcher's mitt. The best I could do for my team was to get beaned.

I was at the bottom of the batting roster, and so my humiliations were brief and far between.

When the other team was up, the coach would send me deep into the outfield. Left out. Emboldened by distance and isolation, I wanted to play. Now I wanted to make a difference. I yearned to hustle. But man is—above all else—an adaptive creature. So I adapted. There was nothing for me to do. So I did nothing. I'd put my mitt over my face, and look at the world through the V of the glove. Ever done that? I liked the cool leather on my cheeks. I liked the smell of neat's-foot oil. I'd dream. I'd breathe deeply. In out. In out. The Zen of baseball.

I might have settled to the ground and taken a nap, but this was frowned upon. I also learned that it was not considered cricket, or baseball, to turn around and look off into the woods. For reasons that mostly escaped me, I was supposed to face home plate.

Bored almost into a coma, I'd squint through the glove at the other players. I'd watch their distant dramas with admirable detachment. *Why are they so excited now?* I'd wonder. *I didn't know there was another Cheever on the team. Why is everyone rushing toward me? Why are their faces crimson? Why are they waving their arms in the air?*

Baseball was not my sport.

Soccer wasn't either.

My position? I played bench. I remember vividly how those benches felt, and the uniforms I had climbed into, the last picked from the barrel, worn out without being at all comfortable. The oversized jerseys billowed around me, the sweat coursed unchecked down my sides.

I wanted to get out there and score a goal. I wanted to show Coach that I had heart. I wanted to show Coach that I could make a difference.

When I was allowed off the bench, it was to fill one of those positions near our own goal. It would have been difficult for me to score, but then I had a lively imagination. I dreamed up a play in which all our attackers stayed back, freeing me, Ben, to dribble adroitly all the way up the field and score.

I was right in the middle of such a reverie, when the ball actually came down into my quiet neighborhood. I tried to get out of the way, but one of the attacking players kicked the ball and hit me a nasty blow to the hand. This hurt, and when I heard the whistle, I assumed they were going to punish the boy who had injured me.

"Hands in the penalty area." That's what the referee called out.

What?

The other team got a free shot at our goal. They scored. We lost that game one point to nothing. Or rather, I lost the game one to nothing. Talk about making a difference.

In the eighth grade at Scarborough I ran the 880. We had a meet with Peekskill Military Academy. They had a 220 track. When my race started, the coach wasn't there.

Now, it happened that three of the runners from PMA were substantially faster than I was. We ran my third lap neck and neck. For the runners from PMA this was not the third lap, but the fourth.

Coach and a knot of others appeared just as the race became a duel. The four of us were thundering around that final curve. "Hustle!" he shouted. "Hustle, Cheever. Dig it out."

In his hoarse cry you I could hear Coach thinking,

What do you know? Maybe I've been wrong about young Cheever.
Then we all crossed the finish. The PMA runners straggled off

the course. I made the turn and headed manfully off for my final lap.

Coaches are supposed to have small and weathered hearts, something on the order of a horse chestnut. But this is the sort of performance that breaks even a chestnut heart.

I couldn't have been much good for my father's vitals either. The man wanted an athlete as a son.

No video games in those days. Not much TV either. So I played everything. Baseball, football, kick-the-can, even pin-the-tail-on-the-donkey.

I played everything, and I played everything woefully.

"Want to go out and toss a ball?" my father would ask me. I guess he hoped that I could be taught.

"Sure."

We'd go outside. He'd throw the ball at me. I'd drop it.

"I'm sorry," I'd say and pick the ball up and throw it back.

He'd throw the ball again. Again I'd fail to make the catch. "Sorry," I'd say and throw it back.

"For Christ's sake, stop apologizing," he'd say.

"Okay," I'd say. "I'm sorry."

Freshman year looked like my breakthrough. I made it onto the varsity squad of Scarborough Country Day School's six-man tackle football team. I was second-string center.

Steve was first-string center. Steve was not his name. I remember his name. I can still picture the way his belly hung over the canvas belt of his uniform. I remember the way he smelled.

Steve wasn't all that big. Nor was he particularly fast on his feet. Steve had quick hands. The moment the ball was hiked, he'd reach across the line of scrimmage, grab the face guard of the opposing center with one hand, and with the other he'd drive the nose he found there back into the face it belonged to.

I'd spend the rest of the play staggering slowly around in circles while the tears that had obscured my vision ran down my face.

But this was football, varsity football, and I, Ben, was playing.

COACH

In his third novel, *Bullet Park*, my father has Tony Nailles threaten to murder a French teacher named Mrs. Hoe, when she arranges to have him cut from the football team.

> He [Tony] had not anticipated this staggering injustice. He would not cry but there was a definite disturbance in his eyeducts. She didn't know what she was saying. She knew, poor woman, much less about football than he knew about French. He loved football, loved the maneuvers, the grass work, the fatigue, and loved the ball itself—its shape, color, odor and the way it spiraled into the angle of his elbow and ribcage. He loved the time of year, the bus trips to other schools, he loved sitting on the bench. Football came more naturally to him than anything else at his time of life and how could they take this naturalness away from him and fill up the breach with French verbs?
>
> "You don't know what you're saying, Miss Hoe."
>
> "I'm afraid I do, Tony. I've not only talked with Mr. Northrup. I've talked with the coach."
>
> "With Coach?"
>
> "Yes, with Coach."

I didn't like French either. Nor did I want to be cut from the team. But Tony and I had nothing else in common. I lacked his finer sensibility. I had no appreciation of the ball itself, its shape or color.

If there was a shape to my football, it was the pendulous gut of Steve, the first-string center. If there was a color, it was the red I saw after Steve had inserted his little fist into my face mask.

My father was an unusually articulate and forthright man. He used to like to say that he and I operated "on a basis of absolute candor." And there was something to this, although he didn't tell me about his bisexuality. Nor did I tell him what it was actually like to play second string for the six-man tackle football team at Scarborough Country Day.

He knew that I—a freshman—was on the varsity squad. That was all he needed to know. He didn't know, for instance, that I was in the running for the coveted position of "least popular man on the squad."

If it hadn't been for Smalls—not his real name either—I would have won the title. Smalls was fat, of course, and uncoordinated. He was covered with black, oily hair. The starters used to joke that Smalls couldn't smoke cigarettes, because if his eyebrows caught fire, his entire body would burn to the ground.

Smalls was not hated for his faults, but for his virtues. Smalls was punctual. The jocks were inevitably late for practice. They forgot their equipment, they goldbricked through drills, counting two laps around the field as three.

Smalls showed up fully suited and he showed up early. Smalls hustled. Smalls dug it out.

Coach finally gave a lecture: "Gentlemen," he said. "If Bill Smalls—who hasn't yet been on the field in a game—can make it to practice early, then I don't see why all you glory hounds can't make it to practice on time."

Next day and the starters caught Smalls while he was changing. They stripped him naked, took a locker out of its place against the wall, removed the shelves, and inserted Bill Smalls. He just barely fit. The locker was like a coffin two sizes too small. Then they closed the door, attached a combination lock, and put the locker back against the wall upside down.

"Where's Bill Smalls?" the coach asked. "I don't know," said Steve. "I guess he's late today."

After practice Smalls was released. His head was the color of a peeled beet.

Was this the sort of squad that Tony Nailles didn't want to be cut from?

And yet it was a fine thing to have won my father's approval. Practice wasn't over until after the last bus had left the school.

My father ordinarily hated the chauffeuring part of parenting, but after football practice, he was pleased, he was honored to pick me up. On the way home, he'd stop and buy me fresh dinner rolls at the Ossining Italian bakery. He had a phrase, a mantra really, "My son the football player."

Fortunately, he never went to a game. I remember him asking me if I had ever caught a pass. I told him no. I hoped he'd think that as in eleven-man football, the center was not eligible to catch a pass.

Fact is, in six-man tackle, the center could catch a pass. Provided, of course, that he could catch a pass.

During one away game, I was sent out to run a button hook. That play was filmed, and afterwards, the whole team got to watch me waddling away from the line of scrimmage, turning uncertainly toward Coach, who operated the camera. The football came flying into the picture, struck my chest, and then hit the ground.

Part of the problem was biological. "There's a high correlation between eye teaming and sports," according to my eye doctor, Alec Perlson of Chappaqua, New York.

"You have exophoria, meaning the tendency for one eye to outward turn. When you look at an object from a distance both eyes are parallel. If I cover one eye then that eye begins to point outward."

The brain can overcome this tendency and align both eyes properly, but this is hard work. So most of the time the brain suppresses the weak eye. This gives me decent vision for a person with one eye. Consequently, I have very little depth perception. This is a limitation.

Coaches don't like to talk about limitations. And God bless them for that. Because sometimes they can overcome the limitations they won't talk about.

Fact of the matter is that most coaches would just as soon not talk at all. Check the Web sometime for the famous quotes uttered by coaches and managers. It's a sobering experience.

What's astonishing about this treasure trove is that it's been preserved at all. With the notable and much-noted exception of Casey Stengel, these men run the gamut from moronic to moronic and cruel.

Leo "the Lip" Durocher—supposed to be a great sage of the baseball diamond—is best known for having said, "Nice guys finish last."

Other Durocher gems include:

"You don't save a pitcher for tomorrow. Tomorrow it may rain."

"Nobody ever won a pennant without a star shortstop."

"In order to become a big league manager you have to be in the right place at the right time. That's rule number one."

If Moses had been this eloquent, the Jews would still be slaves. If Lincoln had coached Little League, we'd be two nations under God.

Nor is Durocher anomalous.

Take Paul "Bear" Bryant, legendary leader of Bama's Crimson Tide. The great football coach got his nickname by wrestling a bear, not in and of itself a demonstration of great good sense.

Here are some of Bear's treasured sayings:

"Get the winners into the game."

"There's a lot of blood, sweat and guts between dreams and success."

What you find in winning coaches is heart. The passion is so naked that there's a tendency to rake leaves over the coals.

Visit the Web site of fabled football coach Vince Lombardi and the quote they hit you with is, "Winning isn't everything—but the will to win is." This has a fine moderate ring to it. Here's the quote Lombardi is known for: "If winning isn't everything, then why do they keep score?"

It's a mistake, though, to judge coaches for talking. I'm a talker. Coaches are not talkers. I held a job once as a sports reporter for the *Crossroads Chronicle* in Vandalia, Ohio. My imagination may be playing tricks on me, but the way I remember it, the high school stadium in Vandalia, Ohio, held more people than actually lived in Vandalia, Ohio.

High school stars were celebrities. The coaches were gods. These were big men, fat men mostly, with thick necks and piercing eyes.

They'd look at this cub reporter in the same way they might look at something that had got caught on their shoe when they went out to get the paper in the morning.

I'd ask questions. They'd nod. "Yup," they'd say, or else, "Maybe."

Try to make a story of out that. Of course I was expected to know the rest. I was expected to know the history of the Vandalia Aviators. I was expected to know how the Smith brothers were doing and that the older boy was at Duke on a full scholarship. I knew none of this.

I was also expected to have my own glorious history in sport. I did not.

My varsity football career had lasted one year. As a sophomore, I went off to boarding school, and yes, I applied for the football team. Is "applied" the correct word here?

All football wannabes lined up in front of the cage. (Cage, for those of you who have not been—as I have—varsity athletes, is the term used for the room or locker in which sporting equipment is left to gather mold and grow fungi.)

A whistle was blown and we rushed the cage. We tore off our street clothes and donned equipment. This was social Darwinism at its purest. The toughest, pushiest boys came up with the best equipment. The shy, uncertain boys made do with what was left.

I managed somehow to secure pants, pads, and a jersey. I was still searching for a helmet when I heard the whistle. We all charged out onto the field.

We were divided into squads. We ran simple drills. Then we were lined up to scrimmage.

The coach noticed me.

Coach: "Yo."

Me: "Yes."

Coach: "Where's your hat, son?"

Me: "My hat?"

Coach: "You gotta have a hat to play ball."

Me: "A hat?"

Coach: "Go back in and get a hat."

Two days later, I was cut from the squad.

I told my father. He was crushed.

I had been out of college for almost a decade before I found a sport I loved. I remember vividly the day I ran my first mile. It wasn't a mile actually, but I did run all the way around the development I lived in. I was wearing a black sweater, jeans, and a pair of conventional sneakers. Afterwards my face was crimson. *I ran a mile,* I thought. *Most people can't run a mile.* Binocular vision had nothing to do with it.

When I'm going up a hill in a footrace, and I'm breathing hard, then I can hear the other men breathing hard as well. A hill for me is also a hill for them.

I run my five miles a day most every day and have done so since 1978. Both sons go out with me, and while I'm still fast, they are faster still. I've done my morning run by the banks of Thames in London, beside the Black Sea in Bulgaria, and along the Seine in Paris. Still a talker, I often find a stranger to fall in step beside. We needn't be from the same country, or culture. We needn't speak the same tongue.

"Pavlo Nurmi," I said to the man I caught up with in Bulgaria. "Pavlo Nurmi," he said back. "The Flying Finn," I said; my new friend smiled and nodded.

I've run marathons in Bordeaux, New York, and Montreal. My wife ran eight of them with me. I've run under fireworks in the Central Park run on New Year's Eve. I've run under the moon at 4 a.m. in the park behind our house.

This is a squad from which I won't be cut. This is a sport for anyplace, anytime, and anybody. Runners don't need a lot of equipment. They don't need a lot of attitude either. You don't need to be picked to run. You won't need a coach at all.

BENJAMIN CHEEVER's most recent book of nonfiction, *Selling Ben Cheever* (Bloomsbury USA, 2001), was excerpted in the *New Yorker,* *Gourmet,* and the *New York Times Book Review*. His last novel, *The Good Nanny* (Bloomsbury USA, 2004), was selected as a new and notable book by the *New York Times Book Review*. He has been a reporter for a daily newspaper, and an editor at *Reader's Digest*. He has taught at Bennington College and the New School for Social Research.

To Althea, From the Net

BY ROBERT LIPSYTE

IN THE SUMMER OF 1972, before the game passed me by completely, as had the Acid Age and the Sexual Revolution, I decided to try again. The country's latest tennis barn had been thrown up only three miles from my house, and the resident teaching pro was . . . Althea Gibson!

I decided to take a lesson from her. Two at the most. For show. When people started name-dropping their pros, I'd ice the conversation. Althea Gibson. I had interviewed her eight years earlier when she was starting out as a tournament golfer, but I was sure she wouldn't remember my name or face. I would be just another anonymous student, as I had been with Claude and Paul and Yale. I made an appointment over the phone for a lesson and met her a week later on a court.

"Hello there, Bob," she sang out, referring to her schedule. "If it's eleven o'clock you must be Bob." She looked up. "You forgot to shave this morning, Bob."

"I'm letting my beard grow."

She looked faintly displeased. I wondered if she was a Lombardi-style teacher. We don't have time to grow beards, Bob. But all she said was, "Take four laps to loosen up, then we'll see what you've got."

Nothing, as it turned out. Althea broke her impassive silence only once, when I rushed to net behind my racket mask.

"What's that?" she yelled. "Now don't tell me you're afraid of getting hit in the face."

I was going to tell her it was one of my ex-pros who was afraid for me, but I was out of breath, a condition that lasted through the next eight months of weekly lessons in which I tried to do what she told me to do, rarely succeeded, but occasionally saw glimmers of the game.

That was a fine season. For the first time in my life there was a self-composed rhythm to my time. Six days a week I worked on a novel called *Liberty Two*, an artistic and political statement that was important to me. And three times a week I played tennis.

At least one of those times I played with an old friend who had sat next to me in kindergarten and roomed with me in college and now lived in the next town. We played a very friendly, relaxed game; we each tried to give the other a strenuous physical workout rather than playing merely to win. I could rush the net without my mask, secure that Mark would never drill me between the eyes just to shake me up.

And once a week, the anchor of my week, I spent an hour with Althea. By winter we were playing mock games, Lipsyte flat out, a foaming retriever who collapsed at the bell, and Gibson just hard enough to make her returns appear effortless. She was loose and graceful, and I had to consciously remember to watch the ball, not her. Every so often I scored a nice point. It would be on a day she had lingered too long over too large a business lunch and her mind was drifty with schemes and she was taking me lightly and preening for the gallery of women and children. I would angle one past her and laugh insanely, then watch in awe as the juices kicked in and turned her briefly back into the monster she had been in the fifties. The monster had to punish me, reclaim the gallery, reassert its omnipotence. If it was my serve, I would lay it in and get my racket up to my face as quickly as possible. If it was her serve there was nothing to do but turn sideways, as in a pistol duel, and wish myself as small as possible. WHOP. A little memo from the champ: Don't get too perky, fool.

Of course, I was never absolutely sure that I had really won the point, that Althea wasn't letting me drop one in now and then to tickle my fantasy and keep me coming.

Althea was more serious about my game than I was. She was very funny about rules, dress, and deportment, and she inspired me to run more, concentrate harder, think creatively about what I was doing on the court. It sometimes seemed absurd, this all-timer concerned with my game, a jet pilot tuning a Volkswagen motor, and it was an incredible luxury, elitist and common at the same time.

The season ended too soon, the novel was finished, and I reluctantly let it go. Althea was off for a summer of appearances and clinics. Before she left, she urged me to enter the club's intermediate singles tournament. She was a great believer in the crucible of competition. I asked her for a preview of my chances. We were fairly relaxed with each other by then. I had even shown her the 1964 feature story and revealed my secret identity to a mild "Well, how about that." She looked me over like a used car, ran her finger down a list of entrants, and guessed I might win half my matches, a pipe dream as it turned out.

Her parting words were, "Got to get out there and see what you're made of, Bob. Only way to learn."

I told her I was going to wear a T-shirt with the message, "I just completed thirty lessons with Althea Gibson." She looked so alarmed I said I was only kidding.

My first opponent was a short, chunky, bowlegged man at least ten years older than I. He was very friendly in the locker room, which made me even more nervous. He told me he hadn't played singles in five years. He wore a red shirt and canvas sneakers. During warm-ups he came to the net with his racket in front of his face and made every backhand shot a long, soft fly to the opposite corner. When the game started, he took a position in the center of the court near the service line, the so-called no-man's-land where Althea had warned me never to be caught, and hit back every shot softly and to my forehand. He never missed. I might as well have been playing a wall. And walls always win.

But I was elated. My first tournament match. True, I was now 0–1, and up ahead was an ambuscade of big servers and fake limpers and cheaters and dink artists and "A" players dropping down to hustle the hardware, but I had been blooded, I had lost one without losing my spirit, when the going gets tough the tough get going, look out for the Comeback Kid.

Two days later Ethel Kennedy called. We had never spoken before. Her voice was high, light, merry, insistent. She began by telling me what a success the first Robert F. Kennedy Pro Celebrity tennis tournament had been. The Comeback Kid was cool although he could not classify himself as either a pro or a celebrity. Mrs. Kennedy trilled on, the second annual Robert F. Kennedy Pro Celebrity tennis tournament would be even a greater smash thanks to Mr. Lipsyte. I thought, resting the racket, get a spare, time for lessons? Mrs. Kennedy said she knew it was a terrible imposition, but so many people had told her how fabulous I was. The Kid felt panicky, would it be him and Althea versus Ethel and Pancho?

Just a few dozen short biographies, she said, one for each of the pros in the tournament, in your own terrific style, you're such a dear, Mr. Lipsyte, it will make the program a veritable collector's item.

ROBERT LIPSYTE, a longtime city and sports columnist of the *New York Times* and now a contributing writer for the paper, is the author of sixteen books, including *In the Country of Illness: Comfort and Advice for the Journey* (Knopf, 1998), *SportsWorld: An American Dreamland*, and such young adult novels as *The Contender, One Fat Summer,* and *Raiders Night.* A former network correspondent at CBS and NBC, Lipsyte won an Emmy in 1990 for on-camera achievement as host of the nightly WNET public affairs broadcast *The Eleventh Hour.* He was also host of *The Health Show,* a weekly live half-hour of medical- and health-related reportage. He is a regular contributor to the op-ed page of *USA Today* and to ESPN. In 1966 and in 1996, he won Columbia University's Meyer Berger Award for distinguished reporting. In 1992, he was a finalist for the Pulitzer Prize in commentary. In June 2001, he won the American Library Association's Margaret A. Edwards Award for lifetime achievement in young adult literature. He lives in Manhattan and on Shelter Island, New York.

Coaching Bob

BY JANE LEAVY

BOB CALLED ME COACH.

I was supposed to teach him how to die.

I don't remember how I got the job; nor do I recall a whole lot of other applicants for the position. My qualifications were limited given that I was neither dead nor dying. My only previous experience—I had lost a best friend once before.

Neither his wife, Maria, nor I remember exactly how it is that I came to be known as Bob's dying coach. Perhaps it grew out of my futile efforts to teach him how to throw a baseball. "It was probably easier to teach Bob how to die than how to throw a ball," she says now, twelve years later.

Coaching is about trying. It's about exhorting and cajoling others to get the most out of their bodies. Mine was a nihilistic task: to give Bob permission not to try, but to let go and let be. There was no winning one for the Gipper. He was the Gipper.

There were no pep talks to give—except his eulogy. There was no playbook, no game plan, no x's and o's to make sense of the inchoate. Only the outcome was certain.

I never knew Bob Lewis when he wasn't dying—an existential truism in every relationship but the defining element of ours. The night we met he told me he was HIV positive. We were at a party in a group house near Dupont Circle in Washington. He was standing on the landing, me a step above. I remember thinking the stairwell was significant. We were headed in opposite directions.

When I left the party that night, I knew I had made a friend for life. I just didn't know how long that would be.

Soon he was introducing me as his new best friend. I was introducing him as my best new friend and architect. We built a house and an aesthetic—I told my husband only I could have a crush on a man dying of AIDS. I was wrong: everybody felt that way about Bob, male and female, except maybe his mother-in-law, who had reservations about her daughter marrying a man who was HIV positive.

My house was the last project he completed before he died. "You know," he told me, "I'm building you the house I'll never be able to build for my family."

"You sonovabitch," I replied. "Now I'll never be able to move." I never have. He shaped the space I live in and he shaped the way I see the world. I live in his colors still. It only took seven years to repaint the walls after he died. The way I looked at it, if Bob could teach me how to see, then the least I could do was to try to teach him how to die.

Athletics long ago appropriated the language of mortality as a means of heightening the importance of trivial struggles. Play-off teams are forever staving off elimination, fighting to stay alive, hoping to prevail in sudden death. It's always do or die; there's no tomorrow.

For Bob it was only a matter of time before real life usurped the athletic idiom. Bob didn't live long enough to witness the advent of "whole life coaching"—of which there are many sub-specialties. Metallica, the rock band, hired a "performance enhancement coach" at $40,000 per month, to prevent them from going the way of the Fab Four. A lawyer I know hired a car coach to tell him what model would be safest for his newborn child. "Volvo," the coach replied. An online search for dying coaches turned up a company offering Soulwork Specialty

Training with a concentration in death and dying. Bob and I were simply ahead of our time.

When Bob first contracted HIV, it was so early in the plague that the test for AIDS had not yet been developed. When he began dating Maria Applewhite, Patient Zero, Gaetan Dugas, the Canadian flight attendant to whom the epidemic is often traced, was still alive. When he and Maria (pronounced like the singer, Mariah) got married in December 1984, all the doctors could tell them for sure was that he had tested positive for the antibodies that caused what was still sometimes called "gay cancer."

When they quit going to the National Institutes of Health where Bob was a member of one of the earliest test groups on AIDS, and where his longevity made him an ideal study subject, the nurse was angry at them, as many of their friends were, for playing Russian roulette with their lives. "They came in and told us they wanted to get married and have kids," Baird said. "I told them, 'You'll be sorry and you'll all be dead.'"

When their daughters were born, medical science did not yet know that if a mother was negative at conception then a child would also be negative. When Dinah, their youngest, shared drooled-upon toys with my infant daughter, the expert manning the hotline at the Whitman-Walker Clinic advised me not to let them play together.

Their marriage was a leap of faith and recklessness. They were looking into the heart of darkness. They just didn't know how dark it was going to be. Bob always said his dying words were going to be "TV movie."

Bob was a "long-term non-progressor" at a time when AZT and other protease inhibitors were first becoming available. He lived twelve years with the virus in his body. He parried it with wit and clothed his fury in gallows humor. Little by little the disease ate away at the things that defined him—his vision, his memory, his sense of space, but never his sense of humor. I asked him once how he wanted to be remembered. He replied,

"For the great body I used to have." Pause. "Until it turned on me."

Not only was I his last coach, I was his first coach. Never a jock, he was always picked last for every team. "I married the scorekeeper," Maria likes to say. But he was buff before the word became fashionable and quit lifting only when the young son of family friends started calling him Popeye. The night we met I couldn't help noticing how well he filled out the little white BVD T-shirt he was wearing.

At first the job was easy. I made a lot of chicken. I laughed at all his jokes. I told him to read A. S. Byatt's novel *Possession* and dwell on what she called "vanishing moments of exquisite pleasure."

There were many of them. But in the winter of 1989, after being hospitalized for meningitis, Bob had to tell his mother, Nola, that his HIV had converted to full-blown AIDS. He was sitting in bed with a thermometer crammed in his yeast-infected mouth. "Oh, Bob," she said. "I think you're just blowing this whole AIDS thing out of proportion."

Understandable coming from a woman who had already buried her husband and oldest son, but enough to send Bob to a shrink. His sole attempt at therapeutic intervention ended in comic failure when the psychologist to whom he had been referred kept forgetting why he felt depressed and kept turning the conversation to his mother. Every week, she needed to be reminded that he had a reason to be depressed and each week seemed surprised. "Oh, well, you're in a crisis situation!"

Turned out she'd had a stroke and lost her short-term memory. Bob thought that was hilarious until he lost his; although, he also liked to point out, he was easier to entertain. "You can just tell me the same stories over and over again."

The day we went to pick the granite tile for my kitchen counters, he finally got angry. We were driving back from Virginia across the 14th Street Bridge in the little white Miata convertible Bob bought himself when his T-cells started going south.

("Pretty soon they'll be as small as my dick," he muttered one day.) Halfway across the span, he started screaming into the wind. Fuck the tile, fuck the kitchen, fuck the bills. He wanted to go to Italy and paint the light while he could still see it.

I reminded him he had a wife and two daughters and no life insurance. I told him if he wanted to paint the light he better start getting up early.

"I have AIDS," he hissed. "I can't get up early."

I told him to set an alarm.

He spent his last summer at the beach on Long Island with Maria and the girls, who were then five and three. He painted the children and the dog and the light, a series of twelve canvasses that chronicle the end of his life. He painted with raging reds and somber purples; teal, ochre, eggplant, brick, and so many shades of resigned gray. One of the canvasses, the best, is a still life of a half-eaten peach, ripe with juice, sitting on a kitchen table. There's a window that gives out onto still waters and in the distance a darkening wood and a cloudless sky tinged with pink. It is a vision of the other side.

It was the summer of hurricane Bob, a portentous storm that marched up the East Coast, sequentially interrupting their beach vacation and then mine. I remember talking to him on the phone from the basement of our rented house in Cape Cod while the eye of the storm passed overhead. He was feverish and chilled; when I saw him next, I felt sick too. His skin was as withered as a child's shriveled balloon.

It was time for some serious coaching. When he was rejected for a clinical study of AZT, I put him in touch with friends in New York who had gotten the medicine from Mexico. When he decided to kill himself before the illness did, I called a sympathetic physician and found out what he had to do. We got the drugs. By the time he was ready to use them, the small legal window of opportunity defined as "being of sound mind" had closed.

It was important to him to make sure his mother was settled

in Washington, near Maria and the girls, before he died. One day he took her shopping at the Design Center where we had picked out all the furnishings for my home. "It was great," he screeched in his inimitable fashion. "You should have seen me looking at wall coverings and floor samples."

He paused. The disease had not yet impaired his comic timing. "Only a mother could hire a blind interior designer."

Instead of Italy, he flew across the country in a two-seater plane with a high school friend as his pilot. In Shreveport, Louisiana, the man who had such spatial acuity that he could spot an eighth-of-an-inch divergence in a level plane got lost while trying to find his way back to his motel room after going down the hall for a Coke. The endgame had begun.

He didn't make it as far as Bolinas, a town north of San Francisco, where a healing center for AIDS patients had been built on a bluff overlooking the Pacific on the grounds of a former RCA laboratory. Native Americans believed that the land was the most electrically charged place on earth and that if you stayed too long you'd go crazy. But the AIDS patients didn't care because they were already crazy and besides the place was so fucking beautiful. His laughter made me brave. We had never talked directly about his death.

I told him I wanted to put together a book for Georgia and Dinah, a collection of letters from friends that would comprise a mosaic of his life, and help them know him. I promised they would be leather-bound. "That's what I'm most worried about," he said, "leaving them a part of me."

He'd been thinking about making a tape but wasn't sure how to go about it. "I think I need you to write it," he said. A statement, perhaps.

A bit awkward, I thought. Bob agreed: "Kind of like a hostage in Lebanon, saying, 'Hi girls, they're treating me fine over here on the other side.'"

"If we could just tape this conversation. That's what you want them to hear."

"I love that idea."

I suggested a videotaped interview. Interviewing is what I do. We could call our movie *Bob Lewis Live.*

We scheduled filming for November 18, 1991, less than two weeks after Magic Johnson announced he was HIV positive. I consulted psychiatrists and grief manuals for suggestions on how to proceed. I reread Elisabeth Kübler-Ross's *On Death and Dying.* What would his children want to know that only he could tell them? What questions would they want to ask that they never could?

The computer printout of the list I made is eight pages long: Tell me about the day the girls were born. First time looked at them. First time held them. Best thing about being a dad. Worst thing about puberty. When lost virginity and to whom. How met Maria? What bugs you about her. Who proposed? Your wedding night. Being sick. Your sexuality. Were you always able to laugh at everything? I warned him I was going to ask about his bisexuality. He hung up on me.

The interview took place in the dining room he designed for us, at the Frank Lloyd Wright table he insisted we buy. My husband, the cinematographer, zoomed in on Bob's face; the hollows filled out by sheer force of personality. The once taut-fitting T-shirt bagged at his chicken neck. Maria wandered in and out of the frame, retreating to the kitchen to make jalapeño cornbread madeleines.

For three exhausting antic hours, Bob was his best self. He answered every question and managed not to curse me or flinch—though he did protest the length of the inquisition. C'mon, c'mon. Last question. Last question. He was worried about being boring. Just keep talking, we said. Now, twelve years later, I realize he was ready for it to be over. We weren't.

He talked about falling in love with the smell of two-by-fours, about coming out after the death of his brother, Johnny, about giving up classical piano in junior high school because he wanted to be cool instead of talented. He described how Georgia came into the world face up, eyes open to every possibility and pulling over on the shoulder of I-95 in tears the night she was born. He said Dinah came out of the womb talking "and hasn't shut up since because she knew around us it was talk or die." He said when he lost his virginity (ninth or tenth grade) and to whom (a congressman's daughter). He talked about his bisexuality without apologizing for it. And, looking straight into the camera, he said pointedly, "In my next life, I want no throwing."

The effort was gallant and depleting. The next morning he called in tears. "Come get me," he said. "I'm blind."

I drove him to the radiologist. The MRI provided unnecessary corroboration of his deterioration. The virus had spread to his brain.

His world dimmed daily. One by one the parts of his brain flickered and died like the lights on the panorama of the battlefield of Gettysburg I visited as a child. First he lost proprioception, the ability to know where the body is in space without visual clues. I looked away as he tried to put a cigarette out in the palm of his hand.

A couple of days later, I watched as he struggled to make his way upstairs, hissing under his breath, "I knew we should have bought a fucking rambler."

I walked behind him and told him it was okay. "Don't leave me," he said. "It's not that okay."

He didn't come downstairs again until my husband carried him out of the house on the day he went to hospice. One afternoon in late January, I was alone with him in the bedroom that had become his world. He lay in a hospital bed, completely exposed. His nakedness embarrassed only me. He was oblivious. "Is that me peeing or are you pouring water?"

It was our last sustained conversation and my last opportunity to ask the questions I had forgotten to include on the videotape. (Q: "What's the funniest thing you can say about AIDS?" A: "It got me off the streets.") Mostly he wanted to talk about the girls whom he called his two little miracles. (There was little hyperbole in that.) How, I wondered, would he toast them at their weddings? "I would congratulate them for surviving both physically and emotionally having me as a father."

In his absence, he wanted me to tell them he understood the risk he had taken with their lives and with their mother's. That he recognized the selfishness of his desire to be a parent. That he took responsibility for his irresponsibility before he died. As a boy he had nightmares about going blind. Now his blindness had helped him see.

More than anything, he wanted me to reassure him that they were okay, that they would be okay. "Are you sure?" he said.

"Yes," I said. "I'm sure."

"Are you sure?" he said.

"Yes, Bobby, I'm sure."

The conversation repeated over and over, a set piece out of a very black comedy. The plain fact is, as Bob lay dying, no one was completely sure his kids would be okay. He died in an agony of ambiguity.

What we did know was that he could no longer remain at home. The girls were in and out of the bed, soiled now with blood and vomit. They liked to play with the buttons that made Daddy go up and down. One Saturday morning, I told my husband to go get him. When he carried Bob down the stairs and out of the house for the last time, Maria ran down the street screaming.

At the hospice, each of the girls had a drawer in his bureau where they kept their crayons and coloring books, water babies and stuffed animals. Their artwork hung on antiseptic walls. Dinah drew a map of the hospice complete with the parking lot and two marked exits and Daddy's corner room all blacked out. Georgia drew a picture of a family picnic. "Daddy loved picnics under trees," the caption read. "He had a blanket so he wouldn't get cold." The sun looks like a spider and the foliage is volcanic. Later, their artwork would be transposed onto Bob's corner of the AIDS quilt that covered the breadth of the National Mall in Washington the last time it was displayed.

Caring for Bob was a team effort. Maria wanted someone with him twenty-four hours a day. The continuity of care was as uninterrupted as the music that played softly from the boom box opposite his bed: Van Morrison's *Hymns to the Silence*. No one thought it ironic.

No one expected him to last as long as he did. But, as his friend Sandy Shapiro once said, "Bob was the first to give a party and the last to leave one."

He was surrounded by friends, clients, cousins, and second cousins, former girlfriends and boyfriends, who signed up for shifts that stretched all day and all night. We left each other notes on the bulletin board updating the next visitor on Bob's condition. Bob had a quiet night. Bob had a very quiet night.

As the days turned into weeks and weeks into another month, the nights became quieter and quieter. On February 7, Richard Mason, an old friend who spent more nights with him than anyone else, reported that Bob's favorite nurse, Mary Callahan, was going to be off for the next three days and wanted to be notified of whatever service there might be for him.

Six weeks later, I was sitting by his bedside when Mary peered through the doorway—the door to Bob's room was always open. Nola was at the head of the bed, fussing over him. Bob was inert except for an occasional twitch, a knee jerk that was purely reflexive.

When I got up to take a break, Mary beckoned to me. "Can't you get his wife and mother to leave him alone?"

"I beg your pardon?"

"He wants to die," she said. "He won't do it with them here. He doesn't want to disappoint them. We see it all the time. Sometimes a family member will sneak out for a cup of coffee or a smoke—thirty seconds or so. And the patient will be dead by the time they come back."

I promised her I'd try, knowing it was impossible for me to banish them from death's sideline.

A day or so later, I began to rethink my strategy. Again Nola and I were alone with him—she swabbing his lips with lemon-scented Q-tips, me reclining in the ubiquitous loved-one recliner—when Dinah appeared at the foot of the bed. She was born as effusive and as blond as Bob. But now she was solemn. "Daddy," she said, climbing on top of her father's inert body. "Daddy?"

She rubbed her cheek against his, stroked his face, twirled his hair around her finger, failing to elicit a response. She whispered to him, hummed to him, cajoled and scolded him, all in the singsong voice of a three-year-old growing up too fast. Then, she gave up. Sliding off the bed, she skipped from the room to go play in the sunny common area where families waited for the inevitable.

I watched Dinah out of the corner of my eye. Peripheral vision was all I could tolerate. But I had seen enough to know I never wanted to see it again. That night I told Maria she needed to consider leaving him alone.

One day not long after, I was sitting at his bedside, thinking about my friend Edie, who had died at age twenty-nine exactly a decade before. I called her every day after her brain tumor was diagnosed until her parents refused to bring her to the phone. They said it was pointless, that she could neither understand me nor be understood. I knew better. One day out of the garble came the word "Janiepus," her private nickname for me.

Her parents, who brought her into the world, shepherded her out of it, retreating into their grief liked a clenched fist. Their sorrow became exclusive and peremptory. I resented it then; as a parent, I understand it better now. I promised myself the next time I would not allow myself to be exiled from friendship.

So I was determined to be Bob's friend as long as I could. I was telling him about the photographers who had come to my house to document his work, and how they marveled at the colors we had chosen—the teals, ochres, and muted grays, the palette of a dying man. How could they reach him, they wanted to know.

That's when I heard his voice, slurred and weak but unmistakably his own. "We just have to get finished," he said.

He was worried about the sink in the powder room.

I started to argue. "What's wrong with the sink? The sink's fine."

"No," he said, emphatically. "We have to get it done."

How slow are the living? My brain couldn't keep up with the simple logic of his. Belatedly, I realized what needed finishing.

"It's all finished," I told him. "There's nothing left to do. You did it all and it's beautiful. It's perfect."

On Thursday, March 28, I was at his bedside again. "I just don't know how to get to the other side," he said suddenly.

This time, I knew where he was headed. I thought about the painting of the half-finished peach on a table in a kitchen looking out onto still waters. "I don't know how you get there," I told him. "I just know you've got to go."

"But how?" he asked.

"I don't know, Bobby. You just have to let go."

On Saturday, before she went home to tuck in the kids, Maria whispered in her husband's ear one last bit of wifely imprecation. "Honey, if you want to let go tonight, it's fine. But Monday is your mom's seventy-fifth birthday. Please don't die on Nola's birthday."

Sometime after midnight Nola went home to get some sleep. By the time she returned five hours later, Bob was dead. He was forty-two years old.

I got to the hospice just in time to see his body wheeled from the room. He looked a lot better dead than alive.

That morning, Maria taught Sunday school at the River Road Unitarian Church where I would give Bob's eulogy six days later. The children sat in a circle at her feet while she delivered her first educational AIDS talk—the urgency of which was made apparent to her when Dinah explained to her classmates that Daddy had gotten HIV from sitting too close to the television.

On Monday, Nola checked into Sibley Hospital in Washington, D.C., not as a patient but as a volunteer. They had a ward full of boarder babies who had been abandoned by their parents. She presented herself to the head nurse and said she wanted to care for the ones with AIDS.

The summer after Bob died, Maria decided it was time to do something about his ashes. Bob had been sitting on her mother's mantelpiece long enough. So she and her girls returned to the rickety bungalow in Southampton where they had spent their last summer as a family. They would fill a rowboat with zinnias the girls picked from the garden, row out into the water Bob had painted, cast the flowers upon the swells, and think nice thoughts about Daddy.

Maria had thought of everything—including extra-pulverized remains, easier to scatter, and a brick to sink the "all-vinyl" box that held them. She didn't want some unsuspecting beachcomber to happen upon an unwelcome souvenir from Rapp's Funeral Home in Washington, D.C.

The flowers were cast, the thoughts thought, the stories told. The afternoon waned. Nola watched from the shore, thinking how pretty it was, the flowers floating on the water illuminated by the setting sun and wondering how Bob would have painted it.

Maria flung the box overboard, turned her back, and headed for shore. She rowed with energy and purpose, exerting herself against the bay's sudden current. The wind came up. The skies darkened. The girls, then four and six, tried to grab her attention.

"Mommy! Mommy!"

She shushed them sharply. The storm was coming up quickly. "But Mommy," Georgia said. "Daddy's following us!"

Sure enough, the unsinkable all-vinyl box was bobbing along in the water, following them back to shore.

*   *   *

COACH

Bob Lewis's mother, Nola, died in January 2004 at age eighty-eight, longer than her two sons combined. She spent the last years of her life working in the Cleveland Municipal School District Adult Literacy program, helping adults acquire their GEDs.

Inspired by Mary Callahan and the other hospice nurses who eased Bob's journey—and aided by her mother-in-law—Maria Applewhite went back to school and got a degree in nursing. She now works as a nursing supervisor at the Cuyahoga County Juvenile Detention Center, where she is once again teaching kids the rude new facts of life about AIDS.

Bob's oldest daughter, Georgia, is a freshman at Lewis and Clark College in Oregon. She hadn't seen the tape since she was eight years old. Maria had put it away in the vault for safekeeping. "Do you still have it?" she asked shyly, and watched it immediately after it arrived overnight by FedEx.

Dinah, a junior in high school, chose not to watch, not wanting to see what she has missed. She is active in the Gay Straight Alliance at Shaker Heights High School and still looks just like her father.

The Bob Lewis Memorial Archive was never realized. In the immediate aftermath of his death, many of his friends told me they were too traumatized to write. The promised book was never delivered—until now.

———————————

JANE LEAVY is the author of the *New York Times* best-seller *Sandy Koufax: A Lefty's Legacy* and the acclaimed comic novel *Squeeze Play*. She is currently working on a literary biography of Mickey Mantle. She lives in Washington, D.C.

The Duel

BY JONATHAN AMES

"PULL YOUR BALLS IN. Create a band of steel from the hips on down."

"Yes, Coach," I said. And I sucked in my balls and I assumed my *en garde* position. Then the coach came at me with his heavy lead bar and I retreated. He swung the bar at my ribs and I parried it with the guard of my sabre. There was a great clang of metal. I held the parry. I was strong, powerful, youthful—the sabre weapon-leader of the Princeton fencing team, 1983–84. These were the days when I was fit, an athlete, my body uncorrupted by age and drinking and adult heartbreak.

The coach attacked me this way up and down the floor of the fencing room. I parried his blows and then I would riposte—return with my counterattacks: chops to his mask, slashes across his belly, cuts to his rib cage, and slices down his shoulders. He was wearing the thick leather suit of a coach so that I wouldn't raise welts on his body. And he was using the lead bar to make me strong, inviolable.

"Commando," he'd say every few minutes to urge me on, to keep me fighting.

The coach and I would practice like this at six in the morning. Just he and I alone, no one else from the team. It was my special commando training to turn me into a champion on the fencing strip. The coach, a Frenchman, had been a commando in the French-Algerian war. And he believed in fitness and combat even more than most fencing coaches. He was in his early fifties, but was still in trim, fighting shape, and he was a good-looking man, even though he was bald. He bore a resemblance to Sean Connery, but his eyes didn't twinkle like Connery's—they were cool and gray, assassin-like and somewhat mad.

After my morning lesson, we'd sit in his office and cool down. My legs would be swollen and exhausted—from fencing you develop incredibly muscular thighs and calves, since in the *en garde* position you are always crouching, always maintaining one's groin in a band of steel. I would drink some water and the coach with his beautiful bald head glistening with sweat would regale me with long-winded war tales from his days in Algeria. He spoke in a thick French accent and often told me the same story—perhaps because of battle trauma he was somewhat repetitive.

"We were making our way through this little village, which we had seized," he would say. "We were checking the buildings for snipers. I was carrying my rifle, of course. Always ready. Always alert. But then suddenly there was a great searing pain in my buttocks. I've been shot, I thought. But then I realized I was flying through the air. I was twenty feet off the ground; I saw my men below me. Was it a mortar? No—it was an electric cable that had come undone and it had whipped through the air and bit me like a black snake. Thousands of volts I received and so I was flying. But I landed, like a cat, on my feet, ready to fight, to survive. A commando."

When I'd leave the coach, I'd jog slowly back to my dorm, furthering my conditioning. Then in my room, I'd do one hundred push-ups, even though my right arm, especially, was aching from parrying the coach's lead bar. I was driving myself like this because I was bent on revenge. I wanted to defeat all my opponents, but I had become fixated most of all on destroying the number one sabre fencer at Columbia—George Leary. For years, he'd been beating me in national competitions when we were both in high school, and he had continued his dominance our first year in college. I had never beaten him in more than a dozen bouts. But now my sophomore year, 1983, I wanted to end his dominance of me. I wasn't going to lose to him again.

What had made his reign over me so dreadful was that he was not an athlete, at least in my arrogant eyes. He was chubby and his face was pasty. He would whine to the judges during his bouts, and then politic with them afterwards. And on the fencing strip, he was savvy and tricky, not graceful. He grew up in New York City and before attending Columbia he had studied with a famous exiled Hungarian sabre master and had learned many exotic moves. So even though Leary was fat and ignoble, he was unbeatable, one of the best in the country. Also, he had snubbed me once at a party at the Junior Olympics in 1981 in Cleveland. Claimed to have forgotten my name. I detested George Leary.

The meet against Columbia was scheduled for late February. The season began in November and I trained hard all those months. And in practice every afternoon, I, as the weapon-leader, challenged my sabre squad to keep up with me. I gave them all nicknames: Sir Gawain, Green Knight, Black Knight, Lancelot, Don Quixote—and myself, I called El Cid. Don Quixote, a lumbering freshman, bore a passing resemblance to Leary and I would take great pleasure in chopping my blade against his ribs and slashing his ample belly.

Against the other teams—the Penns and Yales and Harvards— I was doing very well, winning three-quarters of all my bouts, but always I was aiming toward my confrontation with my Columbia nemesis. The school newspaper, the *Princetonian*, caught wind of my nickname and they would dutifully report that Jonathan "El Cid" Ames had thoroughly vanquished his opponents. And along with my pretentious nickname, I tended to be theatrical on the fencing strip. I was very much caught up in the myth of sword fighting and whenever I struck my foes, I would scream in French, "Et làaa!" which sounded like, "Aye lah!" French is the language of fencing, all its terms are Gallic, and "et là" is often shouted by fencers—it means, "And there!" as in "And there!

Take that, you swine." I just happened to scream "Et là!" louder than most.

Two days before the big Columbia meet it was unusually warm and I took my sabre squad out to our ancient football field, Palmer Stadium. I had us climb to the top of the bleachers, and then over a wall. At the very top, the stadium was surrounded with what looked like the battlements of a castle. I had us duel up there and we engaged in a dangerous free-for-all of three against three. I drove my teammates to the edge of the battlements, slashing at them with mania and bloodlust; it would have been tragic had I sent one of them falling five stories to his death.

Finally, the day of the Columbia meet arrived. The coach, like myself, was particularly anxious for a victory against the Lions. We were the underdogs and this fueled the coach's commando spirit. Also, he and the Columbia coach had once, in their past, been romantic rivals for the affection of a certain lady, and so the lingering effects of this old romantic triangle added to the drama and pathos of the whole thing, which is what sex will always do. Add drama and pathos, that is. In short, my coach wanted to win. He wanted me to win. I sat near him on the van ride up to New York and he told me another war tale: "We were in a marketplace and I saw this Algerian sneaking up on one of my men with a knife; so I moved like a cat and came out with my own knife—one, two, one, two. And he went down. But I didn't kill him. I could have if I wanted to. But I had control of my blade, and we had him arrested. You, 'El Cid,' must control your blade to beat Leary."

When we got to the gym, the Columbia team was nowhere to be seen. We started warming up and then the room was filled with music—Wagner's eerie "Ride of the Valkyries." Then the Columbia team raced into the gym, all of them resplendent in their white uniforms, waving their weapons above their heads, and they circled us. And all the while Wagner's horrible music played. We were supposed to be scared. But in my case, it only made me hate them even more—made me think of them as storm troopers, and Leary as a corpulent Gestapo chief.

The meet began. In fencing there are three weapons: foil, épée, and sabre. In foil only the blunt tip of the blade is used and the target area is the torso. In épée, like foil, only the tip is used, but the whole body is the target. And in sabre one can use the tip, but the primary way to score is to cut and slash. The target area is everything above the waist, including the head and the hands.

We had our opening rounds of all three weapons; in my first bout, I faced the number two Columbia sabre man and I lost. I was too hyped up wanting Leary. Then the second round came and as a team we were behind and we needed a victory. I was scheduled to face Leary. The moment had arrived. Before going on the strip for my bout, I asked a teammate on the épée squad to punch me in the face. He was a strong fellow—he had attended a Texas military high school, which had toughened him up considerably—and he gave me a really good shot to the cheekbone. A little too hard actually. But it got my blood racing and I put on my mask and went out to face my enemy.

As per custom, at the start of the bout, I saluted Leary by bringing my sabre to my mask, though I was leering at him through the iron mesh, and then I saluted the director. Bouts are refereed by a director who determines which fencer has initiated the attack and which fencer has scored. He watches keenly to see if one's blows land or are parried; and when I was fencing, the sabre blades were not yet electronically rigged up, unlike foil and épée, and so the director was aided by four judges. This made sabre fencing at the time the least modern and also the most exciting; it was the closest thing to real dueling.

The director was a Holocaust survivor and a legendary person in the fencing world. He was bald and had a strange lump on his forehead. With his German accent, he began the bout by saying in French, "Allez!"

Leary and I began our dance, our movements back and forth. The first one to score five touches would win. I was deep in my crouch, my band of steel keeping my balls in and lowering my center of gravity so that I could spring out and catch him by surprise. I scored the first touch by feinting to his head and then cutting his exposed ribs. Then I scored the second touch with a beautiful riposte to his head. I was up 2–0, and with each touch I would scream, "Et Làaa!" Then we exchanged touches and I was up 3–1. Leary rallied and tied me, 3–3. Everyone in the gym, about two hundred Columbia fans, were watching our bout and they were cheering against me. My teammates were shouting, "Go El Cid!"

I went ahead 4–3 by chasing Leary down the strip and then executing a beautiful flèche with an attack to his shoulder. Flèche means arrow and that's when you literally leap at your opponent, both feet going in the air, so that ideally you appear like an arrow. Then Leary parried my next attack and cut me across the arm with his riposte. It was tied 4–4. The next touch would end the bout, and when you are at 4–4, the director calls it La Belle, because the next touch is the beautiful touch, the final touch, and in real dueling it would be the death blow.

The coach called time out and came on the strip. He gave me advice in French, and I was too frantic and mad to understand a word of it. But I nodded as if I did, so he walked away from me, but then he turned and looked at me with his cool gray eyes and he said under his breath, "Commando."

I felt like the electric cable had struck me in the ass—I assumed my *en garde* position, I tightened my band of steel. "Allez!" commanded the director. Leary came after me, he pushed me to the end of the strip. I sensed he was going to try his patented attack to cut my left arm. But if I overcompensated with my parry he would then deftly cut my right arm. I waited for him and then he sprang; he was quick and deadly when he needed to be. I met his blade. I didn't overcompensate. The clang of metal was astounding—I had him parried. He was mine. He was off balance and his head was only a foot from our locked blades. All I had to do was move my sabre efficiently and directly to his mask and for once I would beat him. But something primitive happened to me—I reared my arm back like a man lifting an axe over his head to chop wood, and this was foolish, it left me exposed. But Leary didn't react and so I brought my blade down with the tremendous force of a woodcutter on his head and my blade snapped in two. I saw silver glistening in the air as the severed portion went over the hysterical crowd. But it counted, I had broken my blade over his head, and I was bellowing, "ET LÀAAA!!!"

Leary was woozy and I was so passionate that I was pumping my now jagged and dangerous sabre up and down. And later I was told that it looked as if I was going to run Leary through. His father, who had paid for all those lessons with the Hungarian master, was shouting irrationally, "His blade is broken! His blade is broken!"

But I didn't stab Leary, and the ancient director with the odd lump on his forehead shouted above all the screaming and said, "Touch to the left, to Princeton!"

And my teammates lifted me up and I shouted again, "Et là!" It was the most glorious moment of my athletic career, and then from my teammates' shoulders I looked down and saw Leary. His mask was off; his hair was matted with sweat. I reached out my hand and said graciously, "Good bout." I hardly meant it, though, but it was the right thing to do, and Leary shook my hand and then my teammates carried me away. I had my vengeance!

When my teammates lowered me, my coach, maintaining his commando-ish dignity, calmly shook my hand, but I could see that his cool eyes were quite happy.

A few years ago at a dinner party, I reenacted this story using my steak knife as a substitute sabre. A woman at the party said she knew George Leary. She later got in touch with him and when she recounted my story, he claimed not to remember me.

JONATHAN AMES is the author of *I Pass Like Night*, *The Extra Man*, *What's Not to Love?*, *My Less Than Secret Life*, and *Wake Up, Sir!*

Our Miss O

BY CHRISTINE BRENNAN

WE FILLED THE GYM on a bright Saturday afternoon in late May 1998: the high-school girls, now nearing middle age; our graying parents; our children, eager to hear the enchanting stories retold again.

"There's something about a coach. A coach sees you after school, has dinner on the road with you, gets to know your parents on road trips the way other teachers don't, sees you when you win and, more importantly, sees you when you lose."

These were my words. I had been asked to emcee our retirement party for Miss O.

"When Miss O started coaching, it was a different time for girls and women in sports. Title IX had not yet been signed by Richard Nixon. Billie Jean King had not yet beaten Bobby Riggs. We had no buses for our games, no cheerleaders, and only one jersey that our mothers had to wash every night so we could wear it the next day.

"Because it was a simpler time in girls' sports, there was no specialization, so we could play several sports. Many of us ran between the field hockey game and the tennis courts for a match, or between volleyball and basketball games, or softball games and track meets.

"And the best thing was, Miss O was right there, running with us."

* * *

Word was traveling from the high school girls all the way down to us in the seventh grade: Miss O was coming back. I didn't know who Miss O was, much less that she had left for two years to teach somewhere else. But now she was returning, and all the older girls were so excited, sitting on the benches in the musty old locker room, giggling and telling stories about how young Miss O was and how much fun she was and how she acted more like an older kid than a real live teacher. How could any seventh grader not be fascinated by this?

Sandy Osterman was coming back to Ottawa Hills High School, and our adjoining junior high, in a small suburban village just outside Toledo, Ohio, to teach gym class and to coach the high school girls' sports teams. Nowadays, you'd ask which teams she was coming to coach. Back then, the answer was simple. All of them: field hockey, tennis, basketball, volleyball, softball, and track and field.

As best as she can remember, in the first few years she was at Ottawa Hills, she received a total of $300 extra for the entire year to coach all those teams.

It was the fall of 1971 when Miss O walked back into our locker room and entered my life. I was thirteen, she was twenty-five. The older girls were right; she acted more like a high school senior than our teacher. In eighth grade gym class, she played field hockey with us, slapping at the ball with a ferocity and determination that none of us had yet developed. She ran sprints with us—and often beat us. She agonized over the ridiculously narrow width of the balance beam with us. She even had her hair cut like us, in a shag, and giggled with us when we talked about the single male teachers with whom we wanted to fix her up.

She could have passed for an old-looking high school senior, but there was no doubt she was our teacher. She commanded our respect with the shrill whistle that hung around her neck and the often overworked, gravelly voice that could turn in an instant from a mischievous laugh to a no-nonsense bark. Tell a joke during practice, you got the laugh. Call a timeout without her permission in a game, you got the bark—and an invitation to sit the bench for several minutes.

She was, as I came to think of it decades later, the first female sports role model we actually knew. Our mothers may have played intramurals when they were in high school, but they never thought of themselves as athletes.

I certainly thought of myself that way, although there were no organized teams for people like me to play on until freshman year of high school. When I say people like me, I mean half the population of the United States. In other words, women and girls. In the fall of 1971, President Nixon was still nine months away from signing a piece of legislation that would change the playing fields of America, the law known as Title IX. Until he did, girls like me were unable to participate in team sports, and women like Miss O were known mostly as gym teachers, not coaches.

So I played tennis every summer day with my friends and shot baskets by myself on the driveway and cheered on my brother in Little League and dreamed of the day I finally could play with a team. I was never sad about this because I didn't know what I was missing. This was just the way life was for a girl athlete in the 1960s and early 1970s.

I threw myself into sports in many other ways: trading baseball cards with the boys, keeping score of Toledo Mud Hens minor league baseball games on the radio, and clamoring for my father to take us to as many University of Michigan and University of Toledo football games and Detroit Tigers and Mud Hens games as was humanly possible. Dad not only obliged, he bought season tickets.

All around me, sports made heroes of mostly men and boys. The only women I ever saw play sports on TV were Billie Jean King and Chris Evert, and, every four years, Olympians like figure skater Janet Lynn and swimmer Shirley Babashoff. Otherwise, my heroes were Al Kaline and Ernie Banks and Dick

Butkus, athletes who were lucky enough to play on a team and have games every day or week and get covered in the newspaper every day.

Then along came Miss O. She was the first woman any of us knew who was getting paid for a career in sports, although the significance of that certainly didn't dawn on me back then. To us, she just seemed to be having a fun time in sports, and making a life out of it. This was incredibly intriguing.

Miss O herself had been inspired by her high school gym teacher to go to Bowling Green State University in 1964 to become a physical education teacher. When her teacher asked her what she wanted to be, Miss O answered, "Maybe a secretary."

That was not what the teacher wanted to hear. "No," she replied, "you're going to be a teacher."

At Bowling Green, Miss O played on the extramural basketball and field hockey teams. They weren't called interscholastic sports in the 1960s. There were intramural sports involving sororities and dorms, and extramural sports, in which Bowling Green played other universities. The players received food money—"$1.50 for lunch, $2 for dinner," Miss O recalled, and she often came home with a few dollars saved in her pocket.

The basketball Miss O played was the six-woman variety of that bygone era, in which two players stayed on one half of the court, two on the other, and two played as rovers. She didn't remember any games particularly, or any scores. "When the year was finished, that was it," she said. "There was no recognition, there were no letters or awards given to us. You played, your season was over, you went on. But we had fun."

After graduating in 1968, Miss O came to Ottawa Hills the first time, stayed a year, then went to teach at high schools in Florida and Michigan before returning to us in 1971.

By the 1972–73 school year, my freshman year, she was not just my gym teacher, but also my coach.

*   *   *

Seven seconds remained on the clock. The junior varsity girls' basketball game was tied, 16–16. We were in the tiniest gym at Ottawa Hills, which was saying something because OHHS was a particularly small school with no more than a hundred students in each graduating class. The few parents who came for the Tuesday afternoon game on February 13, 1973, found a seat on the end of our bench or leaned against the wall. My parents were there, as they almost always were. My dad often was the only father, taking time from the industrial truck company he owned to come watch us. Other fathers weren't able to get away from work, so they never saw their daughters play because we never played at night like the boys did.

As a freshman who already was one of the tallest girls in the school at 5′11″, I was playing on the junior varsity, occasionally moving up to the varsity to play for a quarter of the game.

At the end of this game against rural Lake High School, Miss O signaled for a timeout. We gathered around her. She had a notepad and a magic marker in her hand. She was talking fast and scribbling even faster.

"We're going to try a trick play," she began with a smile. "Cathy Collins is going to inbound the ball to Chris," Miss O said, looking to me. "Chris, you'll be at half-court, and you're going to lob the ball to Susan Secor, who's going to be running toward the basket. You hit her here," Miss O said, marking a spot to the right of the basket on her notepad.

"Now here's the tricky part," she said, lowering her voice. "When you come out, Chris, you pretend you're going to throw it to the other side, and start saying it's going to the left, okay? Say that so Lake hears you. And Susan, you act like we're not throwing it to you, pretend you don't care where it's going, like you're not involved. Say it's not coming to you so the girl guarding you hears it. And I'll keep yelling it's going to the left. Okay? Let's fake 'em out."

We nodded excitedly. We broke the huddle. As she walked back onto the court, Susan dutifully sulked.

Cathy was given the ball by the referee on the sideline near our bench, beyond half-court. She threw it to me, I heaved it to Susan, whose defender was nowhere to be found, and she put it up under the basket.

The ball bounced around the rim one, two, three times—then fell through the net as time expired.

We won, 18–16.

Miss O came bounding onto the court and hugged Susan, then me, then Cathy. We jumped around in each other's arms for several moments. I don't think I ever was happier on a basketball court.

After the varsity played—and also won—we invited all the girls from Lake down the hall to the Home Ec room for cookies and milk. This was a tradition whether we won or lost; we invited our opponents to a social hour. They often returned the favor when we played at their school. This is a ritual that has long since been done away with in girls' sports, having been swallowed up by the very necessary push for equality with the boys. It's too competitive now, the stakes are too high, scholarships hang in the balance. In that world, there is no room for cookies and milk.

Even as we revel in what girls have now, we still can miss a little of what we had then. "It was a wonderful thing," Miss O said. "There was a club feeling to it all, a sense of friendship and camaraderie, that kids don't have with their opponents anymore. There was something to be said for the social part of sports. We did have fun, didn't we?"

But it wasn't all fun. Miss O was fighting battles we never knew about. Ottawa Hills is an extremely well-to-do suburb in which literally 99 percent of the kids go on to college. It's a place where, even thirty-five years ago, parents hoped for the same success for their daughters as they did for their sons. If equality for girls in sports was going to break out anywhere in the United States in the early 1970s, it would break out there.

But it didn't. Money flowed for the boys and trickled to the girls. Everything the boys had was first-class. Everything the girls had was makeshift. Miss O remembers helping players use masking tape to put numbers on their jerseys in the years prior to my high school days. By the time I was a freshman, we had jerseys—one jersey each. If you were playing two sports in a season, as I did in the winter with basketball and volleyball, you had to take the jersey home at night to have your mother wash it so you could wear it the next day for the next sport. Even the cheerleaders had better uniforms than we did.

Throughout my playing days, we did not have matching shorts for the team, nor matching socks or shoes. We wore whatever we wanted, so one girl on the team looked different from the next.

"The boys even had practice uniforms, yet we didn't have any uniforms other than the jerseys," Miss O said.

It wasn't just the clothes. In the fall, Miss O and some of our team would have to put in the white lines for the field hockey field before a game. If the grass wasn't cut short enough, Miss O would get on the mower and cut it herself so the ball wouldn't get caught in the long grass.

"The football coach walked onto the field, his lights were on, his field was cut, his kids were all put in uniforms, they were washed and ready every time," Miss O said. "And we would go out and line our own field."

There was more. "I had to schedule the games, call referees, put kids in charge of who was bringing what as far as food, and find drivers because we didn't have buses yet," she said. "I even made a medicine kit out of a shoe box."

Miss O often made light of her battles, turning every challenge into a social event for us. It was a delight to help her line the field. We laughed when she jumped onto the mower. Once we got our driver's licenses, we clamored to drive to our games. As kids, we never questioned why we had to do this; it was just the way it was.

I found out decades later that Miss O shielded us from many

difficult moments. "I remember being in tears walking out of budget meetings," she said.

One fight was over the times the boys' and girls' basketball teams got to practice in the big gym. "I didn't understand why the boys' varsity, then the boys' JV, then sometimes the boys' freshman team, all got the gym before we did," she said. "They would go right after school, and we had to come back at 7 or 7:30 at night and practice. That just wasn't fair."

As Miss O was fighting our battles, with the help of some of our parents, she also was dealing with a challenge we never imagined: she, like so many women of her era, was ill-prepared to coach six girls' sports. (Then again, most men of that or any era probably would not have been prepared to coach six boys' sports.)

She came out of Bowling Green with a great knowledge of field hockey and a better-than-average understanding of basketball. That was it. Because women weren't playing sports then as they are now, they were not taught how to coach as they are now.

"I'm the head track coach and I never ran track in college," she said, shaking her head. "I'm the head volleyball coach and I never played volleyball in college."

Miss O took only one or two courses on coaching in college. So she learned as best as she could on the job. "I learned coaching by reading books and watching and talking to other coaches. Ideally my background would have been to come into Ottawa Hills as a beginning teacher and have a varsity coach who was outstanding and learn from that person."

Instead, Miss O invited fathers who had played sports to come to our practices to help. And other coaches offered their advice. The head boys' basketball coach, Dick Kuzma, would take her aside when they were in the gym and teach her plays that she then would teach us.

"It was tough," she said. "I wasn't prepared to be a head coach, especially of all those sports, yet that's what I had to be."

Soon, a demanding yet beloved history teacher, Bob O'Connell, was named to coach the girls' tennis team, and, by 1980, when Miss O stopped coaching and focused strictly on teaching physical education, Ottawa Hills was hiring specialists to coach its various girls' teams.

Despite all the obstacles in our path, we fielded teams that were far better than average. We often defeated schools with far greater enrollments in field hockey and basketball; that was a cause for celebration that once led Miss O to honk her car horn all the way back to school from a game with our down-the-street rival, the Catholic girls' school, St. Ursula.

Another wonderful basketball victory propelled us to Farrell's, an ice-cream parlor, where we told the waitress it was Miss O's eighteenth birthday to get a free sundae.

Although we more than held our own in most sports, we were best in field hockey, which, not coincidentally, was Miss O's favorite sport. She laid the groundwork for what eventually would become a prep dynasty. Under head coach Jo Cooley, now in her twenty-fourth year, Ottawa Hills won three state championships in field hockey in the 1990s. Cooley has sent thirty-six girls off to play collegiate field hockey, with twenty-three receiving Division I scholarships. In the 1970s, this kind of success was unimaginable. College scholarships? For Ottawa Hills girls? To play field hockey?

Even though the experience has become much more competitive for today's girls, with scholarships awaiting them, but no cookies and milk, there remains at Ottawa Hills an air of delight among the athletes and a sensibility among most of the parents that took seed in the days of Miss O.

"I wanted to enjoy what I was doing myself and I wanted all you kids to enjoy what you were doing," she told me. "To have kids be the best they can be and to have me be the best coach or teacher I could be, that was the goal. I always wanted us to come out winners, but even more important, I hoped we had a good experience. I believe in praising kids. I like to give people good feelings."

I played my last basketball game for the Ottawa Hills Green Bears on March 12, 1976. For that one day only, we finally were being treated like the boys. We met at 4 p.m. at Ponderosa for a team dinner. Then we took a bus—the first bus ever for an Ottawa Hills girls' game—for the hour's drive to Defiance, Ohio, to play in the first Ohio Girls' Class A Sectional Basketball Tournament.

When we arrived, our fans, including my mother and my two sisters, bought programs for 10 cents apiece. As we were practicing, my sister Kate got my attention. I went over to look at the program. On the page that included all of our names on the roster, the team nickname also was listed: Green Beans.

Green Beans?

We showed Miss O. We all started to laugh. The person typing the program obviously misread Miss O's handwriting, thinking her "r" was an "n."

"Go Green Beans!" Kate and a friend yelled throughout the game.

The Green Beans had about as much luck as the Green Bears. Our season ended at 4–5 with a 51–33 loss to Tinora, a school we had never played—never even heard of—until that day. I was the team's leading scorer over the past two seasons, averaging more than 15 points a game my senior year, but I managed only 9 that evening. I remember coming out of the game at the end for the last time, the horn sounding signaling a substitution, our fans cheering, and Miss O shaking my hand as I sat down hard on the bench. I wanted to be happy and soak up the scene, but that would have to wait. Frustration was all I felt, and Miss O knew it. She left me alone. We would celebrate another day.

*   *   *

Nearing her fifty-second birthday, Miss O retired from Ottawa Hills High School in 1998. We held a retirement party for her in a new gym in the elementary school next door, a gym in which fourth grade girls now play in travel basketball leagues, a gym that was much grander than the little multipurpose gym we often played in over at the high school.

Miss O's players and students came from Seattle and Washington, D.C., from Chicago and Detroit. If they couldn't make it, their parents showed up to represent them.

My parents and sisters joined me in honoring our coach. My father even gave a small speech, thanking Miss O on behalf of all the parents. My mother and father always adored Miss O, and she them. When they passed away—my mother in 2002, my father in 2003—Miss O was one of the first people in line at both of the wakes.

She is no longer Miss O, but Sandy to us now in our adulthood. She marvels as we do at what has happened to girls' and women's sports in the blink of an eye in our nation's history. She keeps scrapbooks with pictures from our games and all the extracurricular Girls' Athletic Association activities she chaperoned: canoe and tobaggoning trips, mother-daughter field hockey games, father-daughter basketball games. All the sign-up sheets, the permission slips, the candid photos: they're all there as she turns the yellowed pages.

She also is finally receiving the credit she is due for being a pioneer in women's sports. She opened a letter from Bowling Green State University to find out there will be a ceremony in February 2005 to give varsity letters to the female athletes who never received them.

Many would have complained about what they never received or the discrimination they faced as a woman playing sports a bit too early in our nation's history. But not our Miss O. She brought an unfailing wonderment to her work, to her coaching, and, thus, to us.

"Were it not for my experiences playing sports at Ottawa

Hills," I said in front of the crowd at the retirement party, "being encouraged every step of the way by my parents, my siblings, and Miss O, I am certain I would not have taken the path I did in my life. And I am certain most of the women here today would agree that they took a certain path in their lives because of their experiences playing sports and being coached by Miss O."

I turned to look at the only woman I ever called Coach.

"Miss O, you shaped our lives and you changed our lives. Thank you."

—————————————

CHRISTINE BRENNAN is a *USA Today* sports columnist and an ABC News/ESPN commentator. She is the author of five books, including the national best-seller *Inside Edge.*

Making It to the Majors

BY BOB WOLFF

I ALWAYS WONDERED WHY baseball takes such pride in being called "the national pastime." Pastime is defined as something that makes the time pass agreeably. That seems to fit into the category of walking in the park, or looking out the window at kids playing games. A nice way to pass the time.

To me, baseball is far more than a time-killer—it's a passion. The craving to play or watch baseball has never left me.

I was born on November 29, 1920, in New York City. By the age of five when we moved to Long Island, a bat, ball, and glove were my most cherished possessions. My love affair with the game continued to grow. By age seven, I was reading baseball box scores. For some strange reason, I began to focus on the day-by-day results of the Philadelphia Athletics. Lefty Grove and George Earnshaw, the A's' outstanding pitchers, were my out-of-town heroes. There was no tangible reason for this. There was no television. I had never seen a big league game and had never been to Philadelphia.

By the time I was ten, I was aware that local games were on the radio, but I wasn't a listener; I wanted to play.

There were no organized youth teams at that time outside of high school. No Little Leagues, no recreation teams, but baseball was played everywhere—on every lot, every schoolyard, every playing field, backyards, front yards, even the streets. Baseball was the nation's participant sport. Today, those fields are bare. Baseball is now setting major league attendance records as a spectator sport. But in earlier days, there were always games going on. My parents bought a house just a block from the school grounds, and I spent hours playing for any group looking for an extra body. I was a fast runner, could catch fly balls, throw well, and had pretty good hitting ability. Making the older boys' teams was never an obstacle.

At these pickup games, there were no coaches, no umpires, no spectators, no fights, and above all, no parents. No disputes, either. If there was a genuine doubt about a ball or a strike, we'd just throw the pitch over again.

We played purely for the fun of it—the inner glow of getting a hit, or making a good defensive play. If one of the pickup teams was better than the others, we'd just switch players around to maintain balance. There was no talk of possible college scholarships, or pro contracts—that was another world.

The only coach I was aware of at that time was Pop LaRue, the local high school baseball coach at Woodmere Academy, which I attended. He also ran a summer camp on the school grounds. That summer camp featured plenty of baseball, and I persuaded my parents that this would be a terrific place for me. They agreed, and I became one of Pop's campers.

We played other sports as well, and when the weather was poor, we used the gymnasium. I was either fearless or just plain ignorant of the possible consequences when I demonstrated an unusual ability in gymnastics exhibitions.

I lined up volunteer kids kneeling down on hands and knees side by side so that I could see just the tops of their backs. I'd place a soft mat at the end of the lineup, then race down a short runway and dive headfirst with arms outstretched, clearing the bodies and ending up with my head tucked down into a quick somersault, springing right back up!

We would start with four or five kneelers, and after each dive, we'd add another person, until we reached as many as eight squatters. Like a plane coming in for a landing, I'd be just above them with my somersault ending, and oddly, I never considered the consequences of a mishap. As an adult, I shudder about it now.

While I was playing baseball at the camp, Pop LaRue watched me dive in similar fashion for line drives, grabbing them with my glove, then rolling on my back with my shoulder tucked in and springing back up, ready to throw. He also watched me win the camp's running and throwing drills and excel at dodgeball and agility exercises. We would chat from time to time and Pop seemed to take pride in my accomplishments, becoming a frequent visitor to my activities.

When I was in eighth grade and a step from varsity ball, Pop watched me pitch a JV game in which I struck out every batter I faced. It commanded attention, but I understood the reason it happened. The JVs used a baseball slightly smaller than the one used by older players. My fingers would grip the smaller ball, and I could impart enough spin to get a huge break on my pitch.

Using fear as my pitching weapon, I'd throw inside, the batters would jump back to avoid being hit, and the ball would break over for a strike. My fingers could never get the same good grip when I pitched with the larger varsity ball, and I relied more on a fastball.

But pitching was not my position of choice—that was only when needed. Pop asked me where I'd like to play on his varsity team, and I told him center field. "I'll work with you," Pop said, and that was an understatement. Maybe Pop saw the joy I received in playing, maybe he viewed me as a bright prospect to be nurtured, maybe he thought I'd help his team win, or maybe he just wanted to do a good deed; whatever, we never discussed why, but day after day when regular practice was over, Pop would hit me hundreds of fly balls until the daylight disappeared and we were forced to go home. The training sessions and his praise provided the greatest encouragement, motivation, and inspiration a young kid could have.

Pop LaRue physically could have been a poster boy for athletics. Sandy-haired, smiling face, sharp blue eyes, chiseled features, he stood about 5′ 10″ with powerful shoulders and bulging forearms. When he hit, the ball exploded off his bat. He had the grace of a professional pitcher and the velocity to go with it.

I never questioned him as to what level he had played or how he did. Pop was the coach—he had talent and my utmost respect. I was thrilled he was spending time with me.

My greatest fun in high school ball was playing a shallow center field and racing in any direction to flag down a long fly or a short drive. I was off before the crack of the bat, after watching the pitch location and the swing, and then calculating where the ball would be hit. My greatest exhilaration came from playing shallow, sighting the ball when it was hit deep, sprinting with my back to the plate, mentally computing when the ball would descend, glancing back quickly while running at full speed, and then catching the ball over my shoulder or turning to get it while facing the diamond once again. I had complete trust in my mental time clock while not watching the ball. I knew where it was instinctively.

Oddly, when I grew older, now playing Press-TV-Radio games, I found that this skill had departed because my visualization was still based on my youthful running speed and not my middle-aged gait.

At the school sports awards dinner at the end of my JV years, I was rushed from the banquet to the hospital to have my appendix taken out. Mom and Dad were with me, of course, but early the next morning, before they arrived again, Pop LaRue was there to talk sports. He brought me a gift—a book of sports stories about courageous athletes, a book I still treasure. Pop had become more than a coach; he was a treasured member of the family.

In high school, as most kids did in those days, I played three sports, quarterbacking the football team, playing guard on the championship basketball team, and, as a center fielder, making the *New York World Telegram and Sun* list of the top twenty New York metropolitan area baseball players. I hit .583 my senior year by learning that going for line-drive hits on each at-bat was a better approach to hitting success than uppercutting long fly outs. Getting on base and scoring runs became my goals.

The time had come to think about college, and paramount to me was going to a school that had the best record at the time of sending players to the majors. I wanted to test myself against the best, and perhaps in the back of my mind I was dreaming that, if I could make it at the college level, it could be a stepping-stone to the majors.

I told Pop that my selection would be between Duke and Holy Cross, and told him wherever I went, I'd be indebted to him for all his work with me, his encouragement, and his friendship.

My college selection was Duke University. When I wrote to them, I told them of my high school background and my desire to play for Coach Jack Coombs, a former Philadelphia A's pitching star. I enclosed some clippings along with my letter. They accepted me and told me that the coach was pleased I'd be joining him, and he was looking forward to watching me in action.

I found out, after enrolling at Duke, that Coach Coombs held a showcase baseball camp during the summer for top high school prospects who wanted to attain college scholarships before attaining pro contracts. After the coach took the prize recruits for Duke, there was still an ample supply for other scouts to work with other colleges to monitor their progress as potential professionals.

I didn't receive a scholarship, nor did I ask for one, but I was promised financial aid in the form of campus jobs, if needed. I soon discovered how keen an eye Coach Coombs had in discovering professional talent.

Seven of Coombs's players on the freshman team went on to pro contracts. Coach had so many good players stockpiled, he'd change the lineup depending on which pro scouts showed up in Durham, North Carolina, to evaluate the talent.

My teammates, as a freshman, were impressive. Pitcher Bill McCahan not only went on to pitch for the Philadelphia A's, he also came up with a no-hitter for them. Bill Mock also pitched in the pros. Crash Davis, our second baseman, whose name resurfaced in the movie *Field of Dreams,* also went to the A's. Eddie Shokes, as fancy a first baseman as one could ever find, played later at Cincinnati. George Byam played in the Red Sox organization; catcher Austin Knickerbocker made it to Philadelphia. Left fielder Eric Tipton played for the Phils and Cincinnati.

One day in practice, my spikes caught in a rundown play. I toppled over in pain. The diagnosis was a broken ankle. A plaster cast covered the bottom of my foot up to my knee. My playing season was over.

Coach Coombs had watched me in action, though. He had watched me racing for, diving, and grabbing long drives; he had seen me run, and watched me hit. I had earned his confidence as a player. But my skinny frame—I was a shade under six feet tall and barely 150 pounds—didn't measure up to the power-hitting centerfielder type that Duke was grooming for the majors. I could hit line drives, steal bases, play great defense, but Coach Coombs knew the majors would like more home runs from their outfielders than I would provide. I knew that I'd have to talk further with the coach about my future after my ankle had healed.

Meanwhile, I didn't lack for activity. WDNC, the CBS radio station in Durham, broadcast all the Duke baseball games as well as football and basketball. The station asked me to sit with them in the radio booth to comment on my teammates and the games. The station's sports director, Woody Woodhouse, made me part of their broadcast family.

This continued during football and basketball season the following year. In fact, during basketball season, WDNC would have a game almost every night as we broadcast all Duke games home and away, and filled in any Duke off dates with games from the University of North Carolina, N.C. State, Wake Forest, or Davidson. After returning to the campus, I'd get my studying and homework done between midnight and 3 a.m. With some early morning classes, it wasn't a schedule designed for sleep. Oddly, my grades stayed up despite these strange hours. With the basketball season ending and with baseball season approaching and my heart still set on playing, it was time to speak to Coach Coombs.

Coach agreed to meet with me for a private conversation. I told him that my broadcast career was thriving, but I still wanted to play the game. What would he advise? "Bob," he said, "you've proven yourself to me as a ballplayer. I assume you came here to find out whether you can make it to the majors. I know you can do the job defensively, and you can hit for average, but the majors want more home runs from their outfielders than you can give them.

"You have good hands, a good arm, good range—so how would you consider moving to the infield? I'll start you out at shortstop if you want to give it a try. You'd have a better shot at making it up as a middle infielder."

I gave it a try and found that fielding grounders was no easy task compared to settling under a fly ball. I worked on quick, accurate ball release, a straight throw to first, making the pivot at second with the runner sliding in, coming in on topped balls— all part of the many new skills that had to be mastered.

I was gaining confidence, and now Bill Jessup, Coach Coombs's assistant coach, decided to give me a final test. "Couple of hard shots, Bob," he warned, "so get ready." I handled the first high hopper cleanly, then came a wicked grass-cutter that seem destined to stay down. I bent over to keep my glove low, when suddenly the ball jumped off a pebble or clump of grass with a gigantic hop right at my face. I quickly raised my bare hand to shield my eyes, and the ball hit the pinky on my right hand—I felt the pain and the blood and looked down at a broken finger, now at a grotesque angle.

They gave me a tetanus shot at the Duke University hospital for protection against infection in a deep, penetrating wound. The shot had a horse serum base, a prescription no longer used. As they worked to put the finger together, I realized I'd be back in the broadcast booth. This was my throwing hand and healing would take time.

A couple of days later, I collapsed on the way to class. The horse serum in the injection had laid me low. Three more days back in the hospital and I finally left with the stern warning that I never permit anyone to inject horse serum in me again. They suggested I carry a card with me with that notation.

I ended the season back in the CBS broadcast booth, and then an unusual turn of events came about. The regular play-by-play announcer revealed that he was leaving. I was offered increased responsibilities and more assignments if I could fit them into my college schedule.

So back to Coach Coombs for a final discussion. "Bob," he said. "I've heard you on the air. You're good. You're still a young guy and the Durham newspapers that own the radio station have given you terrific write-ups. I think you'll make it to the majors as a broadcaster. Your voice will certainly outlast your arm or legs playing baseball.

"I think you'll get to the top in the next few years, and to me that's a better bet than starting over as an infielder.

"I plan to be listening to you and will be proud to say you played for me. I'll keep your uniform ready in case you can't turn away from the field, but you're in a prime position to make it to the bigs as a broadcaster, and you shouldn't pass that up."

I shook hands with the coach, thanked him for his outstanding support and guidance, and told him he'd be hearing from me on the airwaves.

There was a slight detour after graduation, though. World War II was upon us.

I received a naval commission and was sent to Harvard for training as a navy supply officer. Training at the Seabees base in Virginia followed before we were shipped overseas to the Solomon Islands in the Pacific with the 11th Special Battalion. Finding that what I had been taught at Harvard was applicable only to shipboard routine and not to advance bases, I wrote a manual detailing how to deal with advance-base problems, enclosed before-and-after pictures, and sent this back to the Supply Department in Washington.

Within two weeks, I received a letter of commendation and orders to fly back to the nation's capital, where I was put in charge of rewriting the navy advance-base regulations and putting together new instructional material for publications and training movies.

In 1945, with the war coming to a close, while I was still in uniform, the *Washington Post* radio station hired me to be their sportscaster. That year I married Naval Officer Jane Louise Hoy, a beautiful navy nurse I had met while training with the Seabees. In 1946 came another big step up the broadcast ladder. I became Washington's first telecaster, hired by DuMont's WTTG. In 1947 came the giant step. I was selected as the television play-by-play caller for the Washington Senators. I had made it to the majors—as a big league broadcaster.

I count my blessings. All the breaks were good ones. I was so fortunate to have had two coaches whose personal support was vital to my development. Pop LaRue's faith in me, his tireless work with me, and his positive spirit added both enjoyment and motivation in my quest to succeed. At the college level, Coach Coombs's frankness, evaluation and concern for my future was always there. His sensitivity in speaking to me, advising me, making sure that I took advantage of the sportscasting opportunities I was offered, while never diminishing the pride I had in my playing ability, was coaching at the finest level.

Two coaches put me on the right road and kept me there. I'll always be indebted to them.

BOB WOLFF has continued on that right road. It brought him to Cooperstown in 1995 for induction into the broadcast wing of the Baseball Hall of Fame. The longest-running TV sportscaster in history, in 2003 Wolff was installed in both the National Association of Sportscasters and Sportswriters Hall of Fame and the Madison Square Garden Walk of Fame. His early versatility also proved important. Wolff became the first sportscaster to do play-by-play of the four major professional championships—the World Series, the NFL championship, the NBA championship, and the Stanley Cup championship.

Back to Basics

BY IRA BERKOW

As I THOUGHT about the special basketball coaches I have known, I recalled a particularly significant one for me, Edwin Turner, my college coach. I imagined that Coach Turner now would be more than eighty years old, if in fact he was still alive.

I had not seen or been in touch with Turner since my playing days at Roosevelt University, a commuter school in downtown Chicago. I wrote to him in care of the school, and about a week later I received a response, with a return address of Highland Park, Illinois, an exclusive northern suburb of Chicago, which I knew to be decidedly white and primarily Jewish. But Edwin Turner, a black man, was always difficult to categorize and always his own man.

I had asked Coach Turner if I could come for a visit. He responded that he was pleased to hear from me and would look forward to my stopping by. He signed the letter, "Edwin Turner, Coach." He underlined "Coach" twice.

He could have underlined it a third time, and he would have been justified in my view, as I thought back on the year I had played for him at Roosevelt University. It was the season of 1958–59, my sophomore year at Roosevelt, the year I turned nineteen.

Edwin Turner was then in his forties, tall—about 6-foot-3—with a wiry, athletic build. He had a mustache and gentle but aware eyes. His wife, Gladys, was the head of the school library.

I imagined that Coach Turner could have worked there, too, for he had a quiet way about him and was one of those people whom others either don't quite take notice of the first time around or, if they do, may underestimate. He was not bluster, like some coaches, and not given to pronouncement, either. But when challenged, his eyes blazed.

Once, when a player gave him back talk in practice, Turner stopped practice and walked onto the court with a stride so determined that everyone was rooted in his place. He stopped in front of the player. "If there is going to be any dictator here," he said, "I'm the dictator. We don't do what you want to do—you do what I want you to do." He did not raise his voice, but he said this so firmly that it ended discussion.

Edwin Turner was the first black coach I had ever had. And with black players on the team, I didn't know how that was going to work out. How would I be treated? How would he treat them? Would he give me playing time? There was something else occurring that didn't dawn on me at that time—I imagine I was just too self-involved to consider it. But Edwin Turner was possibly the only black head basketball coach of an integrated team in the country.

Not only was he the head coach, he was the only coach we had. He had no assistants. He was also the coach of the bowling, tennis, soccer, track, and golf teams. He was the entire athletic department of Roosevelt University. He even taught a physical education class. I suppose he also found time to eat a meal once every few weeks or so.

I had enrolled at Roosevelt after flunking out of the University of Illinois in Chicago—by a fraction, I hasten to add, after just one semester. I would have been given another semester to prove myself at Illinois if I hadn't entered the school on probation, but I had finished in the bottom quarter of my high school graduating class, and this made me suspect, in the eyes of university authorities, as college material.

On the placement exams for Illinois-Chicago, I had scored

exceptionally high in English and so had been placed into a class for gifted English students. I am pretty sure I was the only one in the class who had been in the lowest quarter of his high school graduating class. But on the same placement exam I scored miserably in math, a class I rarely bothered to attend. To compound matters, I had decided to major in accounting because other friends of mine had, because I thought I would go into business one day, and because I had no real direction. After the first week at Illinois, I knew accounting was a mistake, but my school adviser wouldn't let me get out of it. That—combined with math—all but sealed my fate at that school.

I was embarrassed about flunking out, but I was determined to try again. I applied to Roosevelt and was accepted. Roosevelt was a school known for giving people a second, and a third, chance at a college education. It was a liberal arts school with open admission at a time when open admission in America was barely heard of. If you could come up with the modest tuition, then you would be admitted. If you came to class, you would learn. If you didn't, you wouldn't. It was all up to you. It was a college for adults or for those who looked at education in an adult way.

I wasn't sure how I looked at it. I just didn't want to be a college flunk-out. I wanted another chance. My parents were busy working, and since I was also working and helping to pay the rent while in high school and college, they didn't trouble themselves much with my schooling.

In fact, it wasn't until years later that I told anyone, including my parents, that I had flunked out. I just said I had decided to transfer. That was all.

"Dad," I told my father one day, "I'm going to Roosevelt, and I'm going to major in English."

"English?" he said. "What can you do with it?"

"I don't know, but I like it."

He tried to be helpful. "Do you think you can take another accounting course?"

"I don't think so."

And that was the end of it.

Roosevelt University was hardly a typical college. It was located in the heart of the city, in the old Auditorium Hotel on Michigan Avenue. Hotel rooms and suites had become classrooms. The dining room became the library reading room, and the kitchen and pantries were converted into stacks. As years went on, renovations and reconstructions made it feel like a busy, nicely appointed college that happened to be vertical instead of the more commonplace ivy horizontal.

And most of the students had jobs before or after their classes, as I did. On Sundays, I ran my own belt stand on Maxwell Street, the teeming old-world marketplace where my parents had been born, and on Saturdays and some evenings sold door-to-door religious pictures and sometimes lamps on commission for a clothing, furniture, and jewelry store on the West Side. But all that took a shared place in my life with my new interest in formal education. I hadn't been sure what to expect from the instruction at Roosevelt, but the professors were of a high level, and stimulating. I took four liberal arts courses and made the dean's list, which allowed me to receive a modest academic scholarship the following semester. I was breathing easier. During this time I was still playing basketball in pickup games in Loyola Park, where I had played since the beginning of my high school days, and in a league. But my high school basketball career still bothered me. I thought I could have done better, and that had left me with a sense of unrealized promise. I felt I had bowed to the criticism of my shooting too much and that that sensitivity had handcuffed me. Only later did I learn that developing a hard shell to ward off insecurities is essential in sports and writing alike.

When I came across an item in the Roosevelt University school newspaper that Coach Turner was holding tryouts for the Roosevelt basketball team, I thought, "Why not?" I hadn't even been aware that Roosevelt had a team. I tried out, made the squad, and to my great satisfaction was named to the starting lineup.

Roosevelt played on a Division III level, with no athletic scholarships (though a few years later it moved up to Division II and did offer scholarships to players). It also didn't have a gym. The team used a well-worn recreational facility named Olivet Institute, about four miles from the school building. There were exposed pipes on the ceiling and walls, and not all of the lights were always working, so we sometimes practiced and played games in circumstances that seemed to require miner's helmets.

There were stands in a balcony that could seat several hundred, though for games they were usually more than half empty. We had no band, no cheerleaders, no pom-pom girls, no conference. We just had a basketball team and Coach Turner.

The purpose of the team was to play basketball, and not for any other reason than it was fun or, perhaps, to prove something or other to ourselves to both. There were no illusions of glory. We could quit the team anytime we chose to without financial jeopardy. And some did.

Coach Turner scheduled games against schools like the University of Chicago, teachers colleges, other small liberal arts colleges, junior colleges, as well as the DePaul University freshman team. (That was at a time when freshmen were still not eligible for Division I varsity play.) Our starting five were Jim Malone at center, Louis Campbell and Peter Lutterbeck at forward, and Jim Pazeatopolis and me at guard. It was a proper city mélange: two blacks, a German, a Greek, and a Jew. And a guy named Kelly was sixth man.

Malone and Campbell—who we hoped would dominate the front court—were our most imposing players. Both had been good high school players in Chicago, and I could never figure out why they were playing at Roosevelt instead of at a college on scholarship. It just wasn't something I ever found the opportunity to ask either of them.

In our first game Wilson Junior College beat us by a wide

margin. We lacked cohesion, and I scored eight points. I had
played cautiously and had several turnovers. At the next practice Coach Turner took me aside. "You had shots and you didn't
take them," he said. "I know we can win games, but if we are,
you are going to have to help with scoring."

In our second game, against a team from the Great Lakes
naval training base, we lost by one point, and again I played ten-
tatively. I still felt a constraint about shooting. "If you don't
shoot more," said Turner, "I'm going to put you on the bench.
But I'd rather you helped the team. And I know you have the
shot." There was a decency in the man, and it came out even
when he had possible bad news. But his approach was encouraging, emphasizing my potential.

Looking back, I can see that Turner was obviously sensitive
to inhibitions, self-inflicted or otherwise, even those of an
eighteen-year-old white boy. He had grown up in the segregated South, in the small town of Gilmer, in northeast Texas,
where he was allowed to sit only in the balcony of the local theater; where he was not allowed to attend the grade school a
block from his home but had to travel a mile to the black school.
Despite this and other forms of discrimination, his family—his
father and his uncles—owned five funeral homes in the area,
and he was raised with a sense of independence and dignity.

He attended nearby Texas College, an all-black school,
where has was a standout in basketball, track, and football, making the Negro Colleges' All-America team as a running back and
end in 1934 and 1935. He graduated with honors. He taught
school, and then, when war broke out, became an infantry officer in the U.S. Army—one of only three blacks in his Officer
Candidate School class of 257 at Fort Benning, Georgia, and
ranked third in the class. He served two years in Europe, primarily in Italy, during World War II. I once asked if he had ever
been shot at. "Not to my knowledge," he replied.

In the time I played for Coach Turner, I never saw an opposing coach show any kind of disrespect to him. He was just an-

other coach on the other bench, as I perceived it. It was only later that I learned of what had happened with his golf team.

The Roosevelt golf team was in a conference with eleven other area schools that included Aurora College, Illinois Tech, DePaul, and Loyola. They played on courses primarily in the suburbs. Turner was the only black coach in the conference and the only coach not allowed on the golf courses. Every one of the dozen courses they played on had restrictions against blacks—or, in the terminology of the 1950s, "Negroes." He first learned about it when he walked onto a course in Mt. Prospect. An official of the club told Turner, "You may sit in the clubhouse, but you can't go on the course. Sorry. It's the rules."

So Turner had to sit in the clubhouse and wait for his team to make the turn at the tenth hole. "I'd have to ask them how they were doing," Turner recalled, "where the other coaches could follow their players around and see how they were doing."

And either before matches or after matches, other coaches could play on those courses. All but Turner, who also wanted to play. He liked golf, which he had learned to play as a boy when he caddied at golf clubs in Texas, and caddies were allowed to play on occasion. He decided that for the sake of his team we would not make a protest. "And sometimes you have to pick your spots about when to make a fuss," he said. "Under the circumstances I felt that this just wasn't one of them. Was I angry? Sure. But I know anger isn't good for you. You can't think clearly when you're angry. If you took all of these things seriously, you'd go batty, go crazy. It's very, very frustrating."

After a couple of years, the sense of unfairness on the golf courses in suburban Chicago began to eat at the other college coaches in Turner's conference. I would imagine, too, that, knowing Turner, they had to feel pretty stupid to be involved in something that shameful. And while Turner tried not to get angry, the racism took its toll. Turner, a young, healthy man, suffered ulcers.

"I don't remember how it happened, but one day I found myself playing one of the courses with the other coaches," Turner recalled, "and then I was being allowed to follow my team. And pretty soon, one by one, all the other courses allowed me to do the same."

In our third basketball game, with the bench looming for me, I was concerned and anxious. I had now the same question I'd had for Coach Scher four years earlier after a bad game for Sullivan frosh-soph: Will I ever hit again?

I opened the game by missing a jump shot. I missed a second. But I glanced over to see Coach Turner on the bench clapping his hands with encouragement.

I scored on my third shot and went on to have my best-scoring game in school ball since the frosh-soph. We beat Elgin College 56–53, and I had 18 points—about a third of my team's points— to lead all scorers in the game.

"Nice job," he said with a smile after the game. That was all. That was enough.

In the previous two games I had hustled on defense, I had tried to look for the open man in passing, but I had not gotten the most out of my abilities because I hadn't trusted myself to shoot the ball. And the problem had come from within, a reluctance to throw off the shackles of insecurity. Turner helped me to do so.

In my next game, against the University of Illinois Professional Schools, I did even better, scoring 26 points in a 97–70 victory, hitting 11 baskets, and was 4 for 5 from the free-throw line. The team and I were riding a wave. After we defeated the Chicago Teachers College 86–65, the *Chicago Sun-Times* noted, "Ira Berkow paced the Roosevelt attack with 24 points on 10 baskets and four free throws."

After so many paltry lines in the box scores from my high school days, it was gratifying to see a fat bunch of numbers following my name.

Lou Campbell, our six-foot-four forward, had 23 points in that game against Chicago Teachers. Campbell was a soft-spoken guy who often let his wardrobe do the talking for him. He had a big mustache and a knowing wink, and he invariably showed up for games in a black evening cape. He wore a variety of hats, most black and wide-brimmed, like a gaucho. And when he played, he had a slicing, swooping, birdlike aspect to his moves to the basket—in his cape he also seemed to swoop into the gym. We called him Gull, for seagull.

Our center, Jim Malone, was a broad-shouldered 6-foot-6 senior who worked a full-time job in a factory, as I recall, in addition to going to school, playing ball, and caring for his family, which included a couple of kids. I never remember him looking tired, though he would have had justification. He was an ace rebounder, and what I remember most is people bouncing off him.

But my closest friends on the team were two sometime starters—they started when one of the regulars couldn't make a game. One was a Greek named Mike Simos. He was practical, and he was admiring, in a humorous way. Admiring of himself, that is. The practical: he taught me that when you get into a car on a snowy day, you kick your feet to get off the snow, so you don't create a puddle in the car. The admiring: he would sing a song, "I'm the greatest, I'm too much for words. I'm the greatest, haven't you heard." Usually he would sing it in his car to the rearview mirror.

My other good friend was a black guy named Raymond Tanter. He taught me the best way to win an argument, which was to agree in the gentlest manner with the one you're arguing with. When I heated up on a topic, he would smile and say, "Right again, Ira." Put me at a loss for words.

The Roosevelt team was not exactly one big happy family, however. Not for me, anyway. There was a black substitute player on the team—someone I'll call Baxter—who felt he wasn't playing as much as he should have. I wasn't sure if he resented me or the coach or the world in general. But he was grim and distant. There was a militancy in his eyes before militancy had grown as strong as it would in this country. The Little Rock school-integration crisis had taken place less than a year earlier, and Martin Luther King was still known primarily as a preacher in Birmingham—and then only to those who followed events closely.

I remember one game we won and I scored 17 points and Baxter 5, and by the look on his face, I wasn't sure it was safe for me to leave the gym alone. It was. Baxter had gone his separate way. We said little to each other the rest of the season. He has since disappeared into the mists of my history.

Coach Turner continued to be encouraging, and he suggested I drive more to be effective. "Go in there and get those fouls," he said. "And you can get open more for your outside shot because they start to lay off of you." He was right, but I still found it more comfortable to settle for the jump shot.

For our team, meanwhile, there was no more important game than the one against the DePaul freshman team. These were the scholarship guys, the future hotshots of America. We felt we could best test our skills against them.

I was assigned to guard John Incardone, who had been a widely publicized All-Catholic League high school player in Chicago and became a starter on the DePaul varsity. He was about my height and looked as solidly built as a steel cabinet. On the very first play of the game, he brought the ball downcourt toward me and then suddenly went left. That is, his left shoulder went left, and I followed it. The rest of him went right. Right by me for an easy layup. What a great fake! He didn't make that move off me again and had to settle for a variety of other great moves. The DePaul freshmen beat us, 82–51, but I had my moments. Although we lost, we gave them a battle until they pulled away at the end. It was especially gratifying to me because I scored 15 points and was Roosevelt's high scorer.

I wound up the season with a 15-point average, which I believe was the best on the team. I had come out of my shell as a basketball player—and proved that I could score consistently in interscholastic competition. And in large part I had Coach Turner to thank for it.

The season turned out to be the only one I would play for Roosevelt and for Coach Turner. I had signed up for the six-month National Guard program in order to avoid being drafted for a two-year hitch, and I knew that one day I would be called for active duty for six months. That day came in the spring of 1959.

While in the army that summer, I met Ron Hamilton, who had recently been a star guard on the basketball team at Tennessee State, a black university. Hamilton and I and others played on the grounds at Fort Gordon, Georgia, and one day someone told us about an American Legion hall in nearby Augusta that had a great basketball court. Six of us, including Ron, the lone black, piled into a car to play there. Turned out it was closed. As we were driving back to the camp in the dusk, deep in disappointment, I saw a handsome outdoor court—with nets!—at the side of the road.

In my nineteen-year-old enthusiasm I shouted to the driver, "Stop the car! We've got a place to play!" The guy driving was several years older than I and quicker to comprehend the situation. "I don't think so," he said, and continued driving. Hamilton was silent. Then I realized: if some rednecks had seen white guys playing with a black guy in Georgia in the fifties, we might have been shot. This was the South of separate drinking fountains, separate public toilet facilities, and state-mandated segregated schools. But this was the first time I had felt personally affected by irrational racial attitudes. Though it was a minor episode, I now had some inkling—as trivial as it was—of what it was like for blacks facing discrimination. My game, my pleasure, a kind of liberty, had been taken from me, and there was nothing I could do about it. I was furious about such intolerance and remain so to this day.

Not long ago I tracked down Ron Hamilton, who now lives in

a Chicago suburb and is a sales representative for an educational book company. After he left the army, he played for the Cleveland Pipers of the now-defunct American Basketball League—a team that starred Jerry Lucas and was owned by a young scion of a Cleveland shipping company, George Steinbrenner. Ron never made it to the NBA. He and I talked about going to the American Legion gym to play basketball that summer night, and he went on to tell me how tough it had been for him to serve in the South.

"On the base, I remember that when I was on the chow line, I'd always be picked out to be server, so I stayed in the barracks until almost everybody had gone," he said. "And when I'd go off campus, I'd be wearing my black soldier shoes, and people tried to take advantage of me. I felt like a marked man, like they saw me as a trick. I mean the black folks. They thought because I was in the army that I had money, which was kind of funny because I was only making something like $97 a month. And since the area outside the base was highly segregated, I naturally didn't feel comfortable with whites, either. So I stayed on the base, essentially. It was very hot down there. I remember I just tried to stay out of the way and in the shade."

After the army I returned to Roosevelt for one semester and then transferred to Miami of Ohio, wanting a new experience at a college away from home. But my days at Roosevelt University and playing for Coach Turner were memorable for me. Now, nearly forty years later, I looked forward to visiting him in Highland Park. As I drove there, I saw that the house was in a woodsy, all-white area—Turner told me that he had gotten a good deal from a Realtor who was one of his former students.

When Coach Turner opened the door, he hugged me. I embraced him back. He still looked fit and not at all his age, eighty-two. He said he still played golf, though he had considered giving it up.

"I had arthritis in my back and shoulders so bad that I

couldn't follow through on my swing," he said. "And where once I had a 12 handicap, I now was shooting 98, 99, 102, 105—and I'd never shot over 85 or 86. Once you've done reasonably well in certain sports and you begin to falter, you get a little discouraged, disenchanted, and you lose interest. I told my wife that I was going to quit playing golf. 'You like the game,' she said. 'You just go out there and enjoy yourself.'"

And what happened? I asked.

"I went back out," he said, "and I made adjustments. And then the arthritis got a little better. And I played a little better. Not where I was before, but better than I had been playing."

In the hundreds?

"Oh no," he said. He smiled. "In the high nineties."

When he and Gladys were considering moving into this neighborhood, Coach Turner told me, a vote was taken of the residents in the thirty-nine houses in their development. All but one person voted yes. And that was the family that would be living next door. "Well, we moved in and they didn't speak to us for about three years," said Turner. "And then one day I had picked crab apples from our tree, and I saw the woman and offered her some of our crab apples. She looked hesitant but accepted. A few days later she came over with some tomatoes she had grown. We became friends after that."

He said that they had a fright when they first moved in. "We heard something pinging against our picture window in the living room," he said. "We didn't know what it was, but it sounded like somebody was throwing a rock or something at our window. We wondered if it was, you know, some kind of welcoming committee. Like, get out of here. Well, what happened was, a lot of birds fly around here. And they hit the windows. Sometimes you go out and find them lying on the lawn, their necks broken."

I told Coach Turner that I still play basketball and asked whether he thought I should still be at it.

"If you feel you can do it," he replied. "I don't put any limit on doing things. That's my philosophy of life. About ten years ago I told a friend of mine that I was going to buy a car and that it was going to be my last car. He said to me, 'I won't ever buy anything and call it my last. Even if I want something and I'm almost on my deathbed, I'm going to buy it if I want it. And going to buy top of the line, too.' I thought that made a lot of sense. What are you saving for at this age? So I went out and bought a Cadillac."

"Is it your last?" I asked.

"Oh no," he said, "but ours now is five years old. We're going out shopping for a new one."

IRA BERKOW is a Pulitzer Prize–winning sportswriter for the *New York Times*. He has written numerous books, including the national bestseller, *Red: A Biography of Red Smith; The Man Who Robbed the Pierre*, a finalist for the Edgar Award for best true crime book of the year; and a memoir, *To the Hoop*.

Fit to Be Tied

BY BUD COLLINS

HE TAUGHT ME HOW to tie a bow tie.

Not an inconsiderable coaching feat. This was long after we first met, and well before I knew that successfully wrestling with a narrow thirty-six-inch strip of silk or cotton—preferably polka-dotted—was considered, in most male minds, tantamount to pinning "Killer" Kowalski.

"It's very easy to be ordinary, but it takes courage to excel," he constantly reminded his pupils, on the field or in the classroom. "And we must excel."

He frequently added, "Always reach for a star. You won't get there, but keep reaching anyway. You'll be surprised how far you'll get."

Cravats that draped and "got in the way of an active man" were not his style. And the predominant pre-tied snap-on bow he deemed ordinary—a cop-out. Excelling was getting in there to the jugular with both hands, a two-fisted attack on resistant fabric, coming off with a satisfying win.

That was Edward Leo Finnigan, an ebullient Irishman out of Cleveland's East Side whose smile could melt an iceberg, even a young student rejecting his advice on neckwear or athletic performance.

Eddie Finnigan made much of his excellent reputation in college coaching with a sport about which he had known little: track and field. His first coaching loves were football and basketball. He succeeded at the former, but not at basketball, even though he'd been an All-America in 1933 for Western Reserve (now Case Western) University in Cleveland.

If Eddie, who sent many bow-tie-adorned disciples into the scholastic coaching vineyards throughout Ohio during his thirty years as physical education professor and varsity coach, is remembered for one pupil, it would be a skinny, unimposing hurdler called "Bones."

Unimposing until he burst from the starting blocks, that is. Because Harrison (Bones) Dillard would survive World War II as a combat infantryman in Europe and race on to Olympic gold medals in 1948 and 1952—giving Finnigan, and me, a wonderful ride. Also a place in the headlines for an Ohio college of 1,600 students named Baldwin-Wallace where Finnigan held forth on the cinder track.

It was about eight years into Eddie's Baldwin-Wallace tenure that I became a twelve-year-old disciple. He was a customer, his porch a pitching target on my route for the morning paper, the *Cleveland Plain Dealer*. I was growing up in a house nearby on the leafy B-W campus, in Berea, a drowsy settlement separated from Cleveland by about fifteen miles of farmland. It's all pretty much developed today, and the substantial acreage of weathered Andy Rospaugh, known as "the Bean King of Ohio," has given way to housing and commercial properties.

Eddie had joined the B-W coaching staff immediately on graduation from Western Reserve. But by the time we became acquainted he had lost the head job in basketball. He remained a football assistant, presided over a mediocre track team, carried a full teaching load, and captivated anyone he encountered with that smile and a jovial nature. I first caught sight of him as a rollicking bare-chested tennis player on the college courts, reveling in the challenges of a game new to him.

His life, and the college's, changed in 1941. Then, in the sale of his career—a recruiting coup—Finnigan convinced a shy black teenager from Cleveland's East Technical High that he'd be happier at cozier B-W than gigantic Ohio State. The huge university was also in pursuit of Harrison Dillard, the state's schoolboy hurdling champ. Friendlier, closer to home and the boy's widowed, beloved mother than Columbus. The coach emphasized those selling points on behalf of himself and B-W.

Five years previously Dillard had been entranced by a smile and a wave from national hero Jesse Owens. Also an East Tech grad, Owens, fresh from his golden Berlin Olympics triumphs, was the subject of a celebratory motorcade from downtown Cleveland through his old neighborhood. Dillard, residing in the same turf, ran home to tell his mother all about it, and declare he'd be an Olympic victor, too.

Finnigan assured Harrison that even though Owens had emerged from Ohio State, the same could happen with B-W as the launching pad. And, further, he would be the centerpiece around whom the coach would build a team to attract national attention.

That all came to pass, but at the time the subject of the Olympics was nebulous. Europe was engulfed in war, the 1940 Games had been called off, and who could predict when and if the next edition would appear? Seven years, as it turned out.

If Eddie was up and awake when I made those early rounds with the paper, or when I stopped by for the weekly payment, we would chat. Usually about sports. I, an instant admirer, was proud to be a friend of a college coach, a guy who got his name in the newspapers. Learning that I hoped to be a sportswriter, he approved and was encouraging. He was pleased at landing Dillard, telling me it was the start of big things for the tiny college.

"Harrison will take both of us to the Olympics someday. He'll be great to write about, Bud," promised Eddie, who insisted that I call him by his first name.

That was heady talk to a kid who couldn't envision an Olympics or going abroad, and hadn't yet scored a byline in the high school paper. But I glowed to think about it.

Walking to class, Dillard stood out on a campus with few black students. Even more so at practice. You didn't need to know anything about track to be enthralled by the way he glided over the hurdles. It was a ballet. We were impatient to witness him in competition. However, freshmen weren't eligible for the varsity in that day, so he spent the 1942 season in AAU meets on the road.

Training for the indoor season he often ran on the pavement of Beech Street, a block from my home, simply because the college had no building to accommodate a stretch of three hurdles. Serving as a traffic cop to protect his treasure, Finnigan oversaw those dashes with stopwatch in hand. "Look at that!" he'd exult as Harrison zipped across the barriers. "Olympic gold. Absolutely." That was ever the dream.

If weather kept him off the street, they had to settle for the aged, cramped college gym with room for just one hurdle. A venue to be avoided, if possible, it meant starting from the brick wall at one end, taking the hurdle, and crashing into mats on the wall at the other end.

One of the uncommon times I saw Eddie steaming angry was in the spring of 1948 after Dillard had become the world-record-holding hurdler. *Life* magazine assigned the famed photographer Gjon Mili to do a feature on Dillard in Berea. The weather was bad. Mili wanted to set up his lights, and demanded an indoor location. With the gym as the only possibility, Finnigan demurred. The Olympics was at last in sight, and he wasn't risking possible injury to his "Bones." But the unflappable Dillard said it was okay.

Of course you're familiar with the "Just one more" line of every photographer who ever lived. Mili's encores went on and on, and Finnigan's smile went south. Again and again and again Dillard flew over the hurdle, hurtling into the mats. I thought Eddie would remove his bow tie and strangle Mili with it. Finally it was over, no harm done.

The Olympics seemed farther away, and Dillard's part in it

questionable, as the United States was bombed into World War II at Pearl Harbor, December 7, 1941. Finnigan and B-W got one glorious varsity season out of the sophomore in 1943 before his draft board called. That ended bittersweetly with the Ohio Conference meet at Berea in May, a title that Finnigan had long sought—but was apparently deprived of. Dillard had been inducted into the U.S. Army a few days prior.

It took all of Finnigan's Hibernian charm, blarney and persuasion, and political connections, to retrieve "Bones" on a 48-hour pass. Woozy from the numerous inoculations a draftee endured, he nevertheless reappeared on campus long enough to win the 100- and 220-yard dashes, the high and low hurdles, and anchor a victorious relay team. Truly a one-man gang.

Finnigan won his conference championship, but lost his champion. Almost three long years of wondering ensued, worrying, hoping that "Bones" was all right wherever overseas he was. Olympics? We just hoped he was alive. Would he ever run again?

"That's not the main thing, but I hope so," Eddie said. "He had so much left to do, but you could say that about any number of kids. If he does, Bud, you'll have some terrific stories."

He did, and I would. As the war neared conclusion I was writing for the high school paper, soon to become the sports editor of the weekly *Berea Enterprise* (circulation about 2,000). That amounted to scribbling enough copy to fill eight broadsheet columns, laying out the page, and writing the headlines for the princely sum of five dollars. But it wasn't insignificant for a high school kid at the time. Moreover, it took in coverage of the college's athletes as well, including the most illustrious, Dillard.

I had commenced my professional journalistic career at the *Enterprise* by sweeping floors, emptying trash, and making coffee for the ink-stained wretches who manned the typesetting machines and presses. Even though the editor was a friendly neighbor, he promptly told me that scribbling wouldn't do.

Typewritten copy only. From that command evolved my two-fingered Biblical System—seek and ye shall find—that has sustained me since.

Finnigan was a good source for me as the returned GI, "Bones," picked up right where he'd left off without missing a winning step. He and Eddie were close, working out the finer points of hurdling together. Though Dillard, soft-spoken and extremely modest, wasn't much for quotes, Eddie wowed reporters, filling in the blanks.

Immaculate in his dress, Dillard did not, however, join the coach's bow-tie brigade. The way he ran and competed, and carried Finnigan and B-W to national acclaim, "Bones" probably could have gotten away with tailored sackcloth and ashes. Not a chance. He carried himself as a gentleman who'd been around. Having run in Europe, particularly Scandinavia, he starred on an international circuit during summer vacations, following his return to college for three brilliant campaigns, 1946–47–48.

It was also a time when black athletes were expected to blend in without being showy. A track coach at a Texas college lauded Dillard as "the whitest colored boy I've ever seen"—and it was regarded as a high compliment.

Barely 5-foot-10, short for a high hurdler, Dillard was seen only by Finnigan as potentially the greatest of all hurdlers. Ohio State's coach, Larry Snyder, hadn't been overly concerned when "Bones" said no thanks. But he did experience what he'd missed on bringing his team to Berea for a dual meet in 1947. B-W had little chance in that company, 86–41, but Dillard stood out like a rainbow, scoring 25 points by winning the dashes, 100 and 220, plus the high and low hurdles (the last in world-record time, 22.5 seconds), and completing a half-mile relay win.

Finnigan's vision had taken form. The star Eddie reached for in 1941 had fulfilled his desires and beliefs, Dillard quickly establishing himself as the planetary best, busting records wherever he went, point man for B-W, one of the top small college teams in the country.

I was hanging on to his winged feet, covering the home meets for the *Enterprise*, using up my supply of often overblown adjectives in devoting much of that one page to him. Stealing from accounts and quotes that appeared in the three Cleveland dailies, and briefed by Finnigan, I kept up with his progress away from Berea. (The *Enterprise* was strictly a no-expense-account deal, although I did get a free subscription to the paper.)

As the victories mounted to a record 86 straight wins in hurdles and sprints, Dillard's certification for the U.S. Olympic team was taken for granted. Still, under the U.S. system, he—like every other team member—had to place first, second, or third in his event at the trials to make the boat to London.

No one doubted that he'd win routinely. Least of all me, now a freshman at B-W and the nonpaid sports editor of the college paper, the *Exponent*, as well as the *Enterprise*.

With the trials imminent, my pal Bob Beach, the editor of the *Exponent*, wondered, "Shouldn't we be going to the Olympics to cover our schoolmate?"

Well, sure. But how? Not that I hadn't believed Finnigan's tales of distant Olympic adventures, but, really, a journey to London in 1948 for a couple of college kids wasn't very practical.

"You'll work it out," counseled Finnigan, failing to offer a stowaway position in his luggage. "You have to be there."

He was right, and Beach efficiently plotted, checking out tickets, transportation, lodging. Borrowing from parents and other relatives, demolishing slight savings accounts, we had enough to afford passage on a weary, reactivated troopship called the *Marine Jumper*. It dawdled rather than leaped (nine days, New York–Britain). The *Enterprise* doubled my salary (to $10), but just for the two Olympic weeks.

I talked my father into driving us to Evanston, Illinois, for the trials at Northwestern. It was bliss before the fall. We were still beaming after a large civic banquet at a Cleveland hotel, a tribute to wish Dillard good luck at the Olympics. Lifted by the spirit of the occasion, "Bones" uncharacteristically stepped away from his innate modesty, pledging that he'd bring gold back to his hometown as Jesse Owens had done.

Something went wrong. Who knows why? In the hurdles final the peerless, graceful Dillard was inexplicably out of synch. His leading foot struck the first hurdle, then the second. In seconds the pack was gone, and he stood there, forlornly looking at their backs moving away from him.

I wept.

My father, who had been a track coach himself, tried to console me. "These things happen. He's been winning for years. You have to lose sometime."

"Not now . . . he's the best in the world."

"Not today, son."

Finnigan couldn't explain it. Crushed, he didn't show it. He brought up a silver lining (that later would be gold). "'Bones' is on the boat. Don't forget that. We're all going to the Olympics."

I had forgotten, but the coach cheered me up. Dean Cromwell, the Southern California coach, also overseeing the U.S. Olympic team, assuming, like everybody else, that Dillard was a cinch in the hurdles, had asked Finnigan to enter him in the earlier 100 meters. "If he places fourth we can use him in the 400-meter relay," Cromwell suggested.

Dillard finished third behind Cromwell's Southern Cal ace, Mel Patton, and Barney Ewell, a former Penn State sprinter. By doing so he unexpectedly qualified in that event, and now I— disconsolate me—hoped he might salvage a bronze.

Finnigan and Dillard shifted their outlook, but it never wavered from gold. The prize would come in a different event, that's all.

And it did. Dillard's was one of the more astounding Olympic stories: world's best hurdler wins the 100 instead as an outsider. Incredibly, the "world's fastest human" was himself.

In purchasing tickets well beforehand, Bob Beach and I, and Dale Lucal, a teammate of Dillard's, had splurged for the highest-priced seats on the finish line for the hurdles. We had a good look at "Bones's" prime rival, Bill Porter, take his place at the tape.

For the rest of the days we were in the cheap seats, well across vast Wembley Stadium from the finish lines. Dillard had done well in the heats, qualifying with Patton and Ewell for the six-man final in the 100. On the afternoon of truth, we strained to watch at long distance, heard the gun, peered intently for the 10.3 seconds the mad dash lasted. The climax was a blur of three bodies in white shorts and singlets trimmed in red and blue—two black faces plus that of Patton, the world record holder.

Who breasted the tape? Impossible to tell, but a discouraging indication was Barney Ewell hopping about in a victory dance. Had he done it or was he trying to con the judges? Dillard stood by impassively. It was a seemingly interminable wait, the decision made only after the judges pored over a photo of the finish. We were sure "Bones" had a medal, but which one?

Finally the announcement came: "... first, H. Dillard, United States of America ..."

We shrieked and laughed and shook hands. Mission accomplished. It was a long way from Berea, my first glimpse of Dillard in 1941, and Finnigan's prophecy that he and I would bear witness.

Dillard, Ewell, and Patton stood on the victory podium, "The Star-Spangled Banner" was played, and we set off to find the dressing room. I've often thought, in this day of high and onerous security, how simple it was in 1948. We merely asked directions from a uniformed bobby, and at the door said, "We're friends of Mr. Dillard."

"Go right in, gentlemen," said that cop pleasantly.

Finnigan and some reporters surrounded Dillard, who held the medal. He asked if we'd like to see it. Beach was so nervous that he dropped it and the gold started rolling across the concrete floor. We scrambled for it, embarrassed, but "Bones" was grinning placidly. The medal and order were restored, and Eddie said to me, "We waited a long time for this, didn't we?"

Dillard said he had felt the tape, known he'd won, and congratulated Ewell and Patton. He added another gold as a partner in the triumphant 400 meter relay team, the sideline that had saved his boat ticket.

I devoted almost the entire *Enterprise* sports page to the story, accompanied by a Beach photo of the American trio on the victory stand. It was published a week late, dispatched from London at the cost of an air mail stamp. Perennially shaky financially, the *Enterprise* wasn't about to pay cable charges. But things moved more slowly then, and there was a certain cachet in having a correspondent on the scene. Surely ten bucks worth.

Eddie, Harrison, Bob Beach, and I returned to B-W. Eddie changed gears to football as backfield coach and his classes. There were classes for us, too. Dillard needed a few more hours to graduate with the seniors of '49, whose yearbook was dedicated to him by the editor, Beach. Three years later, at Helsinki, "Bones" completed his unfinished business, remarkably seizing the hurdles gold, age twenty-nine. I wanted to be there, but the U.S. Army had different plans for me. However, my dual typing fingers kept me, a tank company clerk, out of Korean War combat.

Although a history major, I took as many classes from Coach Finnigan as I could fit in. A spellbinding lecturer, he strode the room as a stage, his bald head and dark eyes gleaming above the polka-dot bow. Students felt his empathy and concern for them. Maybe it was because he, an only child, yearned for more than the one kid he and his wife produced. Numerous of his athletes called him "the Master."

Eddie's football coaching course attracted not only me and team members but a higher level of pupil: several Cleveland Browns, who were finishing up undergraduate degrees. One, linebacker Lou Saban, would coach the New England Patriots, Buffalo Bills, and numerous other teams. Another student of the same ilk was Elroy "Crazylegs" Hirsch, the extraordinary Los

Angeles Rams receiver who later became athletic director at Wisconsin.

Nobody interviewed me to coach football. But when Eddie was lured back to his alma mater in 1951 to direct the Western Reserve athletic department and coach the football team, he took me along as the press agent.

It was my first real job—$3,000 a year, and all the sweat socks, T-shirts, and meals at the training table that I could scavenge.

I owe him, and treasure the time I spent with him. You could find any number of his friends and students who would say the same thing about Eddie Finnigan. Before a game or a meet he would spur his athletes with, "All you'll get out of this are the memories. Let's make them good ones."

He has been dead for some time. Still, those good memories return whenever I look at the rack holding my bow ties.

ARTHUR (BUD) COLLINS, a native Ohioan, has spent a half-century writing for Boston newspapers, and by this time feels entitled to a New England green card. Since 1963 he has been a *Boston Globe* columnist as well as a TV sports commentator for such networks as PBS, CBS, and, starting in 1972, NBC. Although named to the International Tennis Hall of Fame in 1994 for his self-described "scribbling and babbling" on that game, he has covered a wide variety of sports and events across the United States and the world, including Muhammad Ali's fights, the Vietnam War, and the Olympic Games. In 1999 he received the Red Smith Award for distinguished sports journalism. He was the first sportswriter to appear on TV at a national level. His most recent book is *Total Tennis*, and his Web site is www.budcollinstennis.com

Acknowledgments

This is a book—in its infancy and ultimately—about families. It began when mine, as I first knew it, changed, more than 30 years ago. I thank my entire family, all of them, for all that they have done.

To a team of friends who have helped sustain me. It's an embarrassment of riches, really, and I am humbled by and more grateful than I could ever say to too many of them to mention here. Special thanks to Matthew Jablow, Matthew Saal, Jim Solomon, John Solomon, Andrew Wagner and Naomi Wolfensohn.

To Steven Shainberg, without whom I simply don't know where I'd be, and in whose debt I will always be.

To everyone at Cavaliers Athletic Club, Collegiate School and Brown University who helped along the way.

To Coach Larry Byrnes, who helped inspire this book and helped me in more ways than he knows. On, off the field, everywhere. And to Coach's family. For sharing him with all of us, for all of these years, the two words that he so often reminded us to say to the people who mattered: thank you.

To Bruce Breimer, who was unconscionably valuable to me at a time when I needed it most.

To Mary Kelly, whose love and generosity knows no limit. I am eternally grateful to you and to your family in Ireland.

To all of the writers who have made contributions to this book and made sacrifices to do so; I'm deeply appreciative.

To Senator Bill Bradley, who was always a role model for me, and for whom, despite my being a Celtics fan, I always rooted (and voted).

To Charles M. Schulz and George Plimpton, who were so kind and generous, inspiring and encouraging to me.

To all the coaches who let me call my own plays in my quarterbacking days.

To John Anz, Alexandra Beal, David Black, Madeleine Blais, Roy Blount Jr., Susan Cheever, Robert Coles, Emmett Covello, Mike Danziger, Drummer, David Duchovny, Dick Enberg, Will Eno, Richard Ford, Samuel G. Freedman, Barbara Graham, Lee Gutkind, Greg Habeeb, Sue Halpern, Jonathan Karp, Carl Kawaja, Anita Klaussen, Stephanie LaFarge, Jennifer Levine, Robin Lippert, Bill Littlefield, Michael Lockett, Gil Mason, Derek Medina, Sarah Plimpton, Larry Shainberg, Floyd Skloot, Curt Smith, Gary Smith, Gay Talese, Rick Telander, Alice Tisch, John Updike, Lesley Visser, Lois Wallace and Alec Wilkinson.

Thank you to everyone at Warner Books, especially Laurence Kirshbaum, Jamie Raab, Emi Battaglia, Chris Dao, Les Pockell, Rebecca Oliver, Mari Okuda and Jason Pinter. Special thanks to my editor Rick Wolff. Jamie said that you were born to edit this book, and she was right. You have all done more than I could have ever hoped for and you have helped make a dream come true.

And to Amanda . . . I everything you. Always.